D1255298

Virginia Woolf
and the Androgynous Vision

Virginia Woolf and the Androgynous Vision

by

Nancy
Topping
Bazin

RUTGERS UNIVERSITY PRESS
NEW BRUNSWICK, NEW JERSEY

Permission to reprint previously published material has been granted as follows:

Excerpts from Virginia Woolf's *A Writer's Diary, The Moment and Other Essays, Jacob's Room, Between the Acts, To the Lighthouse, Night and Day, The Voyage Out, Mrs. Dalloway, The Waves, Three Guineas, The Years, Collected Essays,* Vol. I, and *Collected Essays,* Vol. II, are reprinted by permission of Harcourt Brace Jovanovich, Inc. and The Hogarth Press Ltd.; copyright, 1920, by George H. Doran and Company; copyright, 1922, 1927, 1931, 1937, 1941, by Harcourt Brace.

By Faber and Faber Ltd. and Harcourt Brace Jovanovich, Inc., for quotations from T. S. Eliot's "The Waste Land," "The Dry Salvages," and "Little Gidding," in his *Collected Poems, 1909–1962.*

By the *Modern Language Quarterly,* for use of Nancy Topping Bazin's article, "Virginia Woolf's Quest for Equilibrium," in its September 1971 issue. Chapter I of this book is a modified version of that article.

Excerpts reprinted by permission of New York University Press and George Allen & Unwin Ltd. from *Virginia Woolf* by Dorothy Brewster; © 1962 by New York University.

Second Printing

Library of Congress Cataloging in Publication Data

Bazin, Nancy Topping, 1934–
    Virginia Woolf and the androgynous vision.

    Bibliography: p. 236
      1. Woolf, Virginia (Stephen) 1882–1941.
I. Title.
PR6045.072Z543   823'.9'12   72–4198
ISBN 0–8135–0735–9

To Maurice, Michel, and Christine

Contents

Illustrations

Acknowledgments

Most of all, I wish to thank Wilfred Stone, Sylvia Feldman, Richard Scowcroft, and Lucio Ruotolo for reading and criticizing my manuscript. I am grateful to Leonard Woolf for answering a number of questions. I am indebted to the New York Public Library for permission to consult unpublished manuscripts by Virginia Woolf located in the Berg Collection. Furthermore, I wish to thank Josephine Schaefer and the following publishers for permission to quote: Hogarth Press, Harcourt Brace Jovanovich, Inc., George Allen & Unwin Ltd., New York University, and Faber and Faber Ltd. I am indebted to the Research Council of Rutgers University for a research grant awarded to me. Chapter I of *Virginia Woolf and the Androgynous Vision* is a modified version of my article, "Virginia Woolf's Quest for Equilibrium," published in the September 1971 issue of the *Modern Language Quarterly*.

Abbreviations

AROO	*A Room of One's Own* (1929)
AWD	*A Writer's Diary* (1954)
CE I	*Collected Essays*, Vol. I (1966)
CE II	*Collected Essays*, Vol. II (1966)
CE III	*Collected Essays*, Vol. III (1967)
CE IV	*Collected Essays*, Vol. IV (1967)
JR	*Jacob's Room* (1922)
N&D	*Night and Day* (1919)
TG	*Three Guineas* (1938)
VO	*The Voyage Out* (1915)

NOTES

Unless otherwise indicated, references to Virginia Woolf's works are to editions published by the Hogarth Press.

To distinguish between the series of three periods used by Virginia Woolf and an ellipsis indicating an omission of words, her periods are not spaced (. . .) but those indicating an omission are (. . .).

Virginia Woolf
and the Androgynous Vision

The truth is, a great mind must be androgynous.
                              —COLERIDGE

CHAPTER I

A Quest for Equilibrium

Virginia Woolf would have agreed with D. H. Lawrence that human beings have two ways of knowing, "knowing in terms of apartness, which is mental, rational, scientific, and knowing in terms of togetherness, which is religious and poetic."[1] As we shall see, Virginia Woolf associated these two ways with the two sexes. In *A Room of One's Own* she suggests that every mind is potentially bisexual. But she finds that among writers, and particularly among her contemporaries, most men tend to develop only the analytic, "masculine" approach, what Lawrence calls "knowing in terms of apartness," and most women only the synthetic, "feminine," that is, "knowing in terms of togetherness." In her opinion, however, to be truly creative one must use the "whole" mind. In keeping with this, the greatest writers are "androgynous": they use and harmonize the masculine and feminine approaches to truth (pp. 147-148, 156-157). They do not suffer from what T. S. Eliot calls the "dissociation of sensibility" or what Carl Jung calls the "split consciousness" of modern man;[2] for, in Jungian terms, they have discovered the "self," "a point midway between the conscious and the unconscious" in which there is a reconciliation of opposites.[3] Like Jung, Virginia Woolf felt that neither an individual nor an age can find its point of equilibrium without frankly confronting and understanding the exact nature of the opposing forces. Thus, her interest in what it means to be a male or a female was related to her quest for the self or the

3

point of balance that would stabilize her personality and give her the sense of wholeness and unconsciousness which characterizes the androgynous writer.

Virginia Woolf's interest in the accepted versus the real differences between the sexes was aroused when she was quite young, for she perceived and resented the fact that her father, Leslie Stephen, expected more of his sons than of his daughters.[4] Moreover, she became increasingly aware of the limitations which society placed upon the freedom of women. Her brother Thoby served as a model for Jacob Flanders in her third novel, *Jacob's Room.* Jacob's life of intellectual contacts, friendships, sexual experiences, and travels is contrasted with his sweetheart's dull life of tea and supper parties. Like Katharine Hilbery in *Night and Day* (1919), Virginia Stephen was not satisfied with the role of perfect mother and perfect hostess expected of the women of her class; for just as Katharine pursued mathematics, Virginia wanted to write professionally. Leslie Stephen allowed her to read and practice writing as she wished (CE IV, 79-80). However, after his wife's death in 1895, he felt so miserable and sorry for himself that his demands upon his children for pity and devotion were almost unbearable.[5] Thus, thinking of him in 1928, twenty-four years after his death, she wrote in her diary, "His life would have entirely ended mine. What would have happened? No writing, no books;—inconceivable" (AWD, p. 138). His death freed her from his egotistical demands and, by providing her with an adequate income, made her financially independent.[6] It is significant that in *The Years* Eleanor gives up a life of her own to care for her aging father.

Yet in 1904, when she began a new way of life at 46 Gordon Square in Bloomsbury with her sister Vanessa and her brothers Adrian and Thoby, she discovered that she was only partially liberated. Confronted frequently with Thoby's friends, she found herself extremely shy, wondering if she were capable of speaking as an equal with university graduates; moreover, she was constantly fearful that they were reacting to her, not as a human being, but as a female.[7] Confronted with a blank page in those early years, she felt similarly shy and fearful as a writer. In a paper read in 1931 to the Women's Service League, later published as "Professions for Women," she tells how she had to begin by killing that part of her which had learned that a woman should respect what men have to say and repress what she herself might think or feel (CE II, 285). As a female, she believed that her vision, though ideally bisexual, should on the whole be distinctly feminine, that is, "woman-manly" as opposed to "man-womanly" (AROO, pp. 132, 147-48). Looking back at her own work, she felt that she had succeeded in expressing honestly what she wanted to say with one exception: she had been afraid to convey frankly her "own experiences as a body" (CE II, 288).

Actually, she hints at these experiences in her portrayal of Jinny in *The Waves* and of Isa in *Between the Acts;* and, more important, she captures the way in which sexuality permeates even the seemingly nonsexual contacts between men and women, such as the relationships between Mrs. Ramsay and the male characters in *To the Lighthouse* and between Helen Ambrose and St. John Hirst in *The Voyage Out.* In her fourth novel, she suggests the lesbian's experience by describing Mrs. Dalloway's sexual response to Sally Seton (p. 36).

Virginia Woolf's efforts to understand and harmonize the feminine and masculine aspects of her own nature were further complicated by the mental illness from which she suffered. As her husband and as the publisher or copublisher of many important works in the field of psychoanalysis,[8] Leonard Woolf may be believed, I think, when he suggests in his autobiography that her illness, given the general label neurasthenia by her doctors, was, at least in its severest form, manic-depression. Danger signals (headache, insomnia, a tendency for the thoughts to race) would appear when she tired herself mentally, physically, or emotionally. With rest, these symptoms would usually disappear after one or more weeks, and she would again be able to lead a normal life. Four times, however, they did not, and she slipped into insanity. "She had a minor breakdown in her childhood; she had a major breakdown after her mother's death in 1895, another in 1914, and a fourth in 1940." During each of these breakdowns she went through two distinct stages, first mania, then depression.[9]

I believe that Virginia Woolf's experience during mania is related to what she would have considered an essentially feminine vision of life and that her experience during depression is related to what she would have considered an essentially masculine vision of life. Moreover, as I shall explain, *To the Lighthouse* (1927) would seem to suggest that she related her periods of mania to her mother and her periods of depression primarily, although not exclusively, to her father. John Custance, an English manic-depressive born in 1900, described his psychosis in two books, *Wisdom, Madness and Folly* (1952) and *Adventures into the Unconscious* (1954). On the basis of personal experience, he too associated mania with the maternal and depression with the paternal.[10] Moreover, as we shall see, combining the implications of both visions of life, he developed a *Weltanschauung* amazingly similar to Virginia Woolf's.

There are many hypotheses but no certain knowledge as to why some people become manic-depressives. In Virginia Woolf's case, there were genogenic factors.[11] Her grandfather, James Stephen III, was "over-sensitive and nervously irritable."[12] Her father, Leslie Stephen, was hypersensitive both as a child (he cried if reproached, would not hear stories with an unhappy ending, refused to look at any picture of the Crucifixion, adored poetry but shook with emotion when he listened to it) and as an adult (he would not visit hospitals, would not allow the word "dentist" to be mentioned, and during the Boer War refused to look at a newspaper).[13] Moreover, his endless demands for love, sympathy, even adoration, and his exaggerated self-criticism suggest a depressive type of personality.[14] Significant too is the fact that his elder brother's son, James K. Stephen, in the 1880's "became unpredictable in his behavior, veering between the extremes of wild gaiety and deep gloom," and was later committed to an institution.[15] The nature of the physiological defects which perhaps helped cause this instability in the Stephen family is suggested by strong evidence that the autonomic nervous system and the endocrine system to which it is closely related operate in a deranged manner in manic and depressive disorders.[16] However, such disturbances (whatever the physical predisposition) may also be a response to psychological stress. In turn, anxieties may be aggravated by the tendency towards emotional instability. Thus, in manic-depressives there is probably a very complex, continuous interaction between somatic and psychodynamic events.[17]

Certainly, Virginia Woolf was troubled about her relationship with her parents. Her husband described in his autobiography an incident that occurred in 1915:

> Virginia seemed to have recovered from the terrible breakdown which had lasted for the better part of a year. One morning she was having breakfast in bed and I was sitting by the bedside talking with her. She was calm, well, perfectly sane. Suddenly she became violently excited, thought her mother was in the room, and began talking to her. That was the beginning of the long second stage in a complete mental breakdown.[18]

On the date of her father's birthday, twenty-four years after his death and thirty-three years after her mother's death, she recorded in her diary, "I used to think of him and mother daily; but writing the *Lighthouse* laid them in my mind. And now he comes back sometimes, but differently. (I believe this to be true—that I was obsessed by them both, unhealthily; and writing of them was a necessary act)" (p. 138).

The central characters in *To the Lighthouse*—Mrs. Ramsay, Mr. Ramsay, and Lily Briscoe—were inspired by her mother, her father, and herself. On May 14, 1925, Virginia Woolf recorded in her diary her plan for *To the Lighthouse:* It is "to have father's character done complete in it; and mother's; and St. Ives; and childhood; . . . But the centre is father's character, sitting in a boat, reciting We perished, each alone" (pp. 76–77). The exactitude of her portrait of her father is confirmed by writings by and about Leslie Stephen, particularly by a journal he wrote for his children called the "Mausoleum Book," his essay "An Agnostic's Apology,"[19] and F. W. Maitland's *Life and Letters of Leslie Stephen.* The exactitude of the portrait of her mother is indicated by her sister's reaction: "She says it is an amazing portrait of mother; . . . has lived in it; found the rising of the dead almost painful" (AWD, p. 107).

Leonard Woolf, reading the novel in 1927, called it "a psychological poem" (AWD, p. 103). To write this book, Virginia Woolf had to come to terms with the relationship between her parents and to clarify her relationship to them. Similarly, Lily Briscoe cannot complete her abstract painting of "Mrs. Ramsay sitting in the window with [her son] James" (p. 32) until she has experienced the type of relationship Mrs. Ramsay had with her husband. Early in the novel Lily represents Mrs. Ramsay on her canvas as a triangular shape (p. 84), and toward the end of the novel she perceives Mr. Ramsay as part of the triangular form of a sailboat on the sea. Lily senses a disproportion and lack of harmony when she looks either at the "placing of the ships" on the sea or at the way she has arranged the shapes on her canvas. Before she can feel harmony in her mind and attain it in her painting, she realizes that she must "achieve that razor edge of balance between two opposite forces; Mr. Ramsay and the picture" (p. 296). In other words, she must bring into equilibrium the masculine and feminine approaches to life represented by Mr. and Mrs. Ramsay. When she finally succeeds, she draws a line "in the centre" of her picture (p. 320). As Lily admits, this line may not be satisfying aesthetically; yet it seems to symbolize for her the place at which the masculine and feminine forces meet in the "androgynous" mind. So too, in the novel, Virginia Woolf established the validity and interdependence of the two ways of knowing. She momentarily experienced what in *A Room of One's Own* she called "unity of mind" (p. 145). For this reason, *To the Lighthouse* is the happiest and least disturbing of her novels.

After this moment of insight, however, she must have discovered, perhaps only unconsciously, that in terms of her personal development something important had occurred in the course of writing that novel. In oversimplified Freudian terms, she had made the difficult transition from the pre-Oedipal to the Oedipal stage.[20] This shift is symbolized by the behavior of Lily in Part III of *To the Lighthouse*. Mrs. Ramsay has died, and Lily is longing and crying out for her. But then, having successfully pictured her again in her mind's eye, she suddenly longs for Mr. Ramsay, for she wants to share her vision of Mrs. Ramsay with him (p. 310). Virginia Woolf's normal development was undoubtedly upset, or if it had already been upset, the derangement was compounded, when at the age of thirteen she lost her mother. Like the Ramsay children, Cam and James, she belatedly put aside or at least softened her hostility toward her tyrannical, sympathy-seeking father and yielded to his call for love and pity. She seemed to realize in 1927 more than she had before that, despite his weaknesses, his view of life (" 'We perish'd each alone.' 'We are driving before a gale—we must sink.' ") was, in fact, more honest and like her own than her mother's (unpleasant facts should be hidden for the sake of harmony). After publishing *To the*

Lighthouse, she wrote in a letter, "I am more like him than her, I think";[21] and by 1928 she was able to write: "He comes back now more as a contemporary. I must read him someday" (AWD, p. 138). This new interest in her father's vision of life was increasingly reflected in her subsequent novels.

Virginia Woolf's very lifelike portraits of her parents in *To the Lighthouse* reveal to what extent her concepts of the masculine and feminine ways of knowing were influenced by her observations of her parents and to what extent her inability to harmonize the two in any lasting way was related to her manic-depression. As we shall see, Mr. Ramsay prefers to see life steadily, Mrs. Ramsay to see it whole.

Leslie Stephen said in *An Agnostic's Apology* that "man knows nothing of the Infinite and Absolute"; therefore, he should "renounce for ever the attempt to get behind the veil" and be satisfied with "the systematic interrogation of experience" (pp. 40-41). Indeed, this is sufficiently challenging; for even to proceed, symbolically speaking, from A to Q and try to get to R required of Mr. Ramsay "qualities that in a desolate expedition across the icy solitudes of the Polar region would have made him the leader, the guide, the counsellor" (p. 57). Relentless in his pursuit of truth, he represses his intuition that his efforts are ultimately of no importance and goes about quoting and acting like the charging Light Brigade commemorated in Tennyson's poem:

> Stormed at with shot and shell,
> Boldly they rode and well
> Into the jaws of death
> Into the mouth of hell . . .

Indeed, Mr. Ramsay recites poetry just as did Leslie Stephen, who "could absorb a poem that he liked almost unconsciously from a single reading." According to his daughter, "he knew many of Mr. Rudyard Kipling's ballads by heart,

Virginia and Sir Leslie Stephen in 1902. After publishing *To the Lighthouse,* she wrote of her parents, "I am more like him than her, I think."

and shouted Mr. Henry Newbolt's 'Admirals All' at the top of his voice as he went about the house or walked in Kensington Gardens, to the surprise of the nursery-maids and park-keepers." Just as the poetry recited by Mr. Ramsay in *To the Lighthouse* conveys to the listener his own attitude toward life, so too Leslie Stephen memorized what seemed to be "not merely the words of Tennyson or Wordsworth but what he himself felt and knew." "Thus," said his daughter, "many of the great English poems now seem to me inseparable from my father; I hear in them not only his voice, but in some sort his teaching and belief."[22]

In the novel, when Mr. Ramsay unexpectedly comes upon Lily Briscoe and William Bankes in the garden, he is forced to realize that to the detached observer his intellectual struggle must indeed seem ridiculous (p. 44). The Light Brigade was uselessly sacrificed in 1854 at Balaklava in the Crimean War because "Someone had blundered." Reminded of the uselessness of the attack and muttering "Someone had blundered," he, though averting his eyes, bears down upon his wife for comfort. In her presence he silently regains his self-esteem and hence his equilibrium (p. 52). As he recovers, the reader may be reminded of the lines that follow "Someone had blundered" in "The Charge of the Light Brigade":

> Theirs not to make reply,
> Theirs not to reason why,
> Theirs but to do and die.

The difference between Mr. Ramsay's state of mind in Part I and his state of mind in Part III parallels the difference in tone between "The Charge of the Light Brigade" and the poem that haunts him in Part III, Cowper's "The Castaway." The "mate" he has left behind is his wife, Mrs. Ramsay, whose love and sympathy were so important to him. In her own way, she was admirably courageous; yet no power intervened to prevent her death. Mr. Ramsay, like the speaker in "The Castaway," identifies himself with the fate of the one he loved. The lines he quotes are from the last stanza:

> No voice divine the storm allay'd,
>   No light propitious shone,
> When, snatch'd from all effectual aid,
>   We perish'd, each alone:
> But I beneath a rougher sea,
>   And whelm'd in deeper gulf than he.

When William Cowper wrote this poem in 1799, he had had a delusion that he had lost the favor of God. Like Virginia Woolf's father, Mr. Ramsay had long ago accepted, in the words of Leslie Stephen's friend, W. K. Clifford, the "utter loneliness" that accompanies the agnostic's recognition that "the Great Companion is dead."[23] However, he is faced now with the additional loss of his goddess (Mrs. Ramsay is often described in these terms),[24] whose love shielded him from constant terror. Such terror would have reduced to nothing the self-confidence he needed even to get from A to Q. Mr. Ramsay is saved only because Lily, by praising his boots, takes over Mrs. Ramsay's role as ego-protector (p. 237).

Virginia Woolf seems to have been very familiar with F. W. Maitland's biography of her father. The way the sight of Mrs. Ramsay and James at the window reassures Mr. Ramsay may be compared to what Leslie Stephen wrote in his letters to J. R. Lowell after the birth of Laura in 1870 and again after the birth of Vanessa in 1879. Speaking of his wife and their baby in 1870, he claimed that "nothing much more beautiful can be seen on the face of the earth," and then again in 1879, "The sight of wife and child is the best argument I know against the supremacy as well as the existence of the foul fiend."[25] The A-through-Q image, used to convey the way Mr. Ramsay's mind works, was undoubtedly suggested to Virginia Woolf by the fact that during the first nine years of her life, her father was editing the *Dictionary of National Biography*.

It is easy to see life steadily if one is not conscious of the void, but to be aware of the threat of nothingness and at the same time to try to see life "steadily" is to risk falling into a state of spiritual dryness which may in turn lead to psychotic depression. In *The Abnormal Personality* Robert W. White suggests that in the manic-depressive mania may be an attempt to control depression; for, whereas when depressed the patient considers himself worthless, in mania he avoids all thoughts detrimental to his self-esteem (pp. 525–526). Mrs. Ramsay's fertility places a similar check on Mr. Ramsay's spiritual sterility. Mr. Ramsay goes to his wife "to be assured of his genius, first of all, and then to be taken within the circle of life, warmed and soothed, to have his senses restored to him, his barrenness made fertile" (p. 62). As she sits knitting, his demands for entry are answered by an invitation: "she created drawing-room and kitchen, set them all aglow; bade him take his ease there, go in and out, enjoy himself" (p. 63). Restoring her husband's equilibrium; she makes him feel whole again. D. H. Lawrence felt that such an experience is equivalent to a return to the mother.[26] By writing about her parents' relationship in *To the Lighthouse,* Virginia Woolf undoubtedly discovered a new kinship with her father; for when depressed, she too craved the sense of organic unity or wholeness which she must, as a child, have experienced in her mother's presence.

She also shared her father's desire to look unflinchingly at life as it is. This respect for honesty and truth (which she would have labeled masculine) is reflected in the aspect of her aesthetics emphasized in "Modern Fiction": "Let us record the atoms as they fall upon the mind in the order in which they fall, let us trace the pattern, however disconnected and incoherent in appearance, which each sight or incident scores upon the consciousness" (CE II, 107). In her attitude toward life, it meant that she would have been annoyed, as Mr. Ramsay was, when Mrs. Ramsay "flew in the face of facts" (p. 53), a phrase which must have been inspired by one of Leslie Stephen's in *An Agnostic's Apology*. There, reacting to the supposedly soothing statements made during funeral services, he declared: "To suppress these spasmodic efforts to fly in the face of facts would be some comfort, even in the distress which they are meant to alleviate" (p. 4). In the novel, by insisting that it might not rain the next day (thus allowing the trip to the lighthouse), Mrs. Ramsay "made his children hope what was utterly out of the question, in effect told lies" (pp. 53–54). Leslie Stephen felt that "dreams may be pleasanter for the moment than realities; but happiness must be won by adapting our lives to the realities."[27] According to F. W. Maitland, although Leslie Stephen could not stand to hear of dentists or war, he "would receive his own death sentence with the coolest courage, and any of his friends who had to face 'a bad five minutes in the Alps' or elsewhere would have been wise to choose him for a companion. Nor certainly did he allow his vivid realisation of imagined pain to prevent him from 'looking ugly facts in the face' when he was making his estimate of the world." [28] Indeed, resembling her father, Virginia Woolf would not, like Mrs. Ramsay, have covered a "horrid" skull with a green shawl and then said it was like a mountain, a bird's nest, or a garden. Mrs. Ramsay knew the difference too (pp. 177, 95), but Virginia Woolf would have had a harder time pretending it was something other than what it was. Like Mrs. Stephen, Mrs. Ramsay tried to soften the blows and threats to human happiness; but to Virginia Woolf and her father, a fact was a fact.

Yet there were many moments in Virginia Woolf's life when she shared her mother's way of seeing things whole. For instance, she knew the ecstasy of artistic creation. Her mother, like Mrs. Ramsay, practiced the art of bringing people together and then managing them so that momentarily, despite personality differences, they felt themselves to be part of a harmonious whole, one which, in Mrs. Ramsay's words, partook "of eternity" (p. 163). Noel Annan clarifies why Julia Stephen excelled in the art of personal relationships: "She responded to other people's feelings instinctively; she could . . . read thoughts before they were uttered."[29] In writing her novels, Virginia Woolf similarly created out of the material of life a new entity. Moreover, what Virginia Woolf called "design" was not for her, as it may be for many artists, simply a way of ordering her subject matter (AWD, pp. 58, 61, 146). Like Mrs. Ramsay, she intended, I believe, to convey through pattern the peculiar sense of "reality" or oneness which she claimed to perceive and longed to express. She visualized this "reality" as a permanent shape which exists beneath the constant movement and change inherent in life. Thus, in *To the Lighthouse,* Lily saw her painting in this way: "In the midst of chaos there was shape; this eternal passing and flowing (she looked at the clouds going and the leaves shaking) was struck into stability" (pp. 249–250). In her 1928 diary, Woolf described this shape reality as "something abstract; but residing in the downs or sky; beside which nothing matters; in which I shall rest and continue to exist." She added, "I fancy sometimes this is the most necessary thing to me: that which I seek. But who knows —once one takes a pen and writes? How difficult not to go making 'reality' this and that, whereas it is one thing" (AWD, p. 132). This "reality" is obviously related to the oneness (the key to the universe) sometimes revealed to manic-depressives when they are in mania. John Custance, for instance, experienced "a sort of grasp of the whole, a passing beyond the antitheses, an interpenetration of the innumerable watertight compartments of life and experience." During such moments of manic revelation, in Custance's words, "the Eternal Masculine and Feminine are united and there is peace."[30]

Virginia Woolf did not experience this wholeness very often, however; and in her diary she explicitly said that in depression she had a "harassed feeling" because she searched for it without success (p. 86). Yet, as long as this feminine or manic vision of an underlying design at least alternated or coexisted with her "honest" (scientific) masculine vision of apparently meaningless flux, she was able to remain "upright" like her father. After the two were united briefly in Lily Briscoe's painting, however, Virginia Woolf seemed to be more and more sensitive to the "shot and shell" amidst which man has to live. Although sinking into "deeper gulfs," she continued to look for meaning or at least pattern in life, but the odds against finding either appeared to increase. In 1931 she suggested in *The Waves* that the artist's ability to create may be affected by this lack of pattern; for the protagonist Bernard, who wants to write, fails to transform the chaos of life into an artistic whole. But whereas Bernard's enemy is still the void, against which he fights courageously, in *The Years* (1937) and *Between the Acts* (1941) man's enemy is his own behavior. The tone of these last two novels reflects not only Virginia Woolf's increased sense of the meaninglessness of life but also her horror as she observed supposedly sane individuals and nations preparing for another world war. Her horror of war was as great as her father's, but she could not ignore the world wars as her father had the Boer War. Thus, her periods of depression became "deeper and more dangerous."[31] In *Between the Acts* Miss La Trobe's image of the modern age as fragments of the human and inhuman reflected by moving mirrors clearly suggests that a normal sense of psychological wholeness was by 1941 no longer possible for Virginia Woolf.

The duality inherent in Virginia Woolf's illness, her parents' personalities, her own view of life, and her aesthetics may be further illuminated by John Custance's description of his feelings as a manic-depressive. Considering differences in personalities and the limited information we have about Virginia Woolf's experience while ill,[32] we cannot say that her manic-depression was exactly like his. Yet his vision of the world in terms of the masculine and the feminine, his association of the masculine with depression, the feminine with mania, and his feeling that what was wrong with individuals and societies was that they weren't androgynous because they were not feminine enough[33] suggest some basic similarity in the way their minds worked. His descriptions of depression and mania[34] remind us of her portraits of the personalities of Mr. and Mrs. Ramsay respectively.

In depression, Custance was in a universe of horror; in mania, he was in a universe of bliss. In the former he felt miserable and ill; in the latter he had a sense of well-being. In depression, he, like Mr. Ramsay, did not notice visual detail; in mania he had, like Mrs. Ramsay, an artist's eye. The difference between Mr. and Mrs. Ramsay's ways of seeing is indicated in this passage: "And looking up, she saw above the thin trees the first pulse of the full-throbbing star, and wanted to make her husband look at it; for the sight gave her such keen pleasure. But she stopped herself. He never looked at things. If he did, all he would say would be, Poor little world, with one of his sighs" (p. 112). In one state, Custance withdrew like Mr. Ramsay into his own ego and felt isolated from others and from God just as Ramsay, in the boat, looked "as if he were saying, 'There is no God' " (p. 318). In the other state, Custance felt, as Mrs. Ramsay sometimes did, a "mystic sense of unity with the All."[35] In one mood, he felt repulsion for the outside world and for himself; in the opposite mood, he felt what Mrs. Ramsay often felt—a protective, indiscriminate love for all men and a sense of godlike power over their lives (pp. 19, 131). While depressed he felt guilty and, like Mr. Ramsay, inadequate and dissatisfied; whereas in mania he felt, as Mrs. Ramsay often did, proud and elated (p. 163). Finally, when a victim of depression, he was, like Mr. Ramsay, cut off from the secret of the universe; metaphorically speaking, he could not reach "Z." But as a manic, he seemed to have "some clue, some Open-Sesame to creation" (p. 52); so too

Lily Briscoe depicted Mrs. Ramsay's heart and mind as containing "tablets bearing sacred inscriptions, which if one could spell them out would teach one everything" (p. 82).[36]

These striking similarities and the preceding discussion of Virginia Woolf's own quest for an androgynous vision help to suggest what Leonard Woolf means when he says in *Beginning Again* (1963): "the connection between her madness and her writing was close and complicated" (p. 81). Indeed, Virginia Woolf wrote in her diary on September 10, 1929: "and these curious intervals in life—I've had many—are the most fruitful artistically—one becomes fertilised—think of my madness at Hogarth—and all the little illnesses—that [illness] before I wrote the *Lighthouse* for instance. Six weeks in bed now would make a masterpiece of *Moths* [later entitled *The Waves*]" (p. 146). The intensity of her quest for the androgynous ideal, reflected in her diary, her essays, and her novels, may be better appreciated when we realize that in her mind it meant the difference between sanity and insanity. Custance envisioned the problem of equilibrium in these terms: "Normal life and consciousness of 'reality' appear to me rather like motion along a narrow strip of table-land at the top of a Great Divide separating two distinct universes from each other"; and he added, "In the condition of manic-depression, this table-land is so narrow that it is exceedingly difficult to keep on it" (p. 29). Virginia Woolf knew that to slip off it, into Heaven or into Hell, meant that she could no longer write or take care of herself.

Worse yet, lurking behind the fear of attacks of manic-depression was the greater fear of incurable insanity; for if a manic-depressive is not permanently cured, with age the attacks often become more and more schizophrenic in nature.[37] During the last two attacks of hypomania described by Custance in *Wisdom, Madness and Folly,* he claimed that he had slipped over the line into schizophrenia (pp. 135, 138). A comparison of this first book with his second suggests the difference between the manic-depressive and the schizophrenic cited by White in *The Abnormal Personality:* to an observer, the manic-depressive appears abnormally speeded up or slowed down "and thus seriously disorganized but not unintelligible or queer"; however, the schizophrenic seems "crazy" (pp. 520–521). Moreover, the schizophrenic's chances for periodic or permanent recovery are much less than the manic-depressive's. For instance, a schizophrenic may have to live forty to fifty years in a mental institution.[38] This illuminates Virginia Woolf's explanatory suicide note, in which she expressed her belief that she was going mad again and that this time she would not recover.[39]

This background of threatened insanity explains somewhat Virginia Woolf's intensity as an artist. Driven by a search for self, she put the "whole of herself"[40] into her novels and remarks about writing. With her temperament she could not have done otherwise. Yet her quest was, in personal terms (not, I believe, in terms of her literary reputation), rather like the charge of the Light Brigade; for as Leonard Woolf noted, "it is significant that, whenever she finished a book, she was in a state of mental exhaustion and for weeks in danger of a breakdown."[41] Ironically, the strain of her quest endangered the equilibrium she sought.

CHAPTER II

The Spherical Vision

Virginia Woolf's experiences as a manic-depressive influenced her vision of reality and, in turn, her aesthetics. Manic-depression is a "cyclic" illness—cyclic in the sense that the manic-depressive moves alternately between two extreme psychological states. Hence, he experiences reality in terms of two opposite perspectives. Psychotic depression involves what Jung describes as the experience of the "shadow." That is, looking into the unconscious, the individual sees his own reflection. He takes a risk in looking, for as Jung says, "The mirror does not flatter, it faithfully shows whatever looks into it; namely, the face we never show to the world because we cover it with the *persona,* the mask of the actor." This confrontation with one's own "helplessness and ineffectuality" opens the door to experiencing what I refer to as the void—what Jung describes as "a boundless expanse full of unprecedented uncertainty, with apparently no inside and no outside, no above and no below, no here and no there, no mine and no thine, no good and no bad." Hence, it is an experience not only of nothingness but also of formlessness.[1] Thus, in depression the manic-depressive sees life as transitory, meaningless, and formless. In mania, on the contrary, he sees life as eternal, significant, and whole. Virginia Woolf embodied in her vision of reality the paradox inherent in her experiences as a manic-depressive; she concluded that life is both transitory (ever changing) and whole (never changing).

21

In "Phases of Fiction" (1929) she suggested that for a writer's vision to be "spherical," meaning "comprehensive," it must be "double." The novelist must see the evanescent details, which exist in time, and intuit the invisible underlying whole, which is timeless. For instance, he must see "two faces to every situation; one full in the light so that it can be described as accurately and examined as minutely as possible; the other half in shadow so that it can be described only in a moment of faith and vision by the use of metaphor" (CE II, 97). In "Mr. Bennett and Mrs. Brown" (1924) she implied that Arnold Bennett was guilty of seeing only the light half. He was excessively concerned with describing and analyzing transitory details; therefore, in his novels that which is eternal, namely, "the spirit we live by, life itself" escapes (CE I, 337). "Life itself" can be seized, she felt, only in a "moment of vision." In an instantaneous revelation one sees through the transitory to the eternal.

In an essay entitled "Reading," Virginia Woolf clarified what happens in a moment of vision: "As with a rod of light, order has been imposed upon tumult; form upon chaos. . . . Through the tremor and vibration of daily custom one discerns bone and form, endurance and permanence. Sorrow will have the power to effect this sudden arrest of the fluidity of life, and joy will have the same power. Or it may come without apparent cause, imperceptibly, much as some bud feels a sudden release in the night and is found in the morning with all its petals shaken free" (CE II, 25). She was conscious of the fact that both Joseph Conrad and Thomas Hardy used the phrase "moment of vision" (CE I, 305, 258).

Except perhaps for *Night and Day,* she seems to have conceived of each of her novels as such a moment, a little "globe" of life[2] which holds in equilibrium life's two opposite qualities—the "shifting" and the "solid" (AWD, p. 141). In 1928 she wrote, "I mean to eliminate all waste, deadness, superfluity: to give the moment whole; whatever it includes. Say that the moment is a combination of thought; sensation; the voice of the sea. Waste, deadness, come from the inclusion of things that don't belong to the moment; this appalling narrative business of the realist: getting on from lunch to dinner: it is false, unreal, merely conventional" (AWD, p. 139).

She associated the masculine with the shifting, the feminine with the solid. For example, as we have seen in *To the Lighthouse,* Mr. Ramsay fixes his attention upon the "shifting," rejecting any human knowledge of timeless absolutes. Mrs. Ramsay, however, prefers to explore the timeless realm of the unconscious, rejecting her existence in time as "simply childish." In the unconscious state "there was freedom, there was peace, there was, most welcome of all, a summoning together, a resting on a platform of stability" (p. 100). Seen comprehensively, life contains both the ever changing masculine and the never changing feminine. If the novelist's vision is "spherical," he perceives and balances these two aspects of reality. As in Lily Briscoe's painting, the masculine and the feminine should be balanced but not fused, for truth requires that the paradoxical nature of life be preserved.

In her novels Virginia Woolf sought to convey what it feels like to live. In order to accomplish this, she wanted to stay as "close to the quick of the mind" as possible. She wanted to retain the ambiguities, paradoxes, and complexities of one's innermost thoughts and feelings and to communicate honestly and exactly "the things people don't say" because they don't want to admit what they feel.[3] Theoretically, she believed she had to describe as accurately as possible what goes on in a character's mind before the thoughts and feelings have been transformed into assumptions and generalizations. She thought she was more likely to seize the "quick of the mind" in this way than if she were less interested in precise detail.

Ironically, the never changing essence must preserve the ever changing character of the mind. Otherwise, she would fail to communicate life; for, as she said in her essay on Montaigne, "Movement and change are the essence of our being; rigidity is death; conformity is death." Pleading for accuracy and honesty, she added, "let us say what comes into our heads, repeat ourselves, contradict ourselves, fling out the wildest nonsense, and follow the most fantastic fancies without caring what the world does or thinks or says."

However, in the sentence which concludes this passage, she recalled the necessity for equilibrium and suggested how difficult the task of finding it would be: "For nothing matters except life; and, or course, order" (CE III, 22). In "The Russian Point of View," she described the inner life as "formless. . . . It is confused, diffuse, tumultuous, incapable, it seems, of submitting to the control of logic" (CE I, 242). To put it into a work of art meant that she had to suggest formlessness within form.

One of the ways by which Virginia Woolf wanted to give form to her novels was to make them "poetic." In her essays and diary, she implied that the poetic novelist first apprehends his material, then detaches himself from it in order to sift out, capitalize on, and give form to what is essential. In order to intensify and formalize he must eliminate all "superfluity" (AWD, p. 139). In "Life and the Novelist" (1926) she claimed: "The writer's task is to take one thing and make it stand for twenty" (CE II, 135). In other words, his material takes on a symbolic value.

Although the poetic novel is not written in verse, it is similar in many ways to the novel-poem as she describes it in "Aurora Leigh":

As we rush through page after page of narrative in which a dozen scenes that the novelist would smooth out separately are pressed into one, in which pages of deliberate description are fused into a single line, we cannot help feeling that the poet has outpaced the prose writer. Her page is packed twice as full as his. Characters, too, if they are not shown

in conflict but snipped off and summed up with something
of the exaggeration of a caricaturist, have a heightened and
symbolical significance which prose with its gradual approach cannot rival. (CE I, 217–218)

As she had already noted in 1923 after reading Joseph Conrad, a novelist by the use of a few well-chosen details can
"light up a whole character in a flash" (CE I, 312). In particular, the minor characters in her novels are often "summed up"
in this manner. For instance, in *Mrs. Dalloway* the admirable
Lady Bexborough "opened a bazaar, they said, with the tele-
gram in her hand, John, her favorite, killed" (p. 7). However,
all of Virginia Woolf's characters are to some extent symbolical. One may say of her what she said of George Meredith:
"He is among the poets who identify the character with the
passion or with the idea; who symbolize and make abstract"
(CE I, 229). To see how this statement applies to Virginia
Woolf, one need only think of Helen Ambrose (fate), Mrs. Dalloway (the "life instinct"), Septimus Smith (the "death instinct"),[4] or Mrs. Manresa (the sensual woman).

Virginia Woolf wanted her characters to be convincing simultaneously as individuals and symbols.[5] Mrs. Ramsay, for
example, is a particular mother, wife, and hostess and, at the
same time, the essence and symbol of femininity. Virginia
Woolf visualized how the novelist moves from the particulars to
the essence in a description of Marcel Proust's use of detail in
relation to character. She was speaking of a scene in a theater
in which Proust's emphasis is upon "a young man's emotions
for a lady in the box below":

With an abundance of images and comparisons we are made
to appreciate the forms, the colours, the very fibre and texture of the plush seats and the ladies' dresses and the dull-
ness or glow, sparkle or colour, of the light. At the same
time that our senses drink in all this our minds are tunnel-

ling logically and intellectually into the obscurity of the
young man's emotions, which as they ramify and modulate
and stretch further and further, at last penetrate too far,
peter out into such a shred of meaning that we can scarcely
follow any more, were it not that suddenly in flash after
flash, metaphor after metaphor, the eye lights up that cave
of darkness and we are shown the hard tangible material
shapes of bodiless thoughts hanging like bats in the prime-
val darkness where light has never visited them before.[6]

Proust begins with visual details of objects seen by his characters (realism), yet simultaneously passes on to a metaphorical
use of such details in order to express the inexpressible (realism transformed by the imagination), and arrives finally at a
level of abstract or nonrepresentational art where realistic detail has been replaced by pure form and color. His "hard tangible material shapes of bodiless thoughts" remind us of Mrs.
Ramsay in *To the Lighthouse,* who would shrink to being herself, "a wedge-shaped core of darkness, something invisible to
others" (p. 99). Of course, as Virginia Woolf created her characters she moved back and forth between the world of details
(the masculine vision of the evanescent) and the world of ab-
stractions (the feminine vision of the eternal). Otherwise, a
balance between the two would have been unobtainable.

However, Virginia Woolf claimed that the essence—the aspect of reality which is eternal—is more "real" or "true" than
the particular (CE II, 105). Therefore, she tried to develop
techniques which would permit her to capture it. Although
she knew it was dangerous to move too far towards poetic abstraction (CE II, 82), she began, nevertheless, to move in that
direction in *Jacob's Room.* When as a result she was accused of
creating characters that do not "survive," she commented in
her diary: "I insubstantise, wilfully to some extent, distrusting
[the representational or descriptive] reality—its cheapness.
But . . . Have I the power of conveying the true reality?" (p.

57). To convey not just a glimpse but the whole of the true reality—the one, she must present and reconcile in her novels all the opposing forces which operate within her innermost being.

In 1923 she discovered another way of making her characters more "abstract" and "symbolic." She adopted and, of course, modified to suit her own purposes Conrad's technique of representing in different characters the selves of which a total self might be composed (AWD, pp. 60–61). For instance, just as Lord Jim is Marlowe's shadow-self, in *Mrs. Dalloway* (1925), Septimus Smith is Clarissa's shadow-self. In "Mr. Conrad: A Conversation," Virginia Woolf wrote: "it is when [novelists] bring these selves into relation—when they simplify, when they reconcile their opposites—that they bring off . . . those complete books which for that reason we call their masterpieces" (CE I, 310). Like Clarissa and Septimus, Mr. and Mrs. Ramsay may be viewed as opposing forces or "selves" which Virginia Woolf brought "into relation" in her novel. Moreover, while the six characters in *The Waves* are clearly individualized, they may also be viewed as aspects of a whole. Virginia Woolf saw them as elements in a complex pattern of interrelationships.

In creating the six characters in *The Waves* (1931), she eliminated all details that were irrelevant to their thoughts, feelings, and visual sensations. Moreover, except in the brief interludes between the nine sections of the book, the reader remains inside the minds of the characters. Through this approach to characterization, Virginia Woolf keeps the reader in constant contact with "life"—life in the sense of what it feels like to live. The characters speak only in the condensed, symbolic, rhythmic prose suitable, in Virginia Woolf's terms, to an intensely poetic novel. Significantly, Virginia Woolf referred to *The Waves* as an "abstract mystical eyeless book" (AWD, p. 137). As such, of all her novels, it is the least "representational."

In 1925, while writing *To the Lighthouse,* Virginia Woolf indicated that she thought of prose and poetry as opposite poles. She believed she had discovered a new theory "about *perspective.* . . . [It has] to do with prose and poetry, in novels; For instance Defoe at one end; E. Brontë at the other. Reality something they put at different distances. One would have to go into conventions; real life; and so on" (AWD, p. 83). A few years later, in "Phases of Fiction," she claimed that both Defoe and Emily Brontë were completely consistent in their perspectives. In Defoe's novels "God, man, nature are all real, and they are all real with the same kind of reality." In Emily Brontë's novels "the whole mood and temper" is poetic (CE II, 59, 96). Defoe conveyed what is eternal by describing what "happens actually before our eyes"; in his novels "emphasis is laid upon the very facts that most reassure us of stability in real life, upon money, furniture, food, until we seem wedged among solid objects in a solid universe" (CE II, 57, 58). Emily Brontë conveyed the eternal by freeing "life from its dependence on facts; with a few touches [she indicated] the spirit of a face so that it needs no body" (CE I, 190). Virginia Woolf equated Defoe's perspective with a representational (predominantly masculine) approach to reality, Emily Brontë's with a nonrepresentational (predominantly feminine) approach.

Night and Day is Virginia Woolf's most representational novel. In her first novel, *The Voyage Out,* and to a greater degree in the novels written between 1919 and 1931 she moved towards and, in *The Waves,* even beyond the pole of poetic abstraction symbolized by Emily Brontë. However, Virginia Woolf moved back towards Defoe's approach to reality in her last two novels.

The rise of Hitler and the growing threat of another world war during the late 1930's made her painfully aware of what was going on in the "outer" world and the influence these developments were bound to have on her "inner" world (CE II,

232). Thus, in *The Years* (1937) and *Between the Acts* (1941) she tried new ways of combining the two perspectives —the outer or representational and the inner or nonrepresentational. While writing *The Years* she commented, "I can take liberties with the representational form which I could not dare when I wrote *Night and Day*—a book that taught me much, bad though it may be" (AWD, p. 193). And in *Between the Acts* she united a more descriptive approach to character with a more complex concept of abstract structure than she had used in her stream-of-consciousness novels—*Mrs. Dalloway, To the Lighthouse,* and *The Waves.* She tried to bring the "shifting" and the "solid" into equilibrium in a new way.

Virginia Woolf thought of structure as "something lasting that we can know, something solid" (CE II, 124). The importance which she gave to the essential or "true" reality and to the abstract structure which expresses it may be explained, I believe, by her mystical experiences. These experiences were probably related to the moments of revelation that occur during mania. Moreover, like the manic experience of oneness, her glimpses of the eternal apparently helped to check the total despair which she frequently felt. For instance, she suggested in her diary that her consciousness of the void was frequently followed by her perception of the abstract whole (p. 132). On one occasion she described the experience of the whole as "a great and astonishing sense of something there, which is 'it'. . . . the thing is in itself enough: satisfactory; achieved. . . . I do fairly frequently come upon this 'it'; and then feel quite at rest" (p. 86).

This aspect of reality has something in common with form. As she explained in *A Room of One's Own,*

It lights up a group in a room and stamps some casual saying. It overwhelms one walking home beneath the stars and *makes the silent world more real than the world of speech* —and then there it is again in an omnibus in the uproar of

Piccadilly. Sometimes, too, *it seems to dwell in shapes* too
far away for us to discern what their nature is. *But whatever it touches, it fixes and makes permanent.* (pp.
165–166, italics mine)

The structure of a novel—what Virginia Woolf referred to as
"design"—also "fixes and makes permanent." According to
Simon Lesser in *Fiction and the Unconscious,* form presents
"everything in a way which emphasizes its wholeness and in-
tactness. By lavishing love and care upon the material, it seeks
to protect from death itself both the material and the object it
commemorates."[7] This concept helps to explain why Virginia
Woolf regarded "design" as the "solid," "permanent" aspect of
the work of art.

She spoke, for instance, of Henry James's novels as "products of 'an inexhaustible sensibility,' all with the final seal
upon them of artistic form, which, as it imposes its stamp, sets
apart the object thus consecrated and makes it no longer part
of ourselves" (CE I, 285). This suggests that Virginia Woolf
saw the use of "design" as a way to seize "life itself" and
make it permanent. Moreover, she saw in her books her
chance for immortality. Leonard Woolf groups her among
those writers who "regard the fate of their books as if it were
the fate of themselves . . . they seem to see in the book shops
and libraries an unending struggle between mortality and immortality." She did not believe in life after death but, as he
says, she "did believe in her life after death in *The Waves,* and
not merely in the life of *The Waves* after her death."[8]

Yet to give the reader the impression that he has seen the
timeless "pattern" which lies beneath the flux, she had to discover how to make him perceive the whole of her design in-
stantaneously. The way in which she resolved this problem reflects the fact that she was visually oriented.

In *Old Friends* Clive Bell said of Virginia Woolf: "In the
strictest sense of the word she is a seer." Moreover, he said

that she "had a genuine and highly personal liking for pictures" and that "she occasionally made drawings, which are said to show considerable talent." He added, "Her sense of visual values revealed itself most clearly, and characteristically, in a feeling for textures and the relations of textures. She would pick up a feather in the fields and set it in an appropriate wine-glass against a piece of stuff carelessly pinned to the wall, with the taste and 'rightness' of a Klee, if not a Picasso" (p. 113).

This "sense of visual values" reflected the talents and interests of the Stephen family. For instance, Virginia Woolf's father

> would twist a sheet of paper beneath a pair of scissors and out would drop an elephant, a stag, or a monkey with trunks, horns, and tails delicately and exactly formed. Or, taking a pencil, he would draw beast after beast—an art that he practised almost unconsciously as he read, so that the fly-leaves of his books swarm with owls and donkeys as if to illustrate the 'Oh, you ass!' or 'Conceited dunce,' that he was wont to scribble impatiently in the margin." (CE IV, 77)

Moreover, since Mrs. Stephen was the prototype for Mrs. Ramsay, it seems probable that, like Mrs. Ramsay, Virginia Woolf's mother was sensitive to visual detail. Also, as a girl, she had been "courted and admired by eminent artists, and chosen by Burne-Jones as the model for his painting of the Annunciation."[9] Whereas she obviously felt at ease in the company of artists, Leslie Stephen once wrote, "I have always been shy with artistic people, who inhabit a world very unfamiliar to me." In the Stephen home, painters as well as writers visited her on Sunday afternoons.[10] Also, Virginia Woolf's sister, Vanessa Bell, became a professional painter. In 1930 when she exhibited her work under the auspices of the Lon-

don Artists' Association, Virginia Woolf wrote, "Berthe Mori-
sot, Marie Laurencin, Vanessa Bell—such is the stereotyped
phrase."[11] As we shall see, Virginia Woolf's interest in painting was also stimulated by Roger Fry and Clive Bell, the
former a close friend, the latter her brother-in-law. As one
might expect, her visual sensitivity and the artistic talent and
interests of family and friends encouraged her to compare the
art of writing to the art of painting. She wrote in "Walter Sickert" (1934): "Painting and writing have much to tell each
other: they have much in common" (CE II, 241).

Virginia Woolf had a painter's eye for shape and design, and
she found this useful while writing her novels. Her sensitivity
to abstract shapes is evident, for instance, in the way she presented many of the scenes in her books. In *The Voyage Out*
the native women in the Amazon jungle are seen "squatting
on the ground in triangular shapes" (p. 348). In *Night and Day*
when Mary Datchet's brother is feeding chickens, we see him
as "a tall figure in gaiters, rising from a fluttering circle of soft
feathery bodies, upon whom the light fell in wavering discs.
. . . Mary dipped her hand in the bucket he carried, and was
at once the centre of a circle also" (p. 196). More important,
however, is the way in which Virginia Woolf used this sensitivity to provide a structure for her novels.

To one degree or another, she visualized all of her novels in
terms of space much as if the novel were a painting. In speaking of her first novel, she said that "the whole was to have a
sort of pattern."[12] As she discovered techniques which enabled her to rely less and less upon story and, hence, upon a
chronological time sequence, she developed what Joseph
Frank calls "spatial form." Spatial form transforms the novel
itself into an image. That is, in Frank's words, it unites "disparate ideas and emotions into a complex presented spatially
in an instant of time."[13]

As Virginia Woolf said in her introduction to the Modern
Library edition of *Mrs. Dalloway,* the reader's interest should

be in "the effect of the book as a whole on his mind" (p. viii). He must, while reading, build up what she called elsewhere "the architecture of the whole" (CE IV, 4). When he finishes the book, he should suddenly see the whole and simultaneously feel the impact of the book in its entirety.

In other words, the reader should experience in a moment of vision what Ezra Pound described in "A Few Don'ts" (1913) as "that sense of sudden liberation; that sense of freedom from time limits and space limits; that sense of sudden growth, which we experience in the presence of the greatest works of art." The reader experiences this sense of liberation in part because he is suddenly conscious of the unity which exists beneath the complexity, in part because, suddenly realizing that the novel is symbolic, he experiences at the same time the impact of its greater significance. *The Waves,* for example, suggests the absurd nature of human existence; *The Years* conveys a loss of faith in human beings; *Between the Acts* reflects the fragmented world of modern man.

"Design" provides the wholeness which makes the reader's moment of vision possible. In Virginia Woolf's novels the design is a harmonious combination of rhythms and patterns. A rhythm may be established by the periodic repetition or variation of a symbol, a phrase, or a theme. In *Jacob's Room,* for example, the ram's skull, the call "Ja-cob! Ja-cob!," and the themes of love and death are used in this way. Patterns may be created by the reactions of different characters to the same sight or sound or by a series of moments of vision. As in many abstract paintings, the patterns and rhythms seem to overlap or may even appear superimposed. For instance, in *Between the Acts* the hate-love relationship between Giles and Isa is interwoven with the pattern made by the village pageant, and both are seen against a backdrop of war. Some patterns may seem to be composed of masses (like the three parts of *To the Lighthouse*), others of geometrical shapes (like those suggested by the plot of *Night and Day*). Of course, whereas the design is in a visual sense abstract, it is composed of the character's experiences and emotions.

In 1921 Virginia Woolf regarded form only as "emotions . . . placed in the right relations to each other." Hence, she rejected at that time Percy Lubbock's suggestion in *The Craft of Fiction* that one should be able to "see" a novel's structure (CE II, 129, 126). However, in 1923, while writing *Mrs. Dalloway,* she discovered her "tunnelling process": "I dig out beautiful caves behind my characters: I think that gives exactly what I want; humanity, humour, depth. The idea is that the caves shall connect and each comes to daylight at the present moment" (AWD, p. 60). The caves reveal the characters' pasts while at the same time recording their reactions to the present. Freed by this technique from the necessity of revealing facts about her characters' lives in chronological order, she could connect the "caves," and hence her themes, by the spatial devices already described. Significantly, while speaking of her new technique, Lubbock's name again came into her mind; and she implied that by working inductively she had discovered her own kind of visual design (AWD, p. 61).

In fact, she had become fascinated by design. On June 19, 1923, she commented about *Mrs. Dalloway:* "The design is so queer and so masterful. I'm always having to wrench my substance to fit it. The design is certainly original and interests me hugely." By December 13, 1924, she was comparing her way of working to that of a painter: "one works with a wet brush over the whole and joins parts separately composed and gone dry." She again used the image of the "canvas" in her diary while she was writing *Orlando, The Waves,* and *Between the Acts* (pp. 118, 124, 171, 358). By 1929 she was looking at novels written in the past in a new manner:

From the first page we feel our minds trained upon a point which becomes more and more perceptible as the book proceeds and the writer brings his conception out of darkness.

At last the whole is exposed to view. And then, when the book is finished, we seem to see (*it is strange how visual the impression is*) something girding it about like the firm road of Defoe's storytelling; or we see it shaped and symmetrical with dome and column complete, like *Pride and Prejudice* and *Emma.* A power which is not the power of accuracy or of humour or of pathos is . . . used by the great novelists to shape their work. As the pages are turned, something is built up which is not the story itself. (Italics mine)

She claimed that this "power . . . accentuates and concentrates and gives the fluidity of the novel endurance and strength, so that no novel can survive even a few years without it" (CE II, 100–101). Similarly, in "How Should One Read a Book?" she noted: "And the book as a whole is different from the book received currently in separate phrases. Details now fit themselves into their places. We see the shape from start to finish; it is a barn, a pig-sty, or a cathedral" (CE II, 8).[14]

We have seen that Virginia Woolf's double vision of reality was a reflection of her psychological experiences as a manic-depressive. Her concept of the novel as a moment of vision in which the reader sees through the transitory to the permanent was based upon her mystical experiences. Her aesthetics, therefore, were rooted in the whole of her being. However, she was also influenced by the aesthetics of the postimpressionist painters; for, when introduced to their work by Roger Fry, she recognized the kinship between their way of seeing and her own.[15]

The art critic Roger Fry (1866–1934) was an intimate friend of Virginia Woolf's. She met him in 1909 (AWD, p. 299), and during 1910 he became one of the circle of friends that met on Thursday evenings in the Stephen home in Blooms-bury.[16] At that time, he was choosing the paintings for the first British exhibition of the French postimpressionist painters. The exhibition was held from November, 1910, until

Self-portrait of the art critic Roger Fry, who influenced Virginia Woolf's concept of "design."

mid-January, 1911. It included a large selection of paintings by Gauguin, Cézanne, and Van Gogh.[17]

In her biography of Roger Fry, published in 1940, Virginia Woolf said that this exhibition sent the British public "into paroxysms of rage and laughter" (p. 153);[18] most people were not prepared to accept colors and shapes which were not, in their opinion, realistic. However, she herself was evidently fascinated by the postimpressionists. She indicated the impact this exhibition had upon her when, in 1924, she stated in "Mr. Bennett and Mrs. Brown": "In or about December, 1910, human character changed" (CE I, 320). The germ of this important essay goes back to 1917, when she referred in a review to a statement Arnold Bennett made in December of 1910:

> I have permitted myself to suspect that supposing some writer were to come along and do in words what these men have done in paint, I might conceivably be disgusted with nearly the whole of modern fiction, and I might have to begin again. This awkward experience will in all probability not happen to me, but it might happen to a writer younger than me. At any rate it is a fine thought.[19]

Virginia Woolf was one of the young writers who wanted to "do in words" what the postimpressionists had "done in paint." She may well have been attentive when Roger Fry was asking in 1911 why "no English novelist . . . took his art seriously? Why were they all engrossed in childish problems of photographic representation?" and when he was complaining that "literature was suffering from a plethora of old clothes. Cézanne and Picasso had shown the way: writers should fling representation to the winds and follow suit."[20] For Virginia Woolf commented in "The Art of Fiction," an essay written in 1927: "If the English critic were less domestic, less assiduous to protect the rights of what it pleases him to call life, the nov-

elist might be bolder too. He might cut adrift from the eternal
tea-table and the plausible and preposterous formulas which
are supposed to represent the whole of our human adventure.
But then the story might wobble; the plot might crumble; ruin
might seize upon the characters. The novel, in short, might
become a work of art" (CE II, 55).

As influential art critics in their day, Roger Fry and Clive
Bell introduced into English thinking what they had discovered in France, namely, a new way of looking at paintings.[21]
Because of Fry's emphasis upon "plasticity" and Bell's emphasis upon "significant form," attention was shifted from the representational or descriptive elements in a painting (images of
people, places, things) to the nonrepresentational elements—
that is, to the design created by a harmonious combination of
lines and colors. The design should communicate the artist's
grasp of a significant, invisible reality. For instance, Cézanne
said, " 'Nature is more depth than surface, the colours are the
expression on the surface of this depth; they rise up from the
roots of the world.' "[22]

Virginia Woolf's reaction to a painting by Walter Sickert indicates that she had learned to look at pictures in this way:

> At first it suggests the husky voice of Marie Lloyd singing a
> song about the ruins that Cromwell knocked about a bit;
> then the song dies away, and we see a scooped-out space
> filled curiously with the curves of fiddles, bowler hats, and
> shirt fronts converging into a pattern with a lemon-col-
> oured splash in the centre. It is extraordinarily satisfying.
> Yet the description is so formal, so superficial, that we can
> hardly force our lips to frame it; while the emotion is dis-
> tinct, powerful, and satisfactory.

Although she was aware that Sickert considered himself "a literary painter," she felt that often the emotion was derived

from "something that had nothing to do with the story"; it is "the effect of those combinations of line and colour" (CE II, 242–243).

Similarly, when she looked at a picture by Cézanne in which there is a representational element (she referred to "a rocky landscape all cleft in ridges of opal colour"), it was the non-representational element that stimulated her:

> no painter is more provocative to the literary sense, because his pictures are so audaciously and provocatively content to be paint that the very pigment . . . seems to challenge us, to press on some nerve, to stimulate, to excite. That picture, for example, . . . stirs words in us where we had not thought words to exist; suggests forms where we had never seen anything but thin air.[23]

Through purely plastic expression, Cézanne communicated something from the impersonalized, abstract, silent depths of his being which gave birth in the novelist's mind to unexpected words and forms. Virginia Woolf referred to Cézanne as a "silent" painter. By this she meant that he expressed those profound, undefined feelings which cannot be described directly but may be evoked only through symbolic equivalents.

The remark made by Terence in *The Voyage Out* that he wanted to write a novel of silence suggests that Virginia Woolf was interested in writing such a novel as early as 1915 (p. 262). Her fascination with the silent depths of the unconscious is already evident in this novel; for example, Rachel feels that "to be flung into the sea, to be washed hither and thither, and driven about the roots of the world—the idea was incoherently delightful" (p. 365). Virginia Woolf's aesthetic concept of "silence" was undoubtedly rooted in her experiences with the unconscious as a manic-depressive.

She found that she profited from these experiences, for her

novels were often conceived or "fertilised" by what she called
her "madness" (AWD, p. 146). For instance, recovering from
one of these periods, she wrote in her 1930 diary:

> Once or twice I have felt that odd whirr of wings in the
> head, which comes when I am ill so often—last year for
> example at this time I lay in bed constructing *A Room of
> One's Own*. . . . If I could stay in bed another fortnight
> . . . I believe I should see the whole of *The Waves*.

She went on to describe the creative process:

> Something happens in my mind. It refuses to go on register-
> ing impressions. It shuts itself up. It becomes chrysalis. I
> lie quite torpid, often with acute physical pain—as last
> year; . . . Then suddenly something springs. . . . I had a
> tremendous sense of life beginning; mixed with *that emo-
> tion which is the essence of my feeling, but escapes descrip-
> tion*. . . . I felt . . . all the doors opening; and this is I be-
> lieve the moth shaking its wings in me. I then begin to
> make up my story whatever it is; ideas rush in me; often
> though this is before I can control my mind or pen. It is no
> use trying to write at this stage. (AWD, pp. 153–154, italics
> mine)

What is implied here and elsewhere by her use of the moth
and chrysalis images helps to tie together what has been said
in chapters I and II. In an unpublished autobiographical
fragment, she associated herself with the moth and her mother
with the chrysalis. She wrote that the chrysalis of her childhood split in two when, by the age of fifteen, she had felt the
full impact of her mother's death. The split had been coming
for two years but was precipitated by the death of her stepsister, Stella.[24] After the chrysalis split, she evidently sought to
recover the wholeness she felt she had lost by devoting herself

to her writing; for, in reflections recorded probably in 1903 about a woman who killed herself by jumping into the Serpentine, Virginia Woolf implied that in her own case she had learned to alleviate her sorrow through her work.[25]

As we have seen, Woolf tried to capture the "eternal" aspect of reality within each of her novels, and the novel itself was to partake of the eternal. In *To the Lighthouse* she associates the maternal with the eternal and with light (pp. 100–101). The image of the fragile moth attracted by a light despite the danger of being burned or killed by its efforts to attain it often appears in her writings.[26] The psychological and aesthetic quest for perfect wholeness, symbolized by light, was equally absorbing and dangerous for her; as we have seen, the quest itself endangered her stability. Yet, however destructive, at the same time the quest was saving her. The light was a substitute for the chrysalis. When she perceived it in art or in life she experienced the wholeness which she had lost when her chrysalis had split, leaving her still attached to the two conflicting parts of which it was composed.[27]

Her descriptions of the creative process reveal how her novels began as an indescribable emotion which at times she experienced in terms of a visualized shape.[28] For example, she spoke of *The Waves* as an "angular shape"—"that fin in the waste of water which appeared to me over the marshes out of my window at Rodmell when I was coming to an end of *To the Lighthouse*" (AWD, pp. 142, 169). The "indescribable" feeling had to be put into the words and form which best express it. The emotion could not, however, be described directly; rather it had to be "suggested and brought slowly by repeated images before us until it stays, in all its complexity, complete" (CE IV, 2). Even the words used had to take on a "mystical" quality. The reader must be able to

grasp what is beyond their surface meaning, gather instinctively this, that, and the other—a sound, a colour, here a

Virginia Woolf in front of a mural by her sister Vanessa Bell. Vanessa did in her paintings what Virginia wanted to do in her novels.

stress, there a pause—which the poet, knowing words to be meagre in comparison with ideas, has strewn about his page to evoke, when collected, a state of mind which neither words can express nor the reason explain. (CE IV, p. 200)

Virginia Woolf believed that ideally the novelist must sink into a kind of impersonal state in order to write (AWD, p. 48). His "ego" (his particular personality) should not be allowed to stand between the emotion or state of mind to be expressed and the symbolic equivalent, namely, the work of art (*cf.* AWD, p. 23). In other words, the reader should not feel the author's presence in the novel.

In her foreword to *Recent Paintings by Vanessa Bell* (1930), Virginia Woolf suggests that her sister succeeded in doing in her paintings what she herself hoped to do in her novels. What she said illuminates still another facet of what she meant by her ideal of silence:[29] "One defies a novelist to keep his life through twenty seven volumes of fiction safe from scrutiny. But Mrs. Bell says nothing. Mrs. Bell is as silent as the grave." Virginia Woolf explained the value of this silence:

That is why they [the paintings] intrigue and draw us on; that is why, if it be true that they yield their full meaning only to those who can *tunnel* their way behind the canvas into masses and passages and relations and values of which we know nothing—if it be true that she is a painter's painter—still her pictures claim us and make us stop. (italics mine)

Although her sister's paintings were "silent," she found them "immensely expressive," charged with emotion—that deep, complex emotion which may be evoked in a painting through rhythms and patterns. Simultaneously, however, Vanessa Bell also conveyed the "shock of emotion" which the "visible world" gave her "every day of the week" (pp. 3–4). Hence,

Virginia Woolf found in her sister's paintings the comprehensiveness which she sought to create in her novels, that is, the continual interrelationship between the visible and the invisible—the evanescent and the eternal.

Virginia Woolf's basic concept of the novel never changed. The dual vision of the evanescent and the eternal and the need to bring the two into equilibrium, appear in all Virginia Woolf's writings. Significantly, she often summed up this duality in visual terms.

She often saw the evanescent in terms of color, transparency, or movement, and the eternal in terms of shape, heaviness, or durability. As early as 1915 she imagined the perfect novel as "fireworks that make figures" (VO, p. 266). In 1925 she praised Proust's novels for being "as evanescent as a butterfly's bloom" yet "as tough as catgut" (AWD, p. 72). She praised Laurence Sterne in 1928 for combining "fluidity" with "permanence" in *A Sentimental Journey* (CE I, 96). In 1935 she wanted to preserve both "movement" and "weight" in the last chapter of *The Years,* and in 1938 she imagined *Between the Acts* as "a rambling capricious but somehow unified whole" (pp. 252, 289–290).

However, her concept of the novel is most clearly visualized through Lily Briscoe's eyes in *To the Lighthouse.* Lily sees that "In the midst of chaos there was shape; this eternal passing and flowing (she looked at the clouds going and the leaves shaking) was struck into stability" (pp. 249–250). Early in the novel Lily envisions her painting as "colour burning on a framework of steel; the light of a butterfly's wing lying upon the arches of a cathedral" (p. 78). Later, in Part III, she thinks: "Beautiful and bright it should be on the surface, feathery and evanescent, one colour melting into another like the colours on a butterfly's wing; but beneath the fabric must be clamped together with bolts of iron" (p. 264).

By the time she was writing *The Voyage Out,* Virginia Woolf already viewed reality in terms of the "shifting" and the "solid." But before she could combine the two successfully, she had to develop the necessary techniques. *The Voyage Out, Night and Day,* and *Jacob's Room* prepared her for writing the three important stream-of-consciousness novels—*Mrs. Dalloway, To the Lighthouse,* and *The Waves*—which provide us with the key for understanding her works as a whole. In them we see the realization of her basic aesthetic concept. Her last two novels, *The Years* and *Between the Acts,* were attempts to bring the representational and the nonrepresentational into equilibrium in a new way. They could never have been written had she not passed through her phase as a stream-of-consciousness writer. These novels reveal that she had slightly modified her aesthetics; however, she continued to conceive of her works in terms of a dual perspective, and the problem continued to be one of balance.

As she wrote in 1929:

It is the gift of style, arrangement, construction, to put us at a distance from the special life and to obliterate its features; while it is the gift of the novel to bring us into close touch with life. The two powers fight if they are brought into combination. The most complete novelist must be the novelist who can balance the two powers so that the one enhances the other. (CE II, 101)

Virginia Woolf's continual quest for this equilibrium is summed up by Lily's efforts in *To the Lighthouse.* It is significant that Virginia Woolf found that she could best symbolize her aesthetics in terms of a painter and her painting. Lily is trying to balance "the mass on the right" with the "mass on the left." However, she must gain insight into human beings and into human relationships before she can gain insight into the formal relationships in her painting. She learns something about Mrs. Ramsay's art of personal relationships by giving of herself to Charles Tansley and Mr. Ramsay (pp. 143, 237).

Moreover, she is observing Mrs. Ramsay's relationship with William Bankes when she has her first vision: "Yes, I shall put the tree further in the middle; then I shall avoid that awkward space. . . . She took up the salt cellar and put it down again on a flower in pattern in the table-cloth, so as to remind herself to move the tree" (pp. 132–133). Significantly, a tree may be a symbol of bisexuality.[30] It may also symbolize "the reconciliation of opposites" and "the impersonal life."[31] Lily's second vision occurs after she establishes a balance in her mind between the triangle on her canvas (symbolic of Mrs. Ramsay) and the triangle on the sea (Mr. Ramsay in the sailboat). The line which she draws "in the centre" is both the tree and the lighthouse. Thus, the lighthouse, usually associated only with the masculine, functions here as a symbol of a dual reality; for it is a combination of what Mrs. Ramsay sees, "a silvery, misty-looking tower," and what Mr. Ramsay sees, "the tower, stark and straight" (p. 286). Moreover, Mrs. Ramsay is identified with the light, while Mr. Ramsay is identified with the lighthouse (pp. 311, 318). The light represents to Mrs. Ramsay the essence of her being, which partakes of the eternal (pp. 100–101). The lighthouse which stands on a "dwindling" island, represents to Mr. Ramsay the fact that he will someday be swallowed up by the sea. Indeed, the island on which the lighthouse stands is a symbolic equivalent for the "dwindling" island on which he lives (p. 110).

By uniting the feminine, that which is timeless, with the masculine, that which exists in time, Lily Briscoe creates a symbolic vision of the androgynous work of art. Just as Lily finds it difficult to balance the two halves of her painting; so too Virginia Woolf found it difficult to balance the eternal and the evanescent aspects of reality in her novels. As T. S. Eliot says in "The Dry Salvages," "to apprehend/The point of intersection of the timeless/With time, is an occupation for the saint—."

CHAPTER III

The Voyage Out and *Night and Day*

In a letter to Lytton Strachey dated February 28, 1916, Virginia Woolf described her aim in writing her first novel, *The Voyage Out:*

> to give the feeling of a vast tumult of life, as various and disorderly as possible, which should be cut short for a moment by the death, and go on again—and the whole was to have a sort of pattern, and be somehow controlled. The difficulty was to keep any sort of coherence,—also to give enough detail to make the characters interesting.[1]

This statement indicates, in fact, what she wished to accomplish in all her novels: through both theme and structure she wanted to convey simultaneously her vision of life as meaningless chaos, which is what she meant by "tumult," and her perception of a pattern underlying this flux. Her first two novels, *The Voyage Out* and *Night and Day*, reveal that she had not yet developed the techniques which enabled her to fulfill her aim. In these works, however, we see her already altering what she later called the "representational" form of the novel. For instance, Virginia Woolf felt she was "breaking with complete representation" in writing *Jacob's Room*.[2] In 1933 she referred to her use of "the representational form" in *Night and Day*. In 1934 she spoke of the "representational part" of *The Years* (AWD, pp. 193, 225).

The Voyage Out begins with the departure from London of the *Euphrosyne,* a cargo ship bound for South America. On board is the central character of the novel, twenty-four-year-old Rachel Vinrace. She plans to go up the Amazon with her father, Willoughby Vinrace, the ship's owner. Crossing the ocean with them are her aunt Helen and uncle Ridley Ambrose, a friend, Mr. Pepper, and two strangers, Richard and Clarissa Dalloway, who unexpectedly embark in Lisbon. During the voyage a storm drives Richard Dalloway and young Rachel into a cabin, where they find themselves alone. Moved momentarily by the circumstances, Mr. Dalloway kisses her. Her first reaction to being kissed is one of exultation: "Life seemed to hold infinite possibilities she had never guessed at" (p. 85). But later she feels terrified and dreams she is locked in a moist, womblike vault with "a little deformed man" (p. 86). Rachel tells Helen Ambrose she won't dismiss this incident from her mind until she finds out exactly what it means (p. 90). Interested by Rachel's resolution and angry with Willoughby Vinrace for keeping his daughter in ignorance, Helen decides to help Rachel satisfy her curiosity about sex and life. Instead of going on to the Amazon, Rachel accepts Helen's invitation to stay with the Ambroses on Santa Marina Island. There Helen provides Rachel with a room of her own, unrestricted access to the library, and an opportunity to become acquainted with two young men, Terence Hewet, who aspires to write "a novel of Silence" (p. 262), and St. John Hirst, a Cambridge intellectual, who is writing an "indecent" poem on God (pp. 329, 341). Rachel falls in love with Terence; and with him, instead of with her father, she finally takes the river trip that had been promised to her months before. To persuade Rachel to stay over in Santa Marina, Helen had "promised a river"; also, while proposing the visit, Helen was embroidering a scene similar to that which Rachel later sees on the river trip (pp. 98, 95).[3] In the jungle Rachel and Terence become engaged. She has discovered love; yet in the end, death, not Terence, takes the bride-to-be. As we shall see, the fact that Rachel dies a virgin is significant.

Rachel had always been sensitive to the difficulty involved in establishing significant human relationships. As a young girl living with her aunts, she had concluded that

> It was far better to play the piano and forget all the rest. . . . Let these odd men and women—her aunts, the Hunts, Ridley, Helen, Mr. Pepper, and the rest— be symbols,— featureless but dignified, symbols of age, of youth, of motherhood, of learning, and beautiful often as people upon the stage are beautiful. It appeared that nobody ever said a thing they meant, or ever talked of a feeling they felt, but that was what music was for. *Reality dwelling in what one saw and felt, but did not talk about,* one could accept a system in which things went round and round quite satisfactorily to other people, without often troubling to think about it, except as something superficially strange. (P. 35, italics mine)

For Rachel the inner life is real, the outer life "strange." There is, in her opinion, a purity to be found in the impersonal that cannot be found in the personal. Even after she becomes acquainted with Terence, she finds relating to one person less satisfying than relating to the impersonal one—that is, enjoying through her music what Custance calls "a mystic sense of unity with the All."[4]

Although Rachel loves Terence, she resents his instinctive desire to dominate her. She determines that their intimacy shall not interfere with her privacy—that is, with her right to experience a mystical sense of oneness. Terence is jealous of the enjoyment she derives from these experiences; for during these moments she no longer feels any need for him and consequently is no longer in his power (pp. 261, 370).

Yet, while Rachel doesn't want to be dominated, she

Virginia with her husband Leonard Woolf whom she married in 1912. "Their intimacy" did not interfere with "her privacy."

doesn't want to lose her power over Terence either. It is her turn to feel depressed and jealous when he speaks of his writing: "As he talked . . . he had become suddenly impersonal. He might never care for any one; all that desire to know her and get at her, which she had felt pressing on her almost painfully, had completely vanished" (p. 262). As he went on, "his self-confidence astounded her, and he became more and more remote" (p. 263). She continues listening "with a certain amount of bewilderment" and then calls him back to her with " 'I like you; d'you like me?' " (pp. 264–265).

When Rachel and Terence are unable to find the point of balance between a respect for privacy and a demand for intimacy, each regards the other as an enemy. On one occasion, for instance, Terence tells Rachel,

> "What I like about your face is that it makes one wonder what the devil you're thinking about—it makes me want to do that—" He clenched his fist and shook it so near her that she started back, "because now you look as if you'd blow my brains out. There are moments," he continued, "when, if we stood on a rock together, you'd throw me into the sea." (Pp. 364–365)

Ironically, this hostility stimulates their love. Terence remarks: "Our marriage will be the most exciting thing that's ever been done! We'll never have a moment's peace—' " He'll enjoy the battle; yet Rachel warns that ultimately he may not be the victor:

> He caught her in his arms as she passed him, and they fought for mastery, imagining a rock, and the sea heaving beneath them. At last she was thrown to the floor, where she lay gasping, and crying for mercy.
> "I'm a mermaid! I can swim," she cried, "so the game's up." (P. 365)

Rachel seems to be saying, I look human, but in fact I'm a mermaid. I look as if I belong to this "strange" outer world symbolized by the rock, but in fact I belong to the inner, truer reality symbolized by the sea. More particularly, if I'm not human from the waist down, you cannot possess me. I intend to retain both my power over you (your need for me) and my independence (my preference for mystical not sexual experiences). Implicit in Rachel's preference for the "sea" is a wish for death. To die a virgin, as she does, is for her a victory.

The Voyage Out was inspired in part by Virginia Woolf's reading of Sir Walter Raleigh's *The Discovery of the Large, Rich, and Beautiful Empire of Guiana* (1596). Her description of the river trip into the jungle resembles in several details Raleigh's description of the Orinoco River area. For example, she borrowed Raleigh's account of a dense forest that suddenly opens onto plains of short grass decorated with groves of trees and deer feeding by the water's edge.[5] The idea of having a group of English people leave for South America in October with the intention of returning home in June may have been suggested by Raleigh's remark that "the Summer in *Guiane* is in October, Nouember, December, Ianuarie, February, and March, and then the shipps may depart thence in Aprill, and so returne againe into England in Iune, so as they shall neuer be subiect to Winter weather, eyther comming, going, or staying there."[6]

More significant is the contribution Raleigh's work may have made to the themes of conquest and virginity in *The Voyage Out*. Both Raleigh and Virginia Woolf suggest a comparison between going up the river and penetrating a female. For Terence, for instance, the trip has sexual associations:

> In some strange way the boat became identified with himself, . . . He was drawn on and on away from all he knew, slipping over barriers and past landmarks into unknown waters as the boat glided over the smooth surface of the

river. In profound peace, enveloped in deeper unconsciousness than had been his for many nights, he lay on the deck.
(P. 326)

Moreover, just as Raleigh's Guiana still has "her Mayden-
head" so has Rachel. Raleigh writes:

> *Guiana* is a countrey that hath yet her Maydenhead, neuer
> sackt, turned, not wrought . . . It hath neuer been entred
> by any armie of strength, and neuer conquered or possesed
> by any Christian Prince. It is besides so defensible . . . that
> no shippe can passe up. (P. 115)

To prove how easily the queen could defend Guiana, which
"hath but one entraunce by the sea," Raleigh says an enemy
might penetrate only in small or "flatte bottomed boats, and if
he do offer to enter it in that manner, the woods are so thicke
200 miles together vppon the riuers of such entraunce, as a
mouse cannot sitte in a boate vnhit from the banke" (p. 116).
    As a virgin, Rachel can be compared to Elizabeth, the Vir-
gin Queen, for whom Raleigh's work is written. Theoretically,
Elizabeth remained as impenetrable as Guiana. Rachel, like
the queen, may be considered superior to the legendary "Am-
azones," who, despite their masculine qualities, still needed
men "once in a yeere" because they wanted to have children
(p. 28). Raleigh believed that the empire of these Amazon
women lay at the southern border of Guiana; should the
queen take possession of Guiana, even they would look with
respect upon "a virgin, which is not onely able to defend her
owne territories and her neighbors, but also to inuade and
conquere so great Empyres and so farre remoued" (p. 120).
Having rejected the sexual role of a woman, the Virgin Queen
was free to play the masculine role of conqueror.
    Rachel, too, aspires to master a "far remoued" empire—the
impersonal world in which she can experience a mystical sense

of oneness. Shortly before her death, however, she sees clearly
for the first time the dual nature of reality. She recognizes
that, for her, real victory involves the mastery of not just one
but two realms—the impersonal and the personal:

> She thought how often they [she and Terence] would quar-
> rel in the thirty, or forty, or fifty years in which they would
> be living in the same house together, catching trains to-
> gether, and getting annoyed because they were so different.
> But all this was superficial, and had nothing to do with the
> life that went on beneath the eyes and the mouth and the
> chin, for that life was independent of her, and independent
> of everything else. So too, although she was going to marry
> him and to live with him . . . and to quarrel, and to be so
> close to him, she was independent of him; she was indepen-
> dent of everything else. (P. 386)

It is her relationship with Terence which prepared her for the
vision: "it was love that made her understand this, for she had
never felt this independence, this calm, and this certainty until
she fell in love with him and perhaps this too was love. She
wanted nothing else" (p. 386). Nothing else is necessary because, for the moment at least, her vision is androgynous.

Rachel's experience is like Lily Briscoe's in *To the Lighthouse*. Also a virgin, Lily has to learn something about Mrs.
Ramsay's art of personal relationships before she can have her
androgynous vision and thus complete her painting. Yet
Rachel recognizes that such moments of harmony are rare. As
she says earlier, to work out a viable relationship, most of the
time "it will be a fight" (p. 345). But, because she is basically
a "mermaid," Rachel returns to the "sea" and is saved from
having to live with the inevitable conflicts and compromises
which marriage entails.

Significantly, while Rachel is feeling the first symptoms of the
fatal disease she contracted in the jungle, Terence is reading

aloud from Milton's *Comus* (pp. 398–399). He reads the passage in which the Spirit is pleading with the virgin nymph Sabrina to rescue the Lady, who is under Comus' spell:

> Sabrina fair,
>   Listen where thou art sitting
> Under the glassy, cool, translucent wave,
>   In twisted braids of lilies knitting
> The loose train of thy amber dropping hair,
> Listen for dear honour's sake,
>   Goddess of the silver lake,
>   Listen and save![7]

Comus had first tried to conquer the Lady with words. He had listed the arguments against virginity; she had countered with the arguments for virginity. Because she insists upon preserving her virginity, Comus finally fixes her in her chair like a statue. He thinks he has conquered her; but the Lady tells him: "Thou canst not touch the freedom of my minde / With all thy charms, although this corporal rinde / Thou hast immanacl'd" (ll. 663–665). A slightly different but equally relevant theme is emphasized (p. 205) by the passage Rachel reads when she picks up Gibbon's *The Decline and Fall of the Roman Empire:* "The northern countries of Europe scarcely deserved the expense and labour of conquest. The forests and morasses of Germany were filled with a hardy race of barbarians, who despised life when it was separated from freedom." So too Rachel prefers death to being "conquered."

Terence mistakenly thinks he is finally united with Rachel once she is dead:

> This was death. It was nothing; it was to cease to breathe. It was happiness, it was perfect happiness. They had now what they had always wanted to have, the union which had been impossible while they lived. (P. 431)

His will no longer has hers to contend with; however, a moment or so later he becomes aware of the fact that he no longer has her either:

As he saw the passage outside the room, and the table with the cups and the plates, it suddenly came over him that here was a world in which he would never see Rachel again.

"Rachel! Rachel!" he shrieked, trying to rush back to her. But they prevented him and pushed him down the passage and into a bedroom far from her room. Downstairs they could hear the thud of his feet on the floor, as he struggled to break free; and twice they heard him shout, "Rachel, Rachel!" (P. 432)

Rachel's escape through death is foreshadowed earlier in the novel when Mrs. Dalloway identifies Rachel's attitude with that of Shelley in these lines from stanza forty of "Adonais":

He has outsoared the shadow of our night;
Envy and calumny and hate and pain
And that unrest which men miscall delight,
Can touch him not and torture not again . . .

At the end of the book Rachel is, like Adonais, "secure" "from the contagion of the world's slow stain" (pp. 62–63). Rachel's character reflects Virginia Woolf's preference for the mystical. However, Rachel's attitude should not be mistaken for that of Virginia Woolf, whose point of view was both ambiguous and paradoxical. Virginia Woolf has Mrs. Dalloway say of these lines from "Adonais": "How divine!—and yet what nonsense!" (p. 62). Mrs. Dalloway goes on to explain to Rachel why she is critical of Shelley's philosophy:

"I always think it's *living,* not dying, that counts. I really respect some snuffy old stockbroker who's gone on adding

up column after column all his days, and trotting back to
his villa at Brixton with some old pug dog he worships, and
a dreary little wife sitting at the end of the table, and going
off to Margate for a fortnight—I assure you I know heaps
like that—well, they seem to me *really* nobler than poets
whom every one worships, just because they're geniuses and
die young. But I don't expect *you* to agree with me!" (P.
62)

Rachel and Mrs. Dalloway are the embodiment of the death-
versus-life dialogue that seemingly went on in Virginia Woolf's
mind from the time her mother died until her own death by
suicide. As such, they are prototypes for Septimus Smith and
a more complex Mrs. Dalloway in the later novel. Likewise,
they are prototypes for Rhoda and Bernard in *The Waves*.

It is interesting to note again that Virginia Woolf attempted
suicide while she was writing *The Voyage Out*. Yet for Virginia Woolf, Rachel's death is both a victory and a defeat.
Through her death, Rachel, like Mrs. Ramsay, gains in power
and purity. However, her death, like that of Mrs. Ramsay,
also supports Mr. Ramsay's vision of the fragility of life. According to this masculine vision, death does not "save" her, it
annihilates her.

It is Helen Ambrose who most often expresses this point of
view in *The Voyage Out*. She is sensitive to the fragility of
man's happiness and existence:

The little jokes, the chatter, the inanities of the afternoon
had shrivelled up before her eyes. Underneath the likings
and spites, the comings together and partings, great things
were happening—terrible things, because they were so
great. Her sense of safety was shaken, as if beneath twigs
and dead leaves she had seen the movement of a snake. It
seemed to her that a moment's respite was allowed, a moment's make-believe, and then again the profound and rea-

sonless law asserted itself, moulding them all to its liking, making and destroying. (Pp. 321–322)

At times she has presentiments of impending disaster. For example, as she stood among the native women in the jungle,

> The cries of the senseless beasts rang in her ears high and low in the air, as they ran from tree-trunk to tree-top. How small the little figures looked wandering through the trees! She became acutely conscious of the little limbs, the thin veins, the delicate flesh of men and women, which breaks so easily and lets the life escape compared with these great trees and deep waters. A falling branch, a foot that slips, and the earth has crushed them or the water drowned them. Thus thinking, she kept her eyes anxiously fixed upon the lovers, as if by doing so she could protect them from their fate. (Pp. 349–350)

Sometimes Helen sees fate as mischievous, "generally adverse to people in proportion as they deserved well"; occasionally feeling more pessimistic, she sees chaos, not fate, as triumphant: "things happening for no reason at all, and everyone groping about in illusion and ignorance." For instance, "How did she know that at this very moment both her children were not lying dead, crushed by motor omnibuses? 'It's happening to somebody: why shouldn't it happen to me?' " (p. 269). Ironically, her own children are safe in London but Rachel dies in her care. Because of Rachel's illness and death, Terence finally comes to understand what Helen had felt all along:

> He looked at the scattered lights in the town beneath, and thought of Arthur and Susan, or Evelyn and Perrott venturing out unwittingly, and by their happiness laying themselves open to suffering such as this. How did they dare to

love each other, he wondered; how had he himself dared to live as he had lived, rapidly and carelessly, passing from one thing to another, loving Rachel as he had loved her? Never again would he feel secure; he would never believe in the stability of life, or forget what depths of pain lie beneath small happiness and feelings of content and safety. It seemed to him as he looked back that their happiness had never been so great as his pain was now. (P. 421)

As illustrated by the impression the jungle made upon Helen Ambrose, Virginia Woolf often stressed the fragility of man by suddenly shifting the angle of vision away from her characters to nature. For example, Hewet leads Rachel, Helen, St. John, and others to the top of a hill for a picnic:

One after another they came out on the flat space on the top and stood overcome with wonder. Before them they beheld an immense space—grey sands running into forest, and forest merging in mountains, and mountains washed by air, the infinite distances of South America. . . . The effect of so much space was at first rather chilling. They felt themselves very small, and for some time no one said anything. (P. 153)

Virginia Woolf also used two storms to make her characters see themselves in perspective. How disturbing an experience this is is indicated by the relief felt by the voyagers on the *Euphrosyne* when the first storm ends: "Instantly the world dropped into shape; they were no longer atoms flying in the void, but people riding a triumphant ship on the back of the sea. Wind and space were banished; the world floated like an apple in a tub, and the mind of man, which had been unmoored also, once more attached itself to the old beliefs" (p. 80). Likewise, Virginia Woolf would suddenly undermine the importance of a character's emotions by showing them against a backdrop of indifferent nature. For instance, Rachel's excitement after Mr. Dalloway's kiss is contrasted with the peaceful ocean (p. 85). On another occasion, Rachel and Terence are momentarily deluded by their emotions and fail to see themselves in perspective: "Merely to be so close soothed them, and sitting side by side the divisions disappeared, and it seemed as if the world were once more solid and entire, and as if, in some strange way, they had grown larger and stronger." But the spell is broken when they "see themselves in the glass, for instead of being vast and indivisible they were really very small and separate, the size of the glass leaving a large space for the reflection of other things" (p. 371). They shift from a feminine to a masculine vision of themselves; that is, they see themselves first as Mrs. Ramsay would see them (man partakes of the eternal) and then as Mr. Ramsay would see them (man is threatened by the void). In terms of what has been said in Chapter I, this parallels the shift from mania to depression. In relation to Virginia Woolf's illness, it is interesting to note that she describes Rachel's mood as fluctuating between "joy and despair" (pp. 271–273).

However, the shift is sometimes in the opposite direction, from the masculine to the feminine view of life. The two coexist in *The Voyage Out* as in the later novels: juxtaposed with the masculine vision of life as uncertain and meaningless is the feminine vision of a pattern underlying the flux. For instance, at the final tea Rachel sees the details of her life coalesce into a pattern:

> She felt herself amazingly secure as she sat in her armchair, and able to review not only the night of the dance, but the entire past, tenderly and humorously, as if she had been turning in a fog for a long time, and could now see exactly where she had turned. For the methods by which she had reached her present position, seemed to her very strange, and the strangest thing about them was that she

had not known where they were leading her. That was the strange thing, that one did not know where one was going, or what one wanted, and followed blindly, suffering so much in secret, always unprepared and amazed and knowing nothing; but one thing led to another and by degrees something had formed itself out of nothing, and so one reached at last this calm, this quiet, this certainty, and it was this process that people called living. Perhaps, then, every one really knew as she knew now where they were going; and things formed themselves into a pattern not only for her, but for them, and in that pattern lay satisfaction and meaning. When she looked back she could see that a meaning of some kind was apparent in the lives of her aunts, and in the brief visit of the Dalloways whom she would never see again, and in the life of her father. (Pp. 384–385)

At the end of the novel St. John Hirst is not forced to face for very long what is implicit in Rachel's death—the constant threat of the void. He is liberated by a sudden sense of detachment:

He lay back in his chair, half-seeing the others, half-hearing what they said. . . . Without any sense of disloyalty to Terence and Rachel he ceased to think about either of them. The movements and the voices seemed to draw together from different parts of the room, and to combine themselves into a pattern before his eyes; he was content to sit silently watching the pattern build itself up, looking at what he hardly saw. (P. 456)

Just as Rachel sees a pattern inherent in her life, so too Hirst sees her death as part of a pattern. Each is comforted by the discovery that order exists amidst the chaos of life.

On a number of occasions a sense of wholeness is experienced by Terence and Rachel in a different way. Instead of merely perceiving the underlying unity, they become one with it. In the jungle, for example, "it seemed to Terence . . . that existence now went on in two different layers. . . . Here were the Flushings talking . . . somewhere high up in the air above him, and he and Rachel had dropped to the bottom of the world together" (p. 335, cf. p. 346). Rachel often experienced a union with the impersonal (or the unconscious) in this way.

> Inextricably mixed in dreamy confusion, her mind seemed to enter into communion, to be delightfully expanded and combined with the spirit of the whitish boards on deck, with the spirit of the sea, with the spirit of Beethoven Op. 112, even with the spirit of poor William Cowper. (P. 35)

This deeper, rhythmic level of reality diminishes the significance of the "upper," particularized reality by making one see it from another angle. To Rachel "it became stranger and stranger. She was overcome with awe that things should exist at all . . . She forgot that she had fingers to raise." When Helen Ambrose came in to show her an invitation to a picnic, we read, "The utter absurdity of a woman coming into a room with a piece of paper in her hand amazed Rachel." Moreover, the ordinary words of the invitation struck Rachel as "incredible" (p. 145). For Rachel the mystical, nonverbal experience of oneness seems more important and, in that sense, more real than the outer world.

Similarly, pattern is more important than plot in Virginia Woolf's novels, for the abstract (which supposedly embodies and represents the forces that dwell in the unconscious) was more real and pure for Virginia Woolf than the particular. On an unspecified date she wrote to R. C. Trevelyan, "I always think of my books as music before I write them."[8] Already while writing *The Voyage Out,* she evidently wished the novel could be as "pure," as nonrepresentational, as a musical composition. For instance, Rachel asks Terence, " 'Why do you write novels? You ought to write music. . . . music goes straight for things. It says all there is to say at once. With writing it seems to me there's so much scratching on the matchbox.' "[9] Rachel suggests that music enables the listener to experience what is so profound that it cannot be verbalized. And according to another character in the book, "it just seems to say all the things one can't say oneself" (p. 197). Significantly, Terence says he wants to write a novel about "the things people don't say" (p. 262). Furthermore, he tells Rachel specifically,

> "What I want to do in writing novels is very much what you want to do when you play the piano. . . . *We want to find out what's behind things,* don't we? . . . Things I feel come to me like lights . . . I want to combine them . . . Have you seen fireworks that make figures? . . . I want to make figures." (P. 266, italics mine)

Terence's remarks are in accord with what we already know about Virginia Woolf's aesthetics. The following facts recorded in her diary testify to the influence of music upon her work. Seeking "unity" in *The Waves,* she decided to run all the scenes together "by rhythms chiefly" (p. 163). She wrote *The Waves* while listening to "late Beethoven sonatas" (p. 108), and she considered *Music* as a possible title for the novel she later called *The Years* (p. 222). Throughout the scenes of this book she wanted to keep "a kind of swing and rhythm," and she planned at one point to end it with "a chorus, a general statement, a song for four voices" (pp. 234, 221).

Of course, as Dorothy Brewster says of *The Voyage Out:*

> This first novel is in many ways traditional, with its chronological sequence, easily followed flashbacks, central characters fully drawn and others receding into the background, a

narrative diversified with scenes and dialogue, explanations of what goes on in people's minds, but not in stream-of-consciousness technique, description of settings, and so on.[10]

Yet, as we have already seen, the emphasis throughout *The Voyage Out* lies elsewhere—not upon the "outer" details but upon the inner life which they reflect. Also, Virginia Woolf visualized the structure of *The Voyage Out* in terms of rhythms and shapes which are interrelated to form an aesthetic whole.

As Virginia Woolf suggested in her letter to Lytton Strachey, the main rhythm of *The Voyage Out* may be described as the tumult of life, the pause of death, and the tumult of life recommencing. Within the first two movements of this overall rhythm one can sense another three-part rhythm in the life of Rachel: the voyage out (towards a more mature attitude about sex and religion), the voyage in (towards a more significant, more intimate relationship with Terence Hewet), and finally, the voyage out (from the particular and personal to the impersonal realm of death, where the self is not only successfully but permanently negated).

There are two major shapes or blocks of material in *The Voyage Out,* that which occurs on the cargo ship, a symbolic island, and that which occurs on the real island of Santa Marina. On each "island" there is a major emotional event, on the first a kiss, on the second a death. The kiss is preceded by a storm and followed by a dream. The death is preceded by a hallucination and followed by a storm.

The dream and the hallucination are similar in a number of details. Many of these suggest a journey into the womb. Here, for instance, is what Rachel experiences in her dream:

> she was walking down a long *tunnel,* which grew so narrow by degrees that she could touch the *damp bricks* on either side. At length the tunnel opened and became a *vault;* she

found herself trapped in it, bricks meeting her wherever she
turned, alone with a *little deformed man* who squatted on
the floor gibbering, with long nails. His face was pitted and
like the face of an animal. The wall behind him *oozed with
damp,* which collected into drops and slid down. *Still and
cold as death she lay,* not daring to move, until she broke
the agony by tossing herself across the bed, and woke
crying, "Oh!" (P. 86, italics mine)

The hallucination occurs when Rachel is near death. It was
inspired by the figure of Nurse McInnis playing solitaire by
candlelight.

The woman was still playing cards, only she sat now *in a
tunnel* under a river, and the light stood in a little archway
in the wall above her. She cried "Terence!" and the peaked
shadow again moved across the ceiling, as the woman with
an enormous slow movement rose, and they both stood still
above her. . . .
    In order to get rid of this terrible stationary sight Rachel
again shut her eyes, and found herself walking through *a
tunnel* under the Thames, where there were *little deformed
women* sitting in archways playing cards, while *the bricks
of which the wall was made oozed with damp,* which collected into drops and slid down the wall. But the little old
women became Helen and Nurse McInnis after a time,
standing in the window together whispering, whispering in-
cessantly. (Pp. 404–405, italics mine)

Antigone is cited in *The Voyage Out* (p. 46) and is used
more extensively in *The Years* (pp. 54, 145–146, 446). The
use of the brick vault in the dream and the hallucination was
probably inspired by the story of Antigone who was imprisoned in a rock vault because she defied Creon, whose son she
was to have married, and thus the "grave" was made her

"bridal chamber." Rachel's situation is similar; by tradition, she is expected to play a submissive role in her relationship with Terence. Moreover, Antigone both boasts of her choice (death rather than submission) and complains that her "doom" is "unjust."[11] Virginia Woolf's attitude toward Rachel's death reflects Antigone's.

In a sense, the dream and the hallucination reflect Rachel's longing for the oneness associated with the womb. In fact, however, Rachel does not experience there the perfect love and complete security which she seeks in oneness; instead she experiences the terror of confronting her shadow-self. Her shadow-self is represented by a "deformed man" in the dream and by "deformed women" in the hallucination. Just as Virginia Woolf conveys meaning through repetition, this slight variation in the pattern is significant.

The hallucination occurs after Rachel has discovered love; but her dream occurs before that discovery and, at the same time, foreshadows it. In *The Voyage Out* Virginia Woolf implies that intimacy between two individuals becomes possible only when they have lost their self-consciousness. Harmony and wholeness are to be found in the primitive, the impersonal, the unconscious being. Hence, before Rachel and Terence can admit their love, they must travel down the Amazon River (represented in Rachel's prophetic dream by the tunnel) into the heart of the jungle. Virginia Woolf suggests the symbolic import of this journey through her choice of images: they go into "the heart of the night" (p. 325), into "silence" (pp. 331–332). In these depths words are inadequate: "The great darkness had the usual effect of taking away all desire for communication by making their words sound thin and small" (p. 325) and Terence's words "flickered and went out" (p. 327). In the jungle (the vault of Rachel's dream) where men still live as primitive beings, the doubts and conflicts posed by conscious intellect dissolve and a decision to marry becomes possible. After this symbolic descent into the womb, Rachel is closer to having solved the problem of her sexual identity; therefore, in her hallucination she sees herself as feminine instead of masculine. Yet her shadow-self is still "deformed"; for, although she has matured, she is still afraid. She cannot attain wholeness via her love for Terence, despite her androgynous vision, for she still rejects for herself the sexual role of the woman. Hence, immobilized by fear in the dream, she is immobilized by death at the end of the novel. Indeed, to die rather than to establish a relationship may be seen either as courageous or as cowardly. Whereas, in one sense, it preserves the integrity of Rachel's spiritual self, in another sense, it denies the realization of her sexual self.

In the womb of the jungle, she encounters not only the possibility of love but also the probability of death, for Virginia Woolf suggests it is there that Rachel contracts her fever. Virginia Woolf's association of love and death with the womb corresponds to the paradoxical character of the archetypal feminine described by Carl Jung and Erich Neumann. The good mother nourishes but the terrible mother devours. Thus, the feminine may give joy or death.[12]

Forming the basic pattern in the Santa Marina section of the novel are five major events: a picnic, a dance, a chapel service, the river trip up the Amazon, and finally Rachel's death. These major events are interspersed with a number of teas, the most important of which falls between the river trip and Rachel's death. Rachel's thoughts during this final tea represent the height of her personal development and of her love for Terence, which begins at the picnic, blossoms at the dance, and is announced during the river trip.

Like the river trip and the death, the picnic, dance, and chapel service represent means by which one can possibly create or experience a sense of wholeness. Thus, each of these scenes reiterates one of the central themes of the novel: the search for unity. A sense of wholeness may be had either through detachment (perception of a pattern) or through immersion (union with the all). In the river trip and death scenes, as we know, wholeness is sought via immersion into the unconscious; but in the first three scenes, as we shall see, wholeness is sought via aesthetic detachment.

Terence, for example, organizes the picnic and later the dance to challenge his ability to create out of disparate individuals a unique entity which, like a work of art, has a life of its own. We see him as a prototype for Mrs. Dalloway and Mrs. Ramsay when we read: "His invitations had been universally accepted, which was the more encouraging as they had been issued against Hirst's advice to people who were very dull, not at all suited to each other, and sure not to come" (p. 146). Terence regards his guests as elements in an aesthetic composition:

> Hewet, who had gone a little in front, looked up at his guests as if to justify himself for having brought them. He observed how strangely the people standing in a row with their figures bent slightly forward and their clothes plastered by the wind to the shape of their bodies resembled naked statues. On their pedestal of earth they looked unfamiliar and noble, but in another moment they had broken their rank, and he had to see to the laying out of food. (P. 153)

He sees these same guests as a composition of moving objects a few moments later when they declare war upon an army of ants invading their tablecloth.

Similarly, the dance is described in terms of changing patterns within the shape of the room:

> Like the rats who followed the piper, heads instantly appeared in the doorway. There was another flourish; and then the trio dashed spontaneously into the triumphant swing of the waltz. It was as though the room were in-

stantly flooded with water. After a moment's hesitation first
one couple, then another, leapt into mid-stream, and went
round and round in the eddies. . . . The eddies seemed to
circle faster and faster, until the music wrought itself into a
crash, ceased, and the circles were smashed into little separate bits. The couples struck off in different directions,
leaving a thin row of elderly people stuck fast to the walls,
and here and there a piece of trimming or a handkerchief
or a flower lay upon the floor. There was a pause, and then
the music started again, the eddies whirled, the couples circled round in them, until there was a crash, and the circles
were broken up into separate pieces. (Pp. 177–178)

As Hewet and Helen begin to dance, we read, "She seemed to
fade into Hewet, and they both dissolved in the crowd" (p.
178). However, Hirst and Rachel had symbolic difficulties:
"instead of fitting into each other their bones seemed to jut
out in angles making smooth turning an impossibility, and
cutting, moreover, into the circular progress of the other danc-
ers." They decide to stop and, once seated, they see the room
in terms of a color-pattern: "It was still surging, in waves of
blue and yellow, striped by the black evening clothes of the
gentlemen" (p. 179).

The moments of harmony (and hence pattern) enjoyed at
the picnic and dance are not present in the chapel scene. For
instance, Rachel finds herself sitting through the service "in a
state of acute discomfort."

Such was the discomfort she felt when forced to sit through
an unsatisfactory piece of music badly played. Tantalised,
enraged by the clumsy insensitiveness of the conductor,
who put the stress on the wrong places, and annoyed by the
vast flock of the audience tamely praising and acquiescing
without knowing or caring, so she was now tantalised and
enraged. . . . All round her were people pretending to feel

what they did not feel, while somewhere above her floated
the idea which they could none of them grasp, which they
pretended to grasp . . . (P. 278)

Because of the bad conductor (Mr. Bax, the preacher) and the
false emotions, Rachel can neither perceive nor experience
oneness. In the jungle and death scenes, however, Rachel
moves successfully toward the satisfaction of her longing; she
returns to the peaceful silence of the womb.

Rachel's mother had died when Rachel was eleven (p. 32).
Rachel's association of ideas as she sits in her room on the
Euphrosyne suggests a relationship between the death of her
mother—or perhaps more precisely the day of her mother's
funeral—and her decision to seek the impersonal through
music and "forget all the rest" (pp. 33–35). Significantly, the
death of a parent is a common factor in suicide cases. Moreover, those who lose a parent as adolescents are often unconsciously convinced that they can overcome this imposed separation through death (or on a symbolic level, through a return
to the womb), thereby recapturing the security and love lost
with the parent.[13] This theory may apply to Virginia Woolf.

Leonard Woolf sensed in Virginia Woolf "some strange, irrational sense of guilt,"[14] which may be related to her initial
failure to feel grief when her mother died (AWD, p. 224). A
childish sense of rivalry for her father's love may account, at
least in part, for this reaction (compare, for instance, in *To
the Lighthouse* James Ramsay's jealousy of his father and his
desire to knife him). Delia's relationship with her mother and
father in *The Years* is relevant here. Just as in the Stephen
family Virginia was "the darling, the pet,"[15] Delia is Colonel
Pargiter's "favorite daughter" (pp. 13, 14). She actually longs
for the death of her mother, whom she "had loved and hated
so" (p. 92). Moreover, when she is confronted with the death,
her experience recalls Virginia Woolf's note in her diary: "Remember turning aside at mother's bed, when she had died,

and Stella took us in, to laugh, secretly, at the nurse crying. She's pretending, I said, aged 13, and was afraid I was not feeling enough" (AWD, p. 224). So too Delia believed those who showed grief at her mother's death were pretending: "She could see two nurses standing with their backs to the wall opposite. One of them was crying—the one, she observed, who had only come that afternoon" (p. 48). Delia's father reacts to his wife's death just as Virginia's father must have done, for the same pattern is used for Terence in *The Voyage Out* and for Mr. Ramsay in *To the Lighthouse*. In Delia's eyes even his grief is suspect:

> there was a stir, a shuffle of feet in the bedroom and out came her father, stumbling.
> "Rose!" he cried. "Rose! Rose!" He held his arms with the fists clenched out in front of him.
> You did that very well, Delia told him as he passed her. It was like a scene in a play. She observed quite dispassionately that the raindrops were still falling. One sliding met another and together in one drop they rolled to the bottom of the window-pane. (P. 49)

As Freud implies in speaking of Dostoevsky, the full significance of the loss later dawns upon the child, who is then horrified by his previous thoughts. Freud suggests that because of the subsequent guilt, the child wants to see himself dead like the parent, for whose death he feels semiresponsible.[16] In this sense, as well as in a sexual sense, Rachel's death may be significant in terms of Virginia Woolf's psychology. As we shall see, the explanation Virginia Woolf gives for Septimus Smith's suicide also lends support to my theory about her.

Unlike Virginia, Rachel does not attempt suicide; yet, at the same time, she offers no resistance to her destiny, and this is reflected in the pattern of her behavior. As Helen points out, she moves toward love and her subsequent death like a

river sliding toward a waterfall (p. 272). Although Helen has
made Rachel's destiny possible by inviting her to Santa Marina, it is Rachel who forces Helen to promise her "a river" (p.
98). It is she who persuades Helen first to go to the hotel (p.
114, cf. p. 112), then to go to the picnic (p. 146), and finally
to go on the river trip (pp. 320–322). This repeated pattern
helps to unify *The Voyage Out*.[17]

Another important part of the overall pattern of the book is
formed by the relationships of the main characters. For instance, St. John Hirst and Helen Ambrose are strongly attracted to each other despite the difference between their
ages. In a sense, they are opposites; he is frail, ugly, but bril-
liant; she is strong, aesthetically pleasing, but "infinitely"
simpler than he. Yet they share the same cynical view of
life and the same habit of being totally frank in conversation. Terence and Rachel attract each other and often share
an interest in human feelings and a positive attitude toward
life; both are repelled by the cynicism of Hirst and Helen.
At a moment of annoyance Rachel exclaims to her aunt,

> "Thank God, Helen, I'm not like you! I sometimes think
> you don't think or feel or care or do anything but exist!
> You're like Mr. Hirst. You see that things are bad, and you
> pride yourself on saying so. It's what you call being honest;
> as a matter of fact it's being lazy, being dull, being nothing.
> You don't help; you put an end to things." (P. 320)

Moreover, Hirst and Rachel represent opposite poles: Hirst's
thought-oriented approach to life versus Rachel's intuitive approach. He divides, analyzes, labels, while she sees the underlying unity, the oneness, the organic whole. Rachel and St.
John complement each other, for they seek different kinds of
truth, both of which are essential. His is the masculine mind,
hers the feminine. Terence, who is capable of admiring both
minds, tells Rachel: "You don't, and you never will, care with

every fibre of your being for the pursuit of truth! You've no respect for facts, Rachel; you're essentially feminine." Rachel eventually begins to like Hirst; yet "she also pitied him, as one pities those unfortunate people who are outside the warm mysterious globe full of changes and miracles in which we ourselves move about; she thought that it must be very dull to be St. John Hirst" (p. 361). Yet by the end of the novel St. John has learned to share Rachel's interest in love and patterns. The minds of Terence and Helen are a mixture of masculine and feminine qualities. They come closer than Rachel or Hirst to the ideal androgynous mind described by Virginia Woolf in *A Room of One's Own*. Even so, Terence recognizes that a sexual barrier exists between himself and Rachel. The main difference between Terence and St. John lies in their view of people. Whereas St. John is quick to label or condemn an individual, Terence feels it almost impossible to pass judgment upon another human being. Such is the complex pattern of relationships between the four main characters, Rachel Vinrace, Terence Hewet, St. John Hirst, and Helen Ambrose.

There are other antitheses added to this pattern of personal relationships. The young reformer, Evelyn, seeks intimacy with everyone but flees from the love of one individual, whereas Rachel shuns intimacy until she discovers and understands her love for Terence. Mrs. Dalloway and Helen Ambrose are also opposites. Despite her superficiality, Mrs. Dalloway is positive and has a zest for life; she can exclaim, " 'I've never met a bore yet!' " To which the wise but negative Helen can reply, " 'And I should say the world was full of them!' " (p. 58).

The pattern created by the different divisions of the novel, by the repetition and variation of themes and sequences, and by the relationships between the characters indicates, I believe, a conscious attempt by Virginia Woolf to express through an almost visual representation some of the principal psychic forces operating within human beings. Already in *The Voyage*

Out, she saw man as torn between opposite poles—life and death, terror and ecstasy, hate and love, time and timelessness. For her, truth was made up of contradictions. If seen as a whole, it contains both the masculine and the feminine visions of reality, both "tumult" and "pattern."

Like *The Voyage Out, Night and Day* deals with a young woman's quest for the point of equilibrium between the inner and the outer, the feminine and the masculine. Even the title embodies the duality inherent in Virginia Woolf's vision: the inner, feminine world is symbolized by night, the outer, masculine world by day. The central character, Katharine Hilbery, associates the feminine with her mother, the masculine with her father and views life in terms of these two poles. Through her love for Ralph Denham, she finally experiences a sense of balance which she did not experience with her first fiancé, William Rodney.

Like Rachel Vinrace, Katharine continually strives to protect her inner life (pp. 355–356), and she loves mathematics for the same reason Rachel loves music: she prefers the impersonal (which is eternal) to the personal (which is evanescent). Katharine reasons that one "cannot make sure of people," but one "can hold fairly fast to figures" (p. 333). She says, "I want to work out something in figures—something that hasn't got to do with human beings. I don't want people particularly" (p. 203); and the author says of her: "She would not have cared to confess how infinitely she preferred the exactitude, the star-like impersonality, of figures to the confusion, agitation, and vagueness of the finest prose" (p. 40). Moreover, Katharine contends that honesty and intimate human relationships are incompatible (pp. 354, 357). Thus, Ralph Denham wisely suggests special terms for their "friendship" to make it "perfectly sincere and perfectly straightforward." It is to be "unemotional" and neither person is to be "under any obligation to the other" (p. 357).

When Katharine arrives for their rendezvous in Kew Gardens the day this agreement is reached, Ralph recalls Mirabell's description of Millamant in Congreve's *The Way of the World:* "Here she comes, like a ship in full sail" (p. 348; II. ii). In her essay "Congreve's Comedies" (1937), Virginia Woolf wrote, "To read Congreve's plays is to be convinced that we may learn from them many lessons much to our advantage both as writers of books and—if the division is possible—as livers of life" (CE I, 80). Hence in laying down the terms for their friendship, Ralph evidently has in mind the famous scene in which Millamant and Mirabell establish unconventional guidelines for their married relationship (IV.i). Ralph offers voluntarily to Katharine the kind of freedom which Millamant had to demand from Mirabell. The fact that Ralph offers Katharine such a relationship gives her hope that she can find the wholeness she seeks. Friendship with Ralph may enable her to bridge the gap between "night" (the inner, private life) and day (the outer life):

as in her thought she was accustomed to complete freedom, why should she perpetually apply so different a standard to her behaviour in practice? Why, she reflected, should there be this perpetual disparity between the thought and the action, between the life of solitude and the life of society, this astonishing precipice on one side of which the soul was active and in broad daylight, on the other side of which it was contemplative and dark as night? Was it not possible to step from one to the other, erect, and without essential change? Was this not the chance he offered her—the rare and wonderful chance of friendship? (Pp. 358–359)

Ralph and Katharine fall in love; but as they do so, their moods alternate between exultation and despair. In particular, their joy is disturbed by the "interruptions" in their love, what they refer to as their "lapses." At times Katharine destroys

Ralph's romantic vision of her; then Ralph concludes that he "loved only her shadow and cared nothing for her reality" (p. 501). At other times the "lapse" is on Katharine's side:

> it took the form of gradual detachment until she became completely absorbed in her own thoughts, which carried her away with such intensity that she sharply resented any recall to her companion's side. It was useless to assert that these trances were always originated by Ralph himself, however little in their later stages they had to do with him. The fact remained that she had no need of him and was very loath to be reminded of him. (P. 501, *cf.* p. 351)

Doubtful, they ask themselves, "How then, could they be in love? The fragmentary nature of their relationship was but too apparent" (p. 501). Hence, their emotions belong not to the "solid" but to the "shifting" aspect of reality.

In terms of Virginia Woolf's psychology it is significant that Katharine is saved from her masculine vision of the uncertainty of love by her mother. Katharine explains her dilemma thus to Mrs. Hilbery:

> "Always to be finding the other an illusion, and going off and forgetting about them, never to be certain that you cared, or that he wasn't caring for some one not you at all, the horror of changing from one state to the other, being happy one moment and miserable the next—that's the reason why we can't possibly marry [.] At the same time," she continued, "we can't live without each other . . ." (P. 513)

Mrs. Hilbery persuades Katharine that "we have to have faith in our vision" and that therefore she and Ralph should marry (p. 513).

Unlike Rachel's guardian, Helen Ambrose, who represents

what Virginia Woolf calls the "manly" side "of the feminine nature," Mrs. Hilbery represents the "womanly" side.[18] Like
Mrs. Ramsay in *To the Lighthouse* and Mrs. Swithin in *Between the Acts,* Mrs. Hilbery is a unifier. Her husband, Trevor
Hilbery, is just the opposite. While she is out of town, he separates Katharine from Ralph, and Katharine's cousin, Cassandra, from William (who officially is still engaged to Katharine),
because he judges their conduct improper. But as soon as
Mrs. Hilbery returns, the two couples are reunited, for she
values happiness above propriety. Unlike her husband, she is
capable of overlooking differences and difficulties for the sake
of harmony.

Significantly, Katharine studies both Ralph and William in
terms of two poles, the characteristics of which are epitomized
by her parents. She thought Ralph was "a person who judges"
(like her father) but then discovers to her satisfaction that he
is "a person who feels" (like her mother) (p. 316). She first
thinks William Rodney is "half poet and half old maid" but
subsequently changes her mind and declares that he is more
old maid than poet (pp. 64–65). He is unfortunately too
much like Mr. Hilbery, too little like Mrs. Hilbery.

The name William and the word "rod" in Rodney symbolize
the masculine-feminine split in his personality. Mrs. Hilbery,
who adores Shakespeare, identifies Rodney with Shakespeare
by speaking of "*my* William" and Katharine's William (p. 323).
Rodney, in fact, tries to imitate Shakespeare by writing poetic
dramas. However, Rodney's dramas are too much the product
of his intellect, too little the product of his emotions. Mechan-
ically, he composes according to his theory that "every mood
has its meter." Listening to him read his manuscript, Katharine observes: "His mastery of metres was very great; and, if
the beauty of a drama depended upon the variety of measures
in which the personages speak, Rodney's plays must have
challenged the works of Shakespeare." Katharine does not
question his skill, which she refers to as "exclusively mascu-

line," nor does she question the fact that, like her father, he is a "scholar" (p. 143). However, Katharine notes in Rodney a rodlike inflexibility which she considers an undesirable side of the masculine personality. This inflexibility conflicts with his development as a poet. For instance, he values propriety over the honest expression of emotion. Moreover, he suppresses the "night" or "feminine" (nonrational) aspect of human experience (p. 258). Unlike Shakespeare, who is Virginia Woolf's example of *the* androgynous writer, Rodney has neither the "unity" of mind nor the unconsciousness which, according to Virginia Woolf in *A Room of One's Own* (1929), is necessarily found in great writers (pp. 145, 148–150).

Whereas Rodney's approach to poetry is masculine, Mrs. Hilbery's is totally feminine. For instance, Mrs. Hilbery is not, as he is, an expert on Shakespeare (she isn't an authority on dates and she often forgets the characters' names) but she is what is more important, a lover of Shakespeare. He is to her what the "magnanimous hero" is to Katharine (pp. 205, 284) and what Shakespeare is to the main character in *Orlando*,[19] namely, her image of the perfect male. In him she detects something of the divine. Therefore, in her own way, she worships him: when the weather is not "settled enough in the country," she suggests "a jaunt to Blackfriar's to inspect the site of Shakespeare's theatre" (p. 120); when the weather is sunny, she goes to visit Shakespeare's tomb (p. 453). Moreover, she dreams of Shakespeare at night and in the morning reads him, and no doubt often misreads him, to help her forget what Katharine would call "the barren prose of reality" (p. 399):

> "Lovely, lovely Ophelia!" [Mrs. Hilbery] exclaimed. "What a wonderful power it is—poetry! I wake up in the morning all bedraggled; there's a yellow fog outside; little Emily turns on the electric light when she brings me my tea, and says, 'Oh, ma'am, the water's frozen in the cistern, and

cook's cut her finger to the bone.' And then I open a little green book, and the birds are singing, the stars shining, the flowers twinkling—" She looked about her as if these presences had suddenly manifested themselves round her dining-room table. (P. 369)

The kind of inspiration which Mrs. Hilbery receives from Shakespeare sometimes enables her to bring harmony out of a seemingly impossible situation. Significantly, it is just after her visit to Shakespeare's tomb that she so skillfully arranges the reunion of Katharine and Ralph. When she learns from Katharine that Ralph is no longer allowed in their home, she merely asks, " 'Would there be time to send for him before lunch?' " Amazed at how simply her mother righted all that was wrong,

Katharine looked at her as if, indeed, she were some magician. Once more she felt that instead of being a grown woman, used to advise and command, she was only a foot or two raised above the long grass and the little flowers and entirely dependent upon the figure of indefinite size whose head went up into the sky, whose hand was in hers, for guidance. (Pp. 513–514)

Inspired by the magical effect which Shakespeare has upon her, Mrs. Hilbery is also able to help William and Cassandra over their discomfort when they first meet again:

Either Mrs. Hilbery was impervious to their discomfort, or chose to ignore it, or thought it high time that the subject was changed, for she did nothing but talk about Shakespeare's tomb.

"So much earth and so much water and that sublime spirit brooding over it all," she mused, and went on to sing her strange, half-earthly song of dawns and sunsets, of great poets, and the unchanged spirit of noble loving which they

had taught, so that nothing changes, and one age is linked
with another, and no one dies, and we all meet in spirit,
until she appeared oblivious of any one in the room. But
suddenly her remarks seemed to contract the enormously
wide circle in which they were soaring and to alight, airily
and temporarily, upon matters of more immediate moment.
(P. 526)

Likewise, to prepare Mr. Hilbery for the news of the two en-
gagements, Mrs. Hilbery again refers to Shakespeare. As her
husband enters the room, she asks him the date of the first
performance of *Hamlet*. The conversation which follows has a
magical effect upon the group:

> In order to answer her Mr. Hilbery had to have recourse
> to the exact scholarship of William Rodney, and before he
> had given his excellent authorities for believing as he be-
> lieved, Rodney felt himself admitted once more to the so-
> ciety of the civilized and sanctioned by the authority of no
> less a person than Shakespeare himself. The power of litera-
> ture, which had temporarily deserted Mr. Hilbery, now
> came back to him, pouring over the raw ugliness of human
> affairs its soothing balm, and providing a form into which
> such passions as he had felt so painfully the night before
> could be moulded so that they fell roundly from the tongue
> in shapely phrases, hurting nobody. He was sufficiently sure
> of his command of language at length to look at Katharine
> and again at Denham. All this talk about Shakespeare had
> acted as a soporific, or rather as an incantation upon
> Katharine. (Pp. 528–529)

Virginia Woolf was probably inspired by Shakespeare in
choosing the framework for her novel. In *The Three-fold Nature of Reality* Josephine Schaefer has pointed out the similarities between the plot of *Night and Day* and that of *Twelfth*

Night. Whether or not *Twelfth Night* is the immediate source for the plot of *Night and Day* remains questionable. However, Schaefer's parallels are valuable for suggesting the elements of Elizabethan (or Shakespearean) comedy such as disguise, mistaken identity, coincidence, and the last-minute happy ending present in this, the most complicated of Virginia Woolf's plots:

> Like Orsino and Olivia, Rodney and Ralph begin courting people they will inevitably not marry. The humor of the shifts and devices by which the couples are realigned is similar: the plight of Rodney courting Cassandra under the cloak of his engagement to Katharine resembles the situation of Olivia trying to woo Viola while she is an ambassador from Orsino. Viola's masculine disguise is comparable to the practical mask Katharine assumes, but with one real difference: when Katharine reveals to Ralph the real person beneath the disguise, she is simultaneously revealing that person to herself, whereas Viola is not experiencing a self-revelation. (P. 51)

Schaefer goes on to show the similarity between the Viola-Sebastian relation to Olivia and the Katharine-Cassandra relation to Rodney. Just as Sebastian is the man Olivia thought Viola to be, Cassandra is the woman Rodney thought Katharine to be.

In "Modern Fiction," written in 1919, Virginia Woolf objected strongly to the "tyrant" who demands that the writer provide a plot (CE II, 106). Feeling that "the greatest infliction that Elizabethan drama puts upon us" is plot (CE I, 56), she seemingly used a Shakespearean-type plot in *Night and Day* in playful protest to the continued demand. The way in which she had Mrs. Hilbery resolve the plot as if by magic is a particularly playful touch.

Moreover, the tone of *Night and Day* is, as a whole, rather tongue-in-cheek. For example, Woolf's attitude toward Mrs.

Hilbery's use of Shakespearean magic to resolve difficult situations was paradoxical; she simultaneously believed and didn't believe in it. Ultimately she embraced both Mrs. Hilbery's rather comical faith in love and oneness and Katharine Hilbery's scepticism. Her vision of life was at once feminine and masculine.

Because Mrs. Hilbery believes herself incapable of dealing with practical matters, Katharine for years has had to run the Hilbery household. Therefore, Katharine is keenly aware of not only the uncertainty of human emotions but also the "barren prose" of daily life, both of which threaten to undermine her mother's faith in love. Virginia Woolf tried in *Night and Day* to show the battle between doubt and faith going on within the context of the "barren prose of reality." Details of daily life play a bigger role in *Night and Day* than they did in *The Voyage Out*. In *Night and Day* the quest for a healthy balance between freedom and intimacy is resolved not in an exotic land far from family and work but within the context of the characters' daily activities in England.

In *Night and Day* Virginia Woolf burdens the reader with an unjustifiable number of scenes and details. Not until her next novel, *Jacob's Room*, did she begin to employ seriously the arts of condensation and omission. Perhaps, however, she first had to write a representational novel. She defended *Night and Day* in a remark made to John Maynard Keynes in 1921: "Oh, it's a dull book, I know, I said; but don't you see you must put it all in before you can leave out" (AWD, p. 35). Yet by including so much detail about the ways of life of the Denhams and the Hilberys, the Datchets and Otways, Virginia Woolf blurred the fact that *Night and Day* is actually not a social but a psychological novel.[20] In short, this emphasis upon "outer" details is at odds with the nature of what she wished to express. Technically, she failed to bridge the gap between night (the inner life of her characters) and day (the outer life of households and tea parties). Furthermore, the tension between the modern subject matter (challenging traditional concepts of the male-female relationship) and the Elizabethan type of plot is never satisfactorily resolved. This plot lends an air of artificiality to *Night and Day,* because it relies upon an inordinate number of coincidences, such as chance meetings. The simpler plot of *The Voyage Out* does not rely upon such devices. In regard to two other aspects, however, *Night and Day* is an improvement over her first novel. By using an English rather than an exotic setting, Virginia Woolf eliminated the most artificial element in *The Voyage Out.* Also, the devices used in creating the psychological pattern (as opposed to the action plot) in *Night and Day* are more subtle than those used in her earlier novel. For instance, one hardly notices that the development of the relationship between Mary Datchet and Ralph Denham closely parallels the development of the relationship between Katharine and William: Ralph finally decides to marry Mary and Katharine to marry Rodney, but in each case their willingness is recognized as insincere and the marriage does not take place (pp. 243, 259); the most harmonious moments are experienced by each couple just before breaking up (pp. 243, 306). There are similar parallels between the development of Ralph's love for Katharine and Rodney's for Cassandra. For example, driven by an impetuous urge to communicate with the person he loves, each young man tries with difficulty to compose a letter to his future fiancée (pp. 295–300, 320). But the most important part of the pattern in *Night and Day* is the movement of Mary, then Katharine, then Ralph, towards a moment of vision.

Mary is the first to "hold" her vision, to see her life with aesthetic detachment:

> Strange thoughts are bred in passing through crowded streets should the passenger, by chance, have no exact destination in front of him, much as the mind shapes all kinds

of forms, solutions, images when listening inattentively to music. From an acute consciousness of herself as an individual, Mary passed to a conception of the scheme of things in which, as a human being, she must have her share. She half held a vision; the vision shaped and dwindled. She wished she had a pencil and piece of paper to help her to give a form to this conception which composed itself as she walked down the Charing Cross Road. . . . Her vision seemed to lay out the lines of her life until death in a way which satisfied her sense of harmony. It only needed a persistent effort of thought, stimulated in this strange way by the crowd and the noise, to climb the crest of existence and see it all laid out once and for ever. Already her suffering as an individual was left behind her. Of this process, which was to her so full of effort, which comprised infinitely swift and full passages of thought, leading from one crest to another, as she shaped her conception of life in this world, only two articulate words escaped her, muttered beneath her breath—"Not happiness—not happiness." (P. 273)

Forgetful of self, she possesses the "knowledge of the impersonal life." Realizing that Ralph loves Katharine, Mary renounces for herself the kind of happiness offered to a woman only in marriage. Having been very much in love with Ralph and still feeling that "affection is the only reality" (p. 287), she knows how much she has given up. Made jealous by a confrontation with Katharine, Mary slips for a few moments that afternoon, but then

the thought of her morning's renunciation stung her conscience, and she tried to expand once more into that impersonal condition which was so lofty and so painless. She must check this desire to be an individual again, whose wishes were in conflict with those of other people. She repented of her bitterness. (P. 286)

At the end of the book Katharine and Ralph, now engaged, stand for some moments beneath Mary's window "looking at the illuminated blinds, an expression to them both of something impersonal and serene in the spirit of the woman within, working out her plans far into the night" (p. 536).

Not until Katharine casts aside her doubts and places her faith in her love for Ralph does she have her vision. Katharine "thought, looking at the sky above Chancery Lane, how the roof was the same everywhere; how she was now secure of all that this lofty blue and its steadfast lights meant to her; reality, was it, figures, love, truth?" Katharine is somewhat resentful when Ralph expresses his need to announce their engagement to Mary Datchet that same evening:

> She had no wish to see any one to-night; it seemed to her that the immense riddle was answered; the problem had been solved; she held in her hands for one brief moment the globe which we spend our lives in trying to shape, round, whole, and entire from the confusion of chaos. To see Mary was to risk the destruction of this globe. (P. 533)

Following a long struggle to understand the nature of love and what it should mean for her, Katharine's decision to place her faith in a future with Ralph has completed one phase of her life-pattern. The culmination has rendered the preceding struggle comprehensible, because the struggle now appears to her to have been the obvious path or means for reaching the type of decision she finally makes. During the struggle all had seemed chaotic; now it is obvious to her that some kind of order had been present all the time.

Finally, aided by Katharine's love, Ralph prepares himself for his vision. Fragments from the past begin to coalesce.

"Do you remember Sally Seal?" he asked. . . .
"Your mother and Mary?" he went on. "Rodney and
Cassandra? Old Joan up at Highgate?" He stopped in his
enumeration, not finding it possible to link them together in
any way that should explain the queer combination which
he could perceive in them, as he thought of them. They appeared to him to be more than individuals; to be made up
of many different things in cohesion; he had a vision of an
orderly world. (P. 536)

Katharine understands what is happening in his mind, that he
too will now "hold his globe for a moment round, whole and
entire."

She felt him trying to piece together in a laborious and ele-
mentary fashion fragments of belief, unsoldered and separate, *lacking the unity of phrases fashioned by the old be-
lievers.* Together they groped in this difficult region, where
the unfinished, the unfulfilled, the unwritten, the unre-
turned, came together in their ghostly way and wore the
semblance of the complete and the satisfactory. (P. 537,
italics mine)

Similarly, the reader of *Night and Day* gropes—with difficulty, however, because of Virginia Woolf's still imperfected
techniques—toward just such a moment of vision—one which
embodies Katharine's perception of the "tumult" of life and
Mrs. Hilbery's Elizabethan faith in an underlying harmony.
     Like Shakespeare in his comedies, Virginia Woolf in *Night
and Day* affirmed the importance of love and life. Both Mary
and Mrs. Hilbery tell Katharine that love is the "only reality"
(pp. 287, 512), and Mrs. Hilbery adds that the language of
love is the only "truth" (p. 324). She hopes Katharine and her
husband will have "the same vision and the same power to believe, without which life would be so meaningless" (p. 148).

What Katharine learns, however, is not only to have faith in the future but also to accept life as an exciting adventure. Although in later years Virginia Woolf placed Dostoevsky merely among the great writers,[21] in 1912 she called him the "greatest writer ever born."[22] Significantly, Katharine quotes Ippolit's statement in *The Idiot* that "It's life that matters, nothing but life—the process of discovering—the everlasting and perpetual process, not the discovery itself at all."[23] According to both Dostoevsky and Virginia Woolf, the essence of life is change. In Virginia Woolf's view "rigidity is death" (CE III, 22). In *Notes from Underground* we read, "perhaps the only goal on earth to which mankind is striving lies in this incessant process of attaining, in other words, in life itself, and not in the thing to be attained, which must always be expressed as a formula, as positive as twice two makes four, and such positiveness is not life . . . but is the beginning of death."[24] Virginia Woolf's concept of "life itself," discussed in "Modern Fiction," may well have been inspired by such statements in Dostoevsky.[25] Katharine has to accept the fact that life offers no certainty. She who loves mathematics must learn through her love for Ralph that, in Dostoevsky's words, "Consciousness, for instance, is infinitely superior to twice two makes four. Once you have mathematical certainty there is nothing left to do and to understand."[26] Katharine moves towards a way of thinking that is the opposite of William Rodney's. Significantly, he has not read *The Idiot*, admits he doesn't understand the Russians, and has exhorted Cassandra "to read Pope in preference to Dostoevsky until her feeling for form [is] more highly developed" (pp. 368, 295). Virginia Woolf included these details to indicate what is wrong with William as a poet and as a person.

While re-emphasizing the faith in love and life that she found in Shakespeare and Dostoevsky, Virginia Woolf recognized, as they did, the facts which make this faith difficult to maintain. She did not deny her husband's impression that the "philoso-

phy" of *Night and Day* is "very melancholy." In her diary she
commented on his opinion:

> if one is to deal with people on a large scale and say what
> one thinks, how can one avoid melancholy? I don't admit
> to being hopeless though: only the spectacle is a profoundly
> strange one; and as the current answers don't do, one has to
> grope for a new one, and the process of discarding the old,
> when one is by no means certain what to put in their place,
> is a sad one. (P. 10)

In *Night and Day* we sense the melancholy outlook which
dominates her last novel, *Between the Acts*. Whereas Katharine
merely states that Ralph's problem is to piece together "fragments of belief, unsoldered and separate," in *Between the
Acts* the reader witnesses Miss La Trobe's pageant, which is
the disquieting product of such an effort. In *Night and Day*
Virginia Woolf described Katharine's sense of the void (p.
299); but in *Between the Acts* the threat of the void is evoked
to provide the context in which the action of the novel takes
place. As Virginia Woolf gained progressively in technical
competence, her readers do not simply hear about her vision
of reality, they experience it more and more directly. Thus,
the contrast between her second novel and her last novel illustrates the direction in which we shall see her moving in her
third novel, *Jacob's Room*.

CHAPTER IV

Jacob's Room and *Mrs. Dalloway*

On January 26, 1920, Virginia Woolf recorded in her diary that she had conceived of "a new form for a new novel"—one which would allow "looseness and lightness." She wanted to "get closer [to life itself?] and yet keep form and speed, and enclose everything, everything." Therefore, "I figure that the approach will be entirely different this time: no scaffolding; scarcely a brick to be seen; all crepuscular, but the heart, the passion, humour, everything as bright as fire in the mist." In this new novel, which became *Jacob's Room* (1922), she wished to use techniques which she had experimented with in the short stories, "The Mark on the Wall," "Kew Gardens," and "An Unwritten Novel." Jacob functions in this longer work as the mark does in "The Mark on the Wall" and as the snail does in "Kew Gardens," that is, as the starting point and nexus for the rest of the content. Also, in both "An Unwritten Novel" and *Jacob's Room* Virginia Woolf belittled physical appearance as an important clue to character. She envisaged the novel as these three stories "taking hands and dancing in unity." At this point her vision was only of the form, for as yet she had no idea what the "unity" or "theme" of the novel would be (AWD, p. 23). After the publication of *Jacob's Room* her remarks again emphasized the newness of the form. For instance, she told Lytton Strachey that in writing this book she was "breaking with complete representation" (*Letters*, p. 146).

What she meant by this remark is evident in her handling of Jacob Flanders, the main character. Rarely does she present what Jacob thinks or says. Even when she does, she explains that her knowledge of Jacob is necessarily limited:

> But though all this may very well be true—so Jacob thought and spoke—so he crossed his legs—filled his pipe —sipped his whisky, and once looked at his pocket-book, rumpling his hair as he did so, there remains over something which can never be conveyed to a second person save by Jacob himself. Moreover, part of this is not Jacob but Richard Bonamy—the room; the market carts; the hour; the very moment in history. Then consider the effect of sex —how between man and woman it hangs wavy, tremulous, so that here's a valley, there's a peak, when in truth, perhaps, all's as flat as my hand. Even the exact words get the wrong accent on them. But something is always impelling one to hum vibrating, like the hawk moth, at the mouth of the cavern of mystery, endowing Jacob Flanders with all sorts of qualities he had not at all—for though, certainly, he sat talking to Bonamy, half of what he said was too dull to repeat; much unintelligible (about unknown people and Parliament); what remains is mostly a matter of guess work. Yet over him we hang vibrating. (Pp. 71–72)

The little we know about Jacob is usually provided by the other characters; but the author casts doubts upon what we learn from them. For example, after listing different characters' opinions about Jacob, she states: "It seems that a profound, impartial, and absolutely just opinion of our fellow-creatures is utterly unknown" (p. 70). Moreover, the adjectives the characters use to describe Jacob are so general that they are meaningless: he is "obstinate" (p. 9), "silent" (pp. 58, 70), "extremely awkward" but "distinguished-looking" (p. 69) and "well-built" (p. 29). Moreover, she plays down the importance of such descriptive words and phrases by saying: "It is no use trying to sum people up. One must follow hints, not exactly what is said, nor yet entirely what is done—" (pp. 29, 153).

Thus, the "representation" of Jacob is literally far from "complete." The reader learns this or that about Jacob but never comes to feel that he *really* knows him. By eliminating the convincing descriptions of appearance, thoughts, and actions which make us feel we "know" characters in novels more completely than we know our friends, Virginia Woolf gives the illusion that we are experiencing as we read *Jacob's Room* what we actually experience in life—at least at those moments when we would agree with her that

> life is but a procession of shadows, and God knows why it is that we embrace them so eagerly, and see them depart with such anguish, being shadows. And why, if this and much more than this is true, why are we yet surprised in the corner window by a sudden vision that the young man in the chair is of all things in the world the most real, the most solid, the best known to us—why indeed? For the moment after we know nothing about him.
>
> Such is the manner of our seeing. Such the conditions of our love. (Pp. 70–71)

Although one does not "know" Jacob in the representational sense of the word, he is "real" in an almost abstract, nonrepresentational way. By choosing to depict only fragments of the representational (predominantly masculine) aspect of reality, Virginia Woolf found she could convey the nonrepresentational (predominantly feminine) aspect of reality more easily. As noted by Leonard Woolf, Jacob is ghostly (AWD, p. 47). We hear only at the end of the book that Jacob dies in the war; however, it is as if Virginia Woolf wrote *Jacob's Room* in an effort to recapture someone already dead.

The eeriness which envelops the novel as a whole is, in my opinion, a direct result of Jacob's ghostlike quality. In creating Jacob, she evidently had in mind her brother Thoby, who died of typhoid as a young man. In a letter dated October 9, 1922, Lytton Strachey wrote to her about Jacob: "Of course I see something of Thoby in him, as I suppose you intended." Like Thoby, Jacob goes to Cambridge and later lives in Bloomsbury. Thoby contracted typhoid in Greece; Jacob travels to Greece just before he is killed in the war. But, as the name Flanders implies, she also had in mind all the young men who died during World War I—particularly those of her class. In the *Times Literary Supplement* of August 8, 1918, Virginia Woolf wrote of Rupert Brooke: "One turns from the thought of him not with a sense of completeness and finality, but rather to wonder and to question still: what would he have been, what would he have done?" (p. 371). She undoubtedly hoped to provoke a similar reaction to Jacob. She seems to take us back through Jacob's "room"—in the broad sense of that word—in the hope that she could seize again the essence of those who never returned to their "rooms." The significance of the word "room" is pointed out by Dorothy Brewster:

> The title has a meaning beyond the actual rooms where Jacob lived or worked or visited his friends. His "room" is a bench on a sunny day in Hyde Park; a seat on the upper deck of an Oxford Street bus; a pew in King's College Chapel; a box at the Covent Garden opera. It is the "outer"
> . —"the semi-transparent envelope surrounding us from the beginning of consciousness to the end." It is also the people who touch Jacob's life, intimately or tangentially: his mother; his tutor; his college friend Timothy Durrant; Bonamy, the friend who does not care for women; the several women who love him, each after her fashion. . . . It is the books he reads, and all the beauty and ugliness that we as-

sume he responds to in the world of Cambridge and London and Greece.[1]

Indeed, Virginia Woolf tried to evoke Jacob indirectly, by showing us not so much Jacob as the environment in which he lived. Thus, Jacob appears continually but almost incidentally in the chronologically arranged excerpts from his life. For instance, in the childhood section the focus is not on Jacob but on his mother; in the Cambridge section, the emphasis falls upon details which suggest what life was like at King's College in 1906.[2] The ghostly quality of Jacob is due, in part, to this technique. Making his presence incidental helps to suggest that the reality (the soul or essence) of Jacob exists apart from the actuality (or facts) of his life, yet that one must somehow get at his "reality" through these facts. Thus, Jacob's life is not the subject but the means by which one reaches the real subject of the novel, namely, the "flame"[3] or impulse of life which was annihilated when Jacob (and those like him) died.

Hence, the author conveys what Jacob symbolizes by emphasizing his "reality" rather than his "actuality." Jacob can represent the young men who died in World War I solely in terms of his essence. As a university graduate who has traveled to France, Italy, and Greece, he is typical only of a certain class. As an essence, however, he illustrates the absurd waste of young lives in war.

Each period of Jacob's life is represented by a series of excerpts which are related, yet not usually linked by any obvious transition. By eliminating transitions, the author is able both to intensify and to diversify the content. Thus, our sense of Jacob's reality is the product of a montage of many separate but superimposed impressions which we derive from reading the whole book. Each of these impressions contributes to the central theme, which serves to unify and universalize Jacob's experience. It is basically the same as the controlling theme (the inner versus the outer life) in both *The Voyage Out* and *Night and Day*. However, in *Jacob's Room* it is society, not intimacy, which threatens to interfere with the free and full development of Jacob's self.

Jacob constantly resists the efforts of his elders to impose their will and ideas upon him. Virginia Woolf suggests that,

> whether undergraduate or shop boy, man or woman, it must come as a shock about the age of twenty—the world of the elderly—thrown up in such black outline upon what we are; upon the reality; the moors and Byron; the sea and lighthouse; the sheep's jaw with the yellow teeth in it; upon the obstinate irrepressible conviction which makes youth so intolerably disagreeable—"I am what I am, and intend to be it," for which there will be no form in the world unless Jacob makes one for himself. The Plumers will try to prevent him from making it. Wells and Shaw and the serious sixpenny weeklies will sit on its head. Every time he lunches out on Sunday—at dinner parties and tea parties —there will be this same shock—horror—discomfort— then pleasure, for he draws into him at every step as he walks by the river such steady certainty . . . (P. 34)

It is significant that Jacob's mother, Betty Flanders, dominates the first and last scenes of the novel, for the mother-son relationship is of key importance in *Jacob's Room*. Mrs. Flanders represents all the mothers whose sons were killed in the war—a war made by the "elderly." Her concern for Jacob's safety and well-being injects the theme of maternal solicitude into the novel. Instinctively, she strives to create a feminine world which resists any intrusion from the outer, "masculine" reality—the world of no god perceived by Mr. Ramsay in *To the Lighthouse*. Thus, she insists that Jacob should not take home the ram's skull which he found while playing on the beach. Within the protected haven of her domestic world the skull would be an unwelcome reminder of the "facts." The masculine reality symbolized by the skull is also represented in the first section of *Jacob's Room* by the hurricane raging outside the house. It threatens death and destruction. Against it she holds up for her sleepless son, Archer, her feminine vision of "fairies, fast asleep, under the flowers" (p. 11). She is a prototype for Mrs. Ramsay, who likewise prefers to defy the "facts" by creating her own reality. For James's sake Mrs. Ramsay denies that it will rain the next day, a fact that will make the trip to the lighthouse impossible; for Archer's sake Mrs. Flanders denies the fact that a hurricane is raging outside. For Cam's sake Mrs. Ramsay denies the fact of death by covering the skull that James had found; she then speaks of fairies. Mrs. Flanders speaks of fairies in denying the storm. Neither Mrs. Flanders nor Mrs. Ramsay wants a "horrid" skull in the bedroom. However, being masculine, both Jacob and James refuse to give up the skulls. The opposition of the inner feminine to the outer masculine world is again illustrated in this passage: " [Mrs. Flanders] bent over and looked anxiously at [her servant, Rebecca's] baby, asleep, but frowning. The window shook, and Rebecca stole like a cat and wedged it. The two women murmured over the spirit-lamp, plotting the eternal conspiracy of hush and clean bottles while the wind raged and gave a sudden wrench at the cheap fastenings" (p. 11).

Mrs. Flanders' anxiety for Jacob continues even when he has grown up and gone away to the university, to London, and to foreign countries. She distrusts the outer world and, symbolically speaking, would prefer to call him back to the security of her own womb. For example, while Jacob goes to bed with Florinda in London,

poor Betty Flanders's letter . . . lay on the hall table— poor Betty Flanders writing her son's name, Jacob Alan Flanders, Esq., as mothers do, and the ink pale, profuse,

suggesting how mothers down at Scarborough scribble over
the fire with their feet on the fender, when tea's cleared
away, and can never, never say, whatever it may be—
probably this—Don't go with bad women, do be a good
boy; wear your thick shirts; and come back, come back,
come back to me. (P. 89)

However, the haven Mrs. Flanders believes she offers is, in
fact, a prison; for she wants to be the only woman to possess
and protect Jacob. Thus, despite and because of her love for
him, Jacob cannot go back to his mother's side. He must try
to find elsewhere the sense of wholeness which she offered him
as a child. Ironically, she is, to the extent that she wants to
imprison him, part of the "world of the elderly," whose will he
must resist.

The childhood section of the novel ends appropriately with
an image of what the rest of Jacob's life will be like. The difficulties with which Jacob will be faced outside of the protective maternal "womb" are suggested by the difficulties faced
by an "opal-shelled crab" lifted by Jacob from a tidal pool
and then abandoned in a bucket. "The child's bucket was
half-full of rainwater; and the opal-shelled crab slowly circled
round the bottom, trying with its weakly legs to climb the
steep side; trying again and falling back, and trying again and
again" (p. 12). This image suggests Jacob's repeated efforts to
save his inner being from the "world of the elderly" which en-
circles him. Jacob usually resists with quiet obstinacy. But
once in London he is moved to write an angry article (p. 68).
This anger is provoked by dishonest scholarship. Later, the
Daily Mail angers him because it is dishonest in its reporting
(p. 137). Yet Jacob does not carry his revolt against the world
of the elderly far enough; for he succumbs to its call to war.
Here is Virginia Woolf's picture of that war:

The battleships ray out over the North Sea, keeping their
stations accurately apart. At a given signal all the guns are

trained on a target which (the master gunner counts the seconds, watch in hand—at the sixth he looks up) flames into splinters. With equal nonchalance a dozen young men in the prime of life descend with composed faces into the depths of the sea; and there impassively (though with perfect mastery of machinery) suffocate uncomplainingly together. Like blocks of tin soldiers the army covers the cornfield, moves up the hillside, stops, reels slightly this way and that, and falls flat, save that, through field-glasses, it can be seen that one or two pieces still agitate up and down like fragments of broken match-stick. (P. 155)

Jacob's Room ends as Jacob's confused, helpless mother stands in his room in London after his death, asking, " 'What am I to do with these, Mr. Bonamy?' She held out a pair of Jacob's old shoes." Rightfully, Winifred Holtby says of this final picture, "Its melancholy, its extraordinary desolation, are indefinable."[4] Indeed, it expresses all the horror inherent in Virginia Woolf's *Weltanschauung*. Within a meaningless universe Mrs. Flanders' efforts and longings to protect her son from harm could not save him. For the protective globe of the feminine vision is easily crushed by the masculine reality, in which an indifferent fate "abandons opal-shelled crabs to the mercilessness of children, and abandons children to the mercilessness of war."[5]

Virginia Woolf used several devices which help make *Jacob's Room* into an aesthetic whole. For example, Jacob's death is foreshadowed throughout the book by the unanswered calls of "Jacob! Jacob!" (pp. 6–7, 166–167) and by references to such things as the ram's skull (pp. 8, 9, 12, 69, 176), the falling tree, and the volley of pistol shots (pp. 21, 30; *cf*. p. 41). The periodic reappearance of certain minor characters (Mr. Floyd, Mrs. Pascoe, the Greek women) and the repetition of certain sentences (such as, "Pickford's van swung down the street") also serve to unify the novel. Ultimately, however, whether or not the novel holds together depends upon the

ephemeral personality of Jacob. As the French critic, Jean
Guiguet, insists, Jacob does emerge as a reality—the "something" at the core of his being does get across to the receptive
reader.[6]

Yet other critics of *Jacob's Room* are almost unanimously
dissatisfied with Jacob, and they too are right, although many
have judged without trying first to understand the nature of
Virginia Woolf's vision. Virginia Woolf succeeds in conveying
Jacob in the way she intended. However, since the reader
knows too little of what Jacob says, thinks, or feels to find
him exciting as a character, he isn't sure he cares about Jacob's "essence." *Jacob's Room* would be more interesting had
the author developed the stream of consciousness of the main
characters as she did in her next two novels, *Mrs. Dalloway*
(1925) and *To the Lighthouse* (1927), or if she had at least
developed the stream of consciousness of the characters
around Jacob as she did for those around Percival in *The
Waves*. In *Jacob's Room* the reader's experience is that of an
observer who sees and guesses; but he rarely feels with Jacob
or the other characters, because none of them is sufficiently
developed.

Added to this flaw is a more serious one, namely, the in-
consistency of the author's point of view. Although inten-
tional, Virginia Woolf's alternating point of view is disturbing
and unjustified. Sometimes she writes as if she were detached
and omniscient; at other times, however, she pretends that she
is not omniscient and intrudes upon the scene as observer and
commentator. Occasionally, without explanation, her remarks
imply that both we and she, the unidentified speaker, are
physically present: for example, "The river races beneath us,"
and "There they are again" (pp. 112, 147). Similarly awkward are introductory sentences like "Let us consider letters
—," "For example, take this scene," and "Then here is another scrap of conversation" (pp. 91, 124, 126). She must
have recognized, however, that her intrusion into a serious

work of which she is not the subject is not desirable; for, except in the more subtle role of the central intelligence, she is absent from her later novels.

Despite these serious weaknesses, *Jacob's Room* is a fascinating book, for it is a bold experiment which reveals the origins of the techniques that are of utmost importance in *Mrs. Dalloway* (1925). First, there is the use of time. For example, in the moor scene with Mrs. Flanders and her friend, Mrs. Jarvis, an effort is made to give us a sense of history. On several occasions clock-time is mocked. We find, too, the technique of juxtaposing simultaneous happenings; and she uses clock-time (5:00 towards the end of *Jacob's Room*) to keep a sense of proportion. The two women Jacob loved most, Clara Durrant and Sandra Wentworth Williams, both think in terms of preserving the moment (pp. 70, 160). Also, as mentioned earlier, Virginia Woolf developed her stream-of-consciousness technique while writing *Mrs. Dalloway;* it took her "a year's groping" to discover it (AWD, p. 61). However, the impetus for the discovery is evident in a remark such as this in *Jacob's Room:* "her mind has lost itself tunnelling into the complexity of things" (p. 66); and the incomplete representation of the outer reality in *Jacob's Room* obviously prepares the way for the subsequent shift in emphasis from the "outer" to the "inner" worlds of the characters. In *Mrs. Dalloway* the "outer" facts are mentioned only insofar as they encroach upon the thoughts and feelings of the characters. Thus, the evanescent (masculine) aspect of reality depicted in the later novel is derived from the inner rather than the outer life. Virginia Woolf's extensive use of the multiple point of view in *Mrs. Dalloway* is also foreshadowed here: different characters see the beach at Cornwall or the nature of Jacob's personality in different ways. Similarly suggestive of *Mrs. Dalloway* is one section of *Jacob's Room* in which Virginia Woolf distinguishes the unspoken from the spoken by putting the former in parentheses (p. 71). Another technique introduced in *Jacob's*

Room is that of ironic juxtaposition. While Clara recalls a romantic moment with Jacob, he tells an indecent joke to his friends (p. 70); while Jacob reads *Phaedrus,* a drunken woman in the street batters at the door crying, "Let me in" (p. 108). Interesting too is the way the author handles the activities of Fanny Elmer and Jacob Flanders just before they meet. A paragraph about Fanny ends with "She passed right beneath Jacob's window." The next subsection is about Jacob's activities in his room:

> He filled his pipe; ruminated; moved two pawns; advanced the white knight; then ruminated with one finger upon the bishop. Now Fanny Elmer passed beneath his window. She was on her way . . . to Nick Bramham the painter.

The next section takes place at Nick's studio; then Jacob's activities are brought up to the moment in a paragraph which ends with his walking off towards Holborn. Finally, he arrives at the Empire, where he meets Fanny, who arrived first only because Jacob had stopped five minutes along his way to see the king drive by (pp. 113–116). In *Mrs. Dalloway* the characters from Clarissa's world and those from Septimus' world are linked in time, place, and activity in a similar but more complex manner by the motor car, the airplane, the child, the battered woman, the omnibus, and the ambulance, as well as by the striking of Big Ben. Thus, in *Jacob's Room* Virginia Woolf experimented on a small scale with the techniques which in *Mrs. Dalloway* play a major role in creating the "design" of the novel.

Moreover, in *Jacob's Room* she created a prose style which is "free, conversational, musical."[7] It is better suited to her vision of life than her manner of writing in *The Voyage Out* and *Night and Day.* As she wrote in her diary after she had finished this novel, "There's no doubt in my mind that I have found out how to begin (at 40) to say something in my own

Virginia Woolf's writing table at Monk's House in Rodmell

voice" (p. 47). By eliminating transitions and descriptions, she could now present the characters' sensations directly and record simultaneous thoughts and movements. Because of this and her increased use of rhythm and symbols (for example, the ram's skull, the crab),[8] we begin to find in this third novel the economy and intensity characteristic of poetic prose. Thus, *Jacob's Room* is not only a less "representational" novel than *The Voyage Out* and *Night and Day;* it is also more "poetic." In terms of her concept of opposite perspectives, namely, the representational novel in prose versus the nonrepresentational novel in poetic-prose, she has moved further from Daniel Defoe and closer to Emily Brontë.

During the years 1922–1925 comments in Virginia Woolf's diary reflect her growing interest in "poetic" intensity. She noted with pride that she had "almost too many ideas" to put into *Mrs. Dalloway:* "I want to give life and death, sanity and insanity; I want to criticize the social system, and show it at work, at its most intense" (AWD, p. 57). But while hoping to "pour everything in," she stressed the need for "art" and "design" (AWD, pp. 62, 69, 58, 61). Gaining in technical competence, she tried to visualize the aesthetic whole: "I want to think out *Mrs. Dalloway.* I want to foresee this book better than the others and get the utmost out of it. I expect I could have screwed *Jacob* up tighter, if I had foreseen; but I had to make my path as I went" (AWD, p. 54).

Virginia Woolf provided a tight structure for her fourth novel mainly by adhering to the classical unities of time, place, and action. *Mrs. Dalloway* occurs on a June day in 1923 in London. As in *Jacob's Room,* the author tried to capture the essence of a central character through a montage of diverse impressions. However, the unity of time and place limited the way by which excerpts from Clarissa Dalloway's past could be presented. Major shifts in time and place could only occur within the minds of the characters. There is unity of action in the sense that Mrs. Dalloway's activities on this hot June day are related to the preparations for her large party to be given that evening. At the party the thematic threads which run through the novel are tied together.

The feminine and masculine visions, represented in *Jacob's Room* by Mrs. Flanders and Jacob respectively, are represented more poignantly in *Mrs. Dalloway* by Clarissa Dalloway and Septimus Warren Smith. Symptoms of manic-depression are evident in the personalities of both Clarissa and Septimus but to different degrees: Septimus deviates much more than Clarissa from the central point of equilibrium. Although each shares to some extent the vision of the other, Clarissa's is predominantly feminine and manic, whereas Septimus' is predominantly masculine and depressive. In terms of Virginia Woolf's "ideas," "life" and "sanity" are associated with Clarissa, "death" and "insanity" are associated with Septimus. However, as we shall see, what being alive and sane mean is questioned; moreover, it is studied with respect to "the social system."

Like Mrs. Flanders, Clarissa Dalloway is "purely feminine." She has "that extraordinary gift, that woman's gift, of making a world of her own wherever she happened to be" (pp. 84–85). She too is consciously trying to shut out the "facts" of the masculine reality (such as, isolation, conflict, time, and death). Seeking a sense of oneness, she tries to create her own harmonious, unified worlds. These worlds help her to repress her terror of the void. Clarissa's old friend and admirer, Peter Walsh, sums up her attitude in this way:

> as the whole thing is a bad joke, let us, at any rate, do our part; mitigate the sufferings of our fellow-prisoners . . . ; decorate the dungeon with flowers and air-cushions; be as decent as we possibly can. Those ruffians, the Gods, shan't have it all their own way—her notion being that the Gods, who never lost a chance of hurting, thwarting and spoiling

human lives, were seriously put out if, all the same, you be-
haved like a lady. (Pp. 86–87)

Peter explains that Clarissa developed this "theory" "directly
after Sylvia's death—that horrible affair. To see your own sister killed by a falling tree (all Justin Parry's fault—all his
carelessness) before your very eyes, a girl too on the verge of
life, the most gifted of them, Clarissa always said, was enough
to turn one bitter" (p. 87). Later Clarissa became less sure
there were any "Gods" to blame and so evolved, in Peter's
words, an "atheist's religion of doing good for the sake of
goodness" (p. 87).

Clarissa creates worlds which enable her to play the role
that she wants to play. One of these is her orderly, smooth-
running household. As suggested by the passage below, she
wants a place where she can feel whole and pure again, safe
from the divisions and passions outside. She seeks therein a
sense of oneness similar to that experienced by the religious
mystic. Thus, for her the home functions as a kind of cloister.
After the sunlight outside, Clarissa must adjust her eyes to its
darkness:

> The hall of the house was cool as a vault. Mrs. Dalloway
> raised her hand to her eyes, and, as the maid shut the door
> to, and she heard the swish of Lucy's skirts, she felt like a
> nun who has left the world and feels fold round her the fa-
> miliar veils and the response to old devotions. The cook
> whistled in the kitchen. She heard the click of the type-
> writer. It was her life, and, bending her head over the hall
> table, she bowed beneath the influence, felt blessed and
> purified. (P. 33)

When she feels this sense of security, she is free to be what she
desires to be—"gentle, generous-hearted" (p. 44).

She is also able to be this way when playing the role of the "perfect hostess" at one of her large parties. The characterization of Clarissa Dalloway and Peter Walsh has its roots in that of Clara Durrant and Jacob Flanders in *Jacob's Room*. Both Clara and Clarissa are so busy being perfect hostesses that neither develops her relationship with the man she loves (Jacob, Peter). Moreover, both women seem to fear intimacy. Like Rachel Vinrace in *The Voyage Out*, Clara remains a virgin, and Clarissa rejects Peter's love in order to marry Richard, who allows her to sleep alone on a "narrow" bed in the attic. And, like Jacob, Peter rejects the class of society which regards Clara's and Clarissa's way of life as normal and desirable.

For Clarissa a successful party is like a smooth-running household in that both provide her with an experience which must be described as mystical. The mystical sense of oneness offered by the party cannot eliminate but can at least lessen the sense of isolation and lack of communication (masculine "facts") which Clarissa regards as intrinsic to human existence.

> Here was So-and-so in South Kensington; some one up in Bayswater; and somebody else, say, in Mayfair. And she felt quite continuously a sense of their existence; and she felt what a waste; and she felt what a pity; and she felt if only they could be brought together; so she did it. And it was an offering; to combine, to create; but to whom?
>
> An offering for the sake of offering, perhaps. Anyhow, it was her gift. (Pp. 134–135)

To create a sense of oneness, however illusory, the party must be composed with the same care as a work of art. Clarissa is profoundly annoyed when Mrs. Marsham forces her to invite Ellie Henderson, whom she had purposely omitted from her guest list: "Why should Mrs. Marsham interfere?" Richard could not understand why this upset her so much, "but Richard had no notion of the look of a room" (pp. 130, 132). Septimus is similarly anxious that Rezia, in stitching Mrs. Peters' hat, "be very, very careful, he said, to keep it just as he had made it" (p. 158). Whether or not Clarissa's vision of wholeness is realized, however, ultimately depends upon something indefinable which either does or does not come into being. Clarissa recognizes that it has come into being when she sees a guest, Ralph Lyon, go on talking while beating back a blowing curtain. The party was "something now, not nothing." It has a reality of its own, something more than the sum of its parts.

As part of this reality, she too is transformed:

> Every time she gave a party she had this feeling of being something not herself, and that everyone was unreal in one way; much more real in another. It was, she thought, partly their clothes, partly being taken out of their ordinary ways, partly the background; it was possible to say things you couldn't say anyhow else, things that needed an effort; possible to go much deeper. (Pp. 187–188)

Near the end of the party, for instance, Richard Dalloway manages to tell his daughter that he is proud of her: "he had not meant to tell her, but he could not help telling her" (p. 213). This contrasts with his behavior earlier in the day. He had wanted to tell Clarissa that he loved her but instead gave her flowers, because "he could not bring himself to say he loved her; not in so many words" (p. 130).

Ironically, however, Clarissa does not permit herself to enter into freer, "deeper" relationships with those at the party. It was not possible "for her; not yet anyhow" (p. 188), for her role is to keep the party going. Therefore, she must remain impersonal. For instance, she hasn't time to speak more than a few words to her old friends, Sally Seton (now Lady Rosseter) and Peter Walsh. Through her large, formal party she can partially overcome her loneliness and her terror of the ultimate isolation—death, without having to accept the risks of intimacy. Since she fears the threat which intimacy poses to the "privacy of the soul," such a situation provides her with the kind of impersonal, safe world which she prefers.

Although she creates only orderly households and parties, Clarissa Dalloway is, in her own way, an artist. Like Virginia Woolf, Clarissa uses her "gift" to create artistic substitutes for the secure childhood world that had been shattered by death. The death of a sister (Sylvia) permanently altered Clarissa's vision of life. As explained in Chapter II, Virginia Woolf felt that the death of her stepsister, Stella, had a similar effect upon her. Stella had been a mother to her since Julia Stephen's death two years earlier. When Stella died, Virginia experienced more fully than before what it meant to be motherless. Under the impact of her grief, her world seemed to split in two. Hence, as we have seen, she spoke of being stuck to both halves of her broken chrysalis.[9] The two poles which threatened from then on to tear her apart exist within the two main characters of *Mrs. Dalloway*. Both Clarissa and Septimus experience forms of mania and depression, but, as indicated earlier, Clarissa must be associated more with mania, Septimus with depression.

Significantly, Clarissa creates situations and maniclike states of mind which deny the reality that has driven Septimus insane. Like Virginia Woolf, she has mystical experiences that are related to a sense of the impersonal life. At times she sees herself as part of an underlying essence. Such experiences stand between her and the terror of the void, for they deny the "masculine" (or depressive) concept of death, that is, death as complete and permanent annihilation:

Did it matter then, she asked herself, walking towards Bond Street, did it matter that she must inevitably cease completely; all this must go on without her; did she resent it; or

did it not become consoling to believe that death ended absolutely? but that somehow in the streets of London, on the
ebb and flow of things, here, there, she survived, Peter survived, lived in each other, she being part, she was positive
of the trees at home; of the house there . . . ; part of people she had never met; being laid out like a mist between
the people she knew best, who lifted her on their branches
as she had seen the trees lift the mist, but it spread ever so
far, her life, herself. (Pp. 11–12)

And when she looks at the sky, she finds "something of her
own in it" (p. 204). This outlook permits her to think of death
as an "embrace," a way of "reaching the centre" (p. 202). She
can thus forget at least temporarily that it is, in fact, a horrify-
ing experience that must be faced alone. Similarly, her parties
(another kind of mystical experience) help her to forget the
loneliness provoked by the latter concept of death. When Septimus' suicide is announced at her party, she is upset: "Oh!
thought Clarissa, in the middle of my party, here's death, she
thought" (p. 201). Going off to be by herself, she again
thinks: "What business had the Bradshaws to talk of death at
her party? A young man had killed himself. And they talked
of it at her party—the Bradshaws talked of death" (p. 202).

Having experienced ecstasy (as Clarissa did with Sally, Septimus with Evans), one might welcome death as Othello did
upon being reunited with Desdemona: "If it were now to die, /
'Twere now to be most happy" (II.i.191–192). Clarissa
quotes this line first at Bourton during a moment of intense
love for Sally and again when, having heard of Septimus' suicide, she wonders whether he had plunged "holding his trea-
sure," that is, his sense of elation (pp. 39, 202–203). Virginia
Woolf was undoubtedly interested in this line from *Othello* because the sense of it changes between Act II and Act V. Othello's emotions move from one pole to the other, from elation
to depression. It is not joy but pain which makes him decide

not to kill Iago: "For, in my sense, 'tis happiness to die" (V.ii.290). It is also interesting to note that Septimus finds in Shakespeare justification for loathing both heterosexual relationships and humanity (pp. 98–99). Such feelings of repulsion are known to accompany depression; they make death seem desirable.

According to Dr. William Bradshaw, his patient Septimus Smith suffered from "the deferred effects of shell-shock" (p. 201). Just as Clarissa's behavior is explained mainly in terms of her reaction to the death of someone she loved, Septimus' behavior is explained in terms of his reaction to the death of his best friend, Evans. He and Evans had fought together during the war, but just before the Armistice Evans had been killed.

> Septimus, far from showing any emotion or recognising that here was the end of a friendship, congratulated himself upon feeling very little and very reasonably. The War had taught him. It was sublime. He had gone through the whole show, friendship, European War, death, had won promotion, was still under thirty and was bound to survive. He was right there. The last shells missed him. He watched them explode with indifference. When peace came he was in Milan, billeted in the house of an innkeeper with a courtyard, flowers in tubs, little tables in the open, daughters making hats, and to Lucrezia, the younger daughter, he became engaged one evening when the panic was on him— that he could not feel. (P. 96)

Helene Deutsch would have considered Septimus' "panic" justified, for she writes in her article, "Absence of Grief":

> The process of mourning as reaction to the real loss of a loved person *must be carried to completion*. As long as the early libidinal or aggressive attachments persist, the painful

affect continues to flourish [;] and vice versa, the attach-
ments are unresolved as long as the affective process of
mourning has not been accomplished.[10]

According to Deutsch and Freud, absence of grief may be
caused by a previously existing conflict with the person who
has died. The initial failure to experience grief may be due to
an unconscious wish for that person's death. Septimus' relationship with Evans had been that of "two dogs playing on a
hearth-rug" (p. 96). His probable guilt feelings concerning his
sexual attraction to Evans may well have made him glad to
have death end the relationship. His subsequent failure to experience grief may have made him feel semiresponsible for
Evans' death.[11] This seems to explain why, when depressed,
Septimus is haunted by a sense of guilt. He considers himself a
criminal who will be judged and punished:

> So there was no excuse; nothing whatever the matter, ex-
> cept the sin for which human nature had condemned him
> to death; that he did not feel. He had not cared when
> Evans was killed; that was worst; but all the other crimes
> raised their heads and shook their fingers and jeered and
> sneered over the rail of the bed . . . ; how he had married
> his wife without loving her; had lied to her; seduced her;
> outraged Miss Isabel Pole [an ex-girlfriend], and was so
> pocked and marked with vice that women shuddered when
> they saw him in the street. The verdict of human nature on
> such a wretch was death. (P. 101)

In short, the story of Septimus' immediate and subsequent reactions to Evans' death seem to be based upon Virginia
Woolf's immediate and subsequent reactions to her mother's
death, which were described in Chapter II.

Moreover, the symptoms of Septimus' illness are undoubtedly based to some extent upon the author's. In any case, his

symptoms resemble those of the manic-depressive, John Custance, referred to frequently in Chapter I. During mania Septimus feels, as Custance did, that he has an important message which must be reported to the Prime Minister (pp. 75, 162). In *Adventures into the Unconscious,* Custance tells how he actually went to 10 Downing Street to see the Prime Minister (p. 199). Septimus' "supreme secret" is "first, that trees are alive; next, there is no crime; next, love, universal love" and again, "Men must not cut down trees. There is a God. (He noted such revelations on the backs of envelopes.) Change the world. No one kills from hatred. Make it known (he wrote it down)" (pp. 75, 28). The manic experiences an ecstatic state of mind in which he denies sin, guilt, hatred, or loneliness, and he wants those in authority to make the real world like his own.

But Septimus' moments of ecstasy are less typical of his vision of life than his moments of terror. During depression both he and John Custance are terrorized by an abnormal awareness of shapes and patterns. When Custance looks at pillows, he sees the "shape" of Hecate; when he looks at cut wood, he sees devils "in serpent form." On the drawn blinds of a "motor car" Septimus sees "a curious pattern like a tree" and then a "gradual drawing together of everything to one centre before his eyes, as if some horror had come almost to the surface and was about to burst into flames" (p. 18). Just as Custance sees "devils by the hundreds in trees and bushes,"[12] Septimus sees trees come to life and feels "the leaves being connected by millions of fibres with his own body. . . . The sparrows fluttering, rising and falling in jagged fountains were part of the pattern; the white and blue, barred with black branches" (p. 26). Because Septimus Smith and John Custance feel an irrational sense of guilt, even the inanimate world threatens to punish them for their crime and drive them "mad." To resist lunacy, Septimus "would shut his eyes" and vow to "see no more" (p. 26).

Paradoxically, however, Septimus enjoys making his own design. The one time during the novel when he feels peaceful and happy is when, helping his wife, he creates "the design" for Mrs. Peters' hat (p. 158). Significantly, he derives the same satisfaction from his design that Clarissa does from her party. Artistic creation, at least in this instance, is part of the feminine, manic reality, for as Simon Lesser says, "Immersion in artistic form has the curious consequence of quieting anxiety and relieving feelings of guilt." Lesser claims that "our admiration of form is an indirect way of protesting our innocence of destructive impulses, our commitment to life and love. In all of its aspects form affirms its abhorrence of destruction."[13]

Thus, Clarissa's party is to her an affirmation of life and love and one that is very necessary for her if she is to remain "upright." The word "upright" is repeatedly associated with Clarissa. The way in which designing a hat restores Septimus' equilibrium clarifies for the reader the importance of Clarissa's party. As Josephine Schaefer says, "without the presence of Septimus, Clarissa's emotions might seem minor and trivial."[14] His presence serves to point out how slight the barrier is between stability and instability; for although Clarissa is believed to be "sane" and he "insane," their reactions to life are extremely similar. For instance, both feel guilty because of their inability to feel and give love; both wish to protect "the privacy of the soul" against those who would invade it. Clarissa understands what Septimus felt about Dr. William Bradshaw, for she had once been his patient: "He had been perfectly right; extremely sensible. But Heavens—what a relief to get out to the street again!" (p. 201). Finally, both Clarissa and Septimus love "life" but not human beings. Yet because Clarissa has not been subjected to the same pressures (the war and the threat of being committed to a rest home), she has remained "upright" whereas he has "plunged" to his death. Although she does not know Septimus, when she hears about him, she recognizes their kinship: "She felt somehow very like him—the young man who had killed himself" (p. 204).

By allowing the reader to enter the minds of most of the characters in *Mrs. Dalloway,* Virginia Woolf found that her work had become "more analytical and human . . . ; less lyrical" (AWD, p. 62). This, too, was her way of making this novel "more close to fact than *Jacob*" (AWD, p. 52). Because the unspoken thoughts are revealed in *Mrs. Dalloway,* we are no longer confronted with the obstacle of "silence" that Jacob put before us. Hence, the characters in the later novel do not seem "ghostly." Moreover, by imitating the process of thought,[15] Virginia Woolf brings us closer to "life itself." Whereas we *observe* Jacob, we learn how it feels *to be* Clarissa or Septimus.

We learn about Clarissa both through her thoughts and those of Septimus. But we also see her through the minds of Richard Dalloway, Peter Walsh (a rejected suitor), Miss Kilman, and others. Thus, Clarissa is seen from a multiple point of view. There are many contradictions among the views expressed: for instance, Clarissa lacks warmth (p. 36); yet, unlike Peter Walsh, she would not have passed Septimus and his wife in the park without trying to find out why they were unhappy (p. 87). Similarly, Sally blames the sterility of Clarissa's life upon her husband, Richard Dalloway; but then Peter tells us that Clarissa gives her parties not for Richard but "for her idea of him (to do Richard justice he would have been happier farming in Norfolk)" (p. 86). Through a montage of such impressions the author communicates her own ambivalent attitude toward Clarissa: although one must criticize Clarissa, for instance, for caring too much about class and rank, one must also admire her sensitivity and her "perfectly upright and stoical bearing" (p. 12).

Indeed, Clarissa's personality is complex. But Virginia Woolf's aesthetics call for both "life" (which is complex, form-

less, evanescent) and "order." The lifelike flow of thoughts
and impressions must, in fact, contribute to the overall design
of the novel; for it is the "design" which enables the reader in
a moment of vision to experience "the effect of the book as a
whole on his mind."[16]

At the end of the novel, after having isolated herself to reflect upon Septimus' suicide, Clarissa reappears. Her presence
is felt and announced by Peter Walsh:

> What is this terror? what is this ecstasy? he thought to him-
> self. What is it that fills me with extraordinary excitement?
> It is Clarissa, he said.
> For there she was.

Brilliantly, Virginia Woolf thus focuses our attention upon
what Clarissa "is." Theoretically at least, she forces us to see
in a flash the complex image of Clarissa which she has built
up in the course of the novel. The depth of our insight into
Clarissa's character is dependent upon our having grasped the
relationship between Clarissa and Septimus. Since Clarissa
and Septimus never meet, the design of the novel plays a
major role in establishing that relationship.

Just as Virginia Woolf alternated psychologically between
the two poles symbolized by Clarissa and Septimus, so too the
reader of *Mrs. Dalloway* moves alternately from her world
(which includes her family and friends) to his. The eight transitions are marked by something seen or something heard.

As we have seen, in her diary Virginia Woolf described her
"tunnelling process" as digging out beautiful caves behind her
characters: "The idea is that the caves shall connect and each
comes to daylight at the present moment." The eight sights
and sounds noted above—the car, plane, bus, and ambulance,
the child and the old woman, and the clock striking (twice)
—are devices which connect the "caves" of the two worlds
and bring the thoughts back to "the present moment." The

basic framework of the novel may be visualized thus: [17]

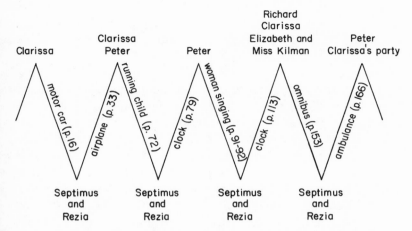

The striking of the clock is also used frequently to mark a shift from one character to the other within Clarissa's world. The exact time is noted at ten irregular intervals.[18] This emphasis upon clock-time serves both to guide the reader through the day and to stress the continual and irrevocable movement of all life towards death.

Time moves Septimus closer to his suicide just as it moves Clarissa closer to her party. In *The Abnormal Personality* Robert W. White says that manic-depressives often need a constant supply of love and moral support.[19] At the end of the novel Septimus feels that he has been deserted, that he will be separated from his wife. Clarissa, on the contrary, feels supported by her husband and friends. Hence, Septimus goes to his window and reluctantly flings himself "vigorously, violently down on to Mrs. Filmer's area railings" (p. 164); whereas Clarissa remains "upright": standing before her window, she sees the old lady opposite and then returns to her husband and old friends, Sally and Peter. Earlier Clarissa had "watched out of the window the old lady opposite climbing upstairs" (p. 139). As Septimus prepares himself to jump,

"Coming down the staircase opposite an old man stopped and stared at him" (p. 164). The use of the old lady and the old man and the repeated use of the words "upright" and "plunge" suggest the basic but precarious difference between Clarissa and Septimus.

Several other words and phrases (such as sun, sea, waves, fear no more) appear repeatedly in the interior monologues of both characters; the similarity in their thinking is thus given emphasis. But of more basic importance, structurally speaking, is the similarity between Lady Bruton's relationship to Clarissa and Dr. Bradshaw's relationship to Septimus. At three points in *Mrs. Dalloway* one or more characters arrive at the Dalloways' home, and each of these occasions marks a significant step in the development of the novel. The first step occurs when Clarissa returns home from her errands. Waiting for her is a message that Mr. Dalloway has departed to have lunch at Lady Bruton's. Clarissa's world is momentarily shattered by this announcement:

> "Fear no more," said Clarissa. Fear no more the heat o' the sun; for the shock of Lady Bruton asking Richard to lunch without her made the moment in which she had stood shiver, as a plant on the river-bed feels the shock of a passing oar and shivers: so she rocked; so she shivered. (P. 34)

Although Clarissa may feel no passion for Richard Dalloway, he is nevertheless a crutch for her without which she could not always stand. Lady Bruton's invitation suggests to Clarissa the possible withdrawal of that crutch and her increasing need for it as she ages. She becomes conscious of how "she feared time itself, and read on Lady Bruton's face, as if it had been a dial cut in impassive stone, the dwindling of life" (p. 34). Lady Bruton makes her feel "shrivelled, aged, breastless" (p. 35). Above all, she feels lonely and regrets that she has failed

Richard again and again. It was neither "beauty" nor "mind" that she lacked but "something central which permeated; something warm which broke up surfaces and rippled the cold contact of man and woman, or of women together" (p. 36). In fact, like Septimus, Clarissa feels attracted to persons of her own sex. Clarissa admits to herself that "she could not resist sometimes yielding to the charm of a woman":

> She did undoubtedly then feel what men felt. Only for a moment; but it was enough. It was a sudden revelation, a tinge like a blush which one tried to check and then, as it spread, one yielded to its expansion, and rushed to the farthest verge and there quivered and felt the world come closer, swollen with some astonishing significance, some pressure of rapture, which split its thin skin and gushed and poured with an extraordinary alleviation over the cracks and sores. . . . But the close withdrew; the hard softened. It was over—the moment. (P. 36)

Virginia Woolf goes on to describe Clarissa's attraction to Sally Seton (pp. 37–40). This explains why she does not seem to need Richard physically; however, emotionally she depends upon his support. Indeed it is he who saves Clarissa from suicide:

> there was the terror; the overwhelming incapacity, one's parents giving it into one's hands, this life, to be lived to the end, to be walked with serenely; there was in the depths of her an awful fear. Even now, quite often if Richard had not been there reading the *Times,* so that she could crouch like a bird and gradually revive, send roaring up that immeasurable delight, rubbing stick to stick, one thing with another, she must have perished. She had escaped. But that young man had killed himself. (P. 203)

Virginia Woolf purposely juxtaposes the accounts of Richard's visit to Lady Bruton and Septimus' visit to Dr. Bradshaw's office. Just as Lady Bruton feels free to separate Richard and Clarissa, Dr. Bradshaw feels free to separate Septimus and Rezia. The cure for Septimus' illness, Bradshaw says, is commitment to a rest home. This means "rest in bed; rest in solitude; silence and rest; rest without friends, without books, without messages; six months' rest . . ." (p. 110). Thus, Septimus regards Bradshaw as an enemy ("Once you fall, Septimus repeated to himself, human nature is on you"), and his wife, Rezia, feels that instead of receiving help, "they had been deserted" (pp. 108–109).

While Septimus and Rezia's world is still shattered, Richard, inspired by the news of Peter's return to London, restores Clarissa's world by buying flowers and making a special trip home in midafternoon to give them to her. He thereby reassures her of his love. Moreover, unlike Peter Walsh, who in his possessiveness demanded "impossible things" of Clarissa (p. 70), Richard offers his love to her without asking that she give up the "privacy" of her soul. Their relationship is similar to Ralph's and Katharine's in *Night and Day*. Unlike Peter, Richard is willing to accept Clarissa's concept of marriage:

> There is a dignity in people; a solitude; even between husband and wife a gulf; and that one must respect, thought Clarissa . . . ; for one would not part with it oneself, or take it, against his will, from one's husband, without losing one's independence, one's self-respect—something, after all, priceless. (P. 132)

Richard's return to the house marks a second important step in the development of the novel.

In the third part of *Mrs. Dalloway* Septimus panics when he suddenly realizes that Rezia is no longer in the room with him. His reaction to her departure parallels Clarissa's earlier reaction to Richard's departure:

> He started up in terror. What did he see? the plate of bananas on the sideboard. Nobody was there (Rezia had taken the child to its mother; it was bedtime). That was it: to be alone for ever. That was the doom pronounced in Milan when he came into the room and saw them cutting out buckram shapes with their scissors, to be alone forever. (Pp. 159–160)

Although he can feel no passion for Rezia, he needs her.

> But he remembered. Bradshaw said, "The people we are most fond of are not good for us when we are ill." Bradshaw said he must be taught to rest. Bradshaw said they must be separated.
>
> "Must," "must," why "must"? What power had Bradshaw over him? "What right has Bradshaw to say 'must' to me?" he demanded. (P. 162)

By imposing his will upon Septimus, he is interfering with the "privacy of his soul." Just as Richard Dalloway reassures Clarissa of his support against the forces (time, Peter Walsh) that would destroy her "self," Rezia reassures Septimus:

> Even if they took him, she said, she would go with him. They could not separate them against their wills, she said. . . . And, she said, nothing should separate them. . . . No one could separate them, she said. (P. 163)

When Holmes, Septimus' regular doctor, arrives that afternoon, Rezia tries to stop him from going up to see her husband; however, she is pushed aside by force. Since, like Bradshaw, Holmes "saw nothing clear, yet ruled, yet inflicted" (p. 163),

Septimus feels he has no choice but to fling himself out the window and thus preserve the "privacy of his soul." Having seen the ambulance that takes Septimus' body away, Peter arrives at Clarissa's house for the party.

Throughout Clarissa's party which makes up the fourth and final section of the novel, the reader is aware of Septimus' fate. When Clarissa hears of his death, she falters but then recovers her equilibrium. Her final appearance seems to confirm what Virginia Woolf claimed to feel in April of 1925: " 'It's life that matters' " (AWD, p. 72). This then is the final impression the reader has of Clarissa. But it conveys not only the victory but the struggle which that victory represents. The party itself also represents a victory, but, similarly, it is a victory which encompasses, rather than strikes out, the satirical statements directed against the individuals of which it is composed.

We see the party mainly through the critical eyes of Peter Walsh. Peter does not even feel awe for the most important guest at the party, the Prime Minister:

> One couldn't laugh at him. He looked so ordinary. You might have stood him behind a counter and bought biscuits —poor chap, all rigged up in gold lace. And to be fair, as he went his rounds, first with Clarissa, then with Richard escorting him, he did it very well. He tried to look somebody. It was amusing to watch. (P. 189)

The others in the room

> went on talking, yet it was perfectly plain that they all knew, felt to the marrow of their bones, this majesty passing; this symbol of what they all stood for, English society. Old Lady Bruton, and she looked very fine too, very stalwart in her lace, swam up, and they withdrew into a little room which at once became spied upon, guarded, and a

sort of stir and rustle rippled through every one openly: the
Prime Minister! (P. 189)

Similarly, others may feel respect and affection for Hugh Whitbread but not Peter. Hugh has a small job at court. Peter
sees him as "a privileged but secretive being, hoarding secrets
which he would die to defend, though it was only some little
piece of tittle-tattle dropped by a court footman which would
be in all the papers to-morrow" (pp. 189–190). Nor does Peter
respect the Bradshaws for their wealth and position. He an-
nounces to Sally that they are "damnable humbugs" (p. 212).
Peter perceives in this society a certain rigidity of manners
and values which means "the death of the soul" (pp. 65–66).
Thus, within the life of this party he perceives death.

Peter perceives a certain rigidity in Clarissa's personality
too; she cares too much about rank and at times is "hard, ar-
rogant, prudish" (p. 66). Yet within what one guest calls her
"damnable, difficult, upper-class refinement" (p. 193), there is a
spark of life. Unlike Peter, she usually looks for the good in
people, and she is kind even to dull guests like Lord Gayton
and Nancy Blow (pp. 194–195). Thus, Peter admires her for
"her courage," "her social instinct," and "her power of carrying things through." He is even obliged to admire the "perfect
manners" that enable her to be the "perfect hostess" (p. 69).
So secure is she in this role that she is able to represent the
force of life itself; for she has "that gift still; to be; to exist; to
sum it all up in the moment as she passed" (p. 191).

Clarissa has created a role for herself which largely satisfies
her own needs and society's demands. However, Peter is too
critical of this society to have accepted a role in it; therefore,
he has spent most of his adult life in India. Society (as represented by the Dalloways, Lady Bruton, and Hugh Whitbread)
considers Peter a failure (pp. 118–119). After Evans' death,
Septimus fails even more than Peter to behave in a way that is
socially acceptable. Because he doesn't have Clarissa's talent

for pretending that the masculine "facts" (like "human cruelty") do not exist, he cannot forget his war experience (p. 155). Nor can he ignore that

> brutality blared out on placards; men were trapped in mines; women burnt alive; and once a maimed file of lunatics being exercised or displayed for the diversion of the populace (who laughed aloud) ambled and nodded and grinned past him, in the Tottenham Court Road, each half apologetically, yet triumphantly, inflicting his hopeless woe. And would *he* go mad? (P. 100)

The appointed representative of the social system, Dr. Bradshaw, declares Septimus too sensitive; he lacks "a sense of proportion." Clarissa's "coldness" is preferable; it allows her to go on giving parties. "Life" and "sanity" are associated with Clarissa but even she recognizes that, because Septimus chose death, he is in a sense more alive and sane than she:

> A thing there was that mattered; a thing, wreathed about with chatter, defaced, obscured in her own life, let drop every day in corruption, lies, chatter. This he had preserved. (P. 202)

Virginia Woolf considered *Mrs. Dalloway* the "most satisfactory" of the novels she had written by 1925 and, indeed, it is (AWD, p. 69). Except for a few passages which succumb, as Reuben Brower has pointed out, to "metaphorical elaboration for its own sake,"[20] *Mrs. Dalloway* is truly an aesthetic whole. The reader's reaction to the book is marred, however, by his reaction to Clarissa. It is difficult to admire and like Clarissa as much as the author intended that he should. Virginia Woolf remarked in her diary, "One must dislike people in art without its mattering, unless indeed it is true that certain characters detract from the importance of what happens to them"

(p. 79). Unfortunately, Clarissa's character does, in my opinion, detract from the importance of what happens to her. Although she is not ghostly like Jacob, she is nevertheless somewhat inhuman in the sense that she is impersonal and cold. In Virginia Woolf's next novel, *To the Lighthouse* (1927), these same qualities are found in Lily Briscoe. However, the central feminine figure, Mrs. Ramsay, is, on the whole, lovable and warm. Our reaction to her influences our reaction to the novel. For this and other reasons, as we shall see, *To the Lighthouse* is a more successful work than *Mrs. Dalloway*.

CHAPTER V

To the Lighthouse and The Waves

In order to understand Virginia Woolf's vision of reality as well as her aesthetics, *To the Lighthouse* is of key importance. I have shown in Chapter I how the dual nature of the author's vision is related to two opposite approaches to truth, the masculine ("knowing in terms of apartness") and the feminine ("knowing in terms of togetherness"). We saw how Mr. Ramsay embodies the masculine approach, Mrs. Ramsay, the feminine; how he emphasizes the "shifting" (evanescence, time) and she, the "solid" (permanence, timelessness). In Chapter II, I pointed out the relationship between Lily Briscoe's role as artist and Virginia Woolf's aesthetics. We saw how Lily's painting symbolizes the androgynous work of art: in it an equilibrium is established between Mr. and Mrs. Ramsay, symbols of the evanescent and eternal aspects of reality.

Lily Briscoe is a "silent" painter in the same manner as Virginia Woolf's sister, Vanessa Bell. As I mentioned earlier, Virginia Woolf perceives in Vanessa's paintings the "shock of emotion" which the "visible world" gives her "every day of the week" and a deep, complex emotion expressed through relations of forms and colors.[1] Similarly, Lily's painting represents "the residue of her thirty-three years, the deposit of each day's living, mixed with something more secret than she had ever spoken or shown in the course of all those days" (p. 84). Lily studies the particular (Mrs. Ramsay and James at the window), but she delves beneath it to the impersonal and ab-

Virginia's sister Vanessa, who married British art critic Clive Bell. Virginia called Vanessa a "silent" painter.

stract. She believes a mother and child, who are "objects of universal veneration," may be "reduced . . . to a purple shadow without irreverence" (p. 85). In her painting she is primarily concerned not with "likeness" but with "the relations of masses, of lights and shadows" (pp. 84, 86). These formal relations represent the essence or symbolic value abstracted from the subject matter. Indeed, like most of Virginia Woolf's characters, Lily is more concerned with the inner than the outer aspect of reality. Yet the latter remains important, because the essence must be reached through the particulars.

So, too, in *To the Lighthouse* the particular and the general are interdependent. For instance, while convincingly lifelike, the main characters simultaneously function as part of the symbolic structure of the novel. Lily Briscoe is both an individual and an exponent of the author's aesthetics; indeed her painting is, as we shall see, an abstract equivalent of the novel itself. When she finally completes her painting, the novel is likewise completed.

The presence of a working artist gives *To the Lighthouse* a dimension not present in *Mrs. Dalloway*. In both novels Virginia Woolf dealt with her "double" vision of reality, but in the later work she also showed its relationship to her aesthetics. Thus, *To the Lighthouse* is richer in content than her previous novel.

It is also a greater technical achievement than *Mrs. Dalloway*, because the author succeeded in making it both more symbolic and more realistic. Only the party, a symbol of unity, plays as important a role in *Mrs. Dalloway* as do the dinner party, island, lighthouse, window, and painting in *To the Lighthouse*. Moreover, the symbolic use of land, sea, and drowning, present in *Mrs. Dalloway*, becomes even more dominant in *To the Lighthouse*, for the novel takes place by and on the sea. While writing *To the Lighthouse*, Virginia Woolf noted in her diary: "I am making more use of symbolism" (p. 101).

To the Lighthouse seems more "realistic" (that is, more life-like) than *Mrs. Dalloway* mainly because the two central characters, representing the masculine and feminine visions, are not merely juxtaposed like Septimus and Clarissa; instead, as husband and wife, they interact. Thus, while a relationship between Septimus and Clarissa can only be suggested, the Ramsays' relationship can be observed. Also, in *To the Lighthouse* Virginia Woolf does not have to invent sights and sounds by which two separate worlds are coincidentally joined. Transitions between the thoughts of different individuals or groups of characters in *To the Lighthouse* seem natural rather than coincidental, both because the characters interact and because they are physically closer together. In the novel as a whole the author abandons unity of time, but she tightens the unity of place. The action takes place in a much smaller area than London, namely, inside or near the Ramsays' summer home.

As indicated earlier, in all her novels Virginia Woolf wanted to give an impression of "tumult" and "pattern" or, in Lily Briscoe's terms, "chaos" and "shape." Thus, like Lily in her painting, she aimed in *To the Lighthouse* "to make of the moment something permanent." Both she and Lily wanted to make life itself "stand still" (pp. 249–250).

To suggest "life itself," which Lily refers to as the "passing and flowing," Virginia Woolf recorded her characters' stream of consciousness. Although the details were carefully selected, she preserved the seemingly aimless pattern of Mrs. Ramsay's thoughts, for example, as well as her contradictory judgments. She recorded Mrs. Ramsay's attitude toward Charles Tansley in this fashion:

he looked so desolate; yet she would feel relieved when he went; yet she would see that he was better treated tomorrow; yet he was admirable with her husband; yet his manners certainly wanted improving; yet she liked his laugh—
(p. 179)

Lily's attitude toward Mrs. Ramsay is similarly complex. Lily admires her, for she

> resolved everything into simplicity; made these angers, irritations fall off like old rags; she brought together this and that and then this, and so made out of that miserable silliness and spite (she [Lily] and Charles squabbling, sparring, had been silly and spiteful) something—this scene on the beach for example, this moment of friendship and liking—which survived, after all these years, complete, so that she dipped into it to re-fashion her memory of him, and it stayed in the mind almost like a work of art. (Pp. 248–249)

But while admiring Mrs. Ramsay as unifier (in a sense, she, too, is an artist), Lily objects to her way of pitying men (p. 132), of being "highhanded" (p. 79), and of insisting that "an unmarried woman has missed the best of life" (p. 80). Just as Virginia Woolf, in order to write, struggled against the limited way society would have her define herself as a woman, that is, as a devoted wife, mother, and hostess, so too Lily, in order to paint and to preserve her independence, struggles against Mrs. Ramsay's view of her as odd (p. 31). Although Lily recognizes Mrs. Ramsay's excellence in the traditional roles of wife, mother, and hostess, she also perceives and resists Mrs. Ramsay's belief that to be normal Lily must likewise excel in those roles and those roles only: Mrs. Ramsay insists that "she must, Minta must, they all must marry . . . but Mrs. Ramsay cared not a fig for her painting" (p. 80). Certainly, Mrs. Ramsay has sacrificed her own interests and ambitions in order to serve her family and friends. She would like to have been "an investigator, elucidating the social problem" (p. 20); she would like to have built a "model dairy and a hospital" on the island (p. 93); but when at the dinner table she speaks excitedly about "the iniquity of the English dairy system . . . her children laughed; her husband laughed; she was laughed at, fire-encircled, and forced to vail her crest, dismount her batteries" (p. 160). Moreover, Mr. Ramsay, watching her read, "exaggerated her ignorance, her simplicity, for he liked to think that she was not clever, not book-learned at all. He wondered if she understood what she was reading. Probably not, he thought. She was astonishingly beautiful" (p. 187). Not only does Mrs. Ramsay allow her own soul to be thus violated, but also she, in turn, violates other souls: she uses her beauty, both consciously and unconsciously, in order to manipulate those she serves (pp. 68–69). She can be charged with "wishing to dominate, wishing to interfere, making people do what she wished" (p. 92). Lily finds such behavior abhorrent. The self is too precious to be either sacrificed or manipulated. Thus, Lily will continue to resist the Charles Tansleys of the world when they insist that "women can't paint, women can't write" (pp. 78, 134, 246, 302); she will avoid the "degradation" of marriage (p. 159); and unlike Mrs. Ramsay, she will never want men to be "trustful, childlike, reverential" in their attitude toward her (p. 15). With both Charles Tansley and Mr. Ramsay, Lily tries to avoid playing the feminine role illustrated by Mrs. Ramsay's "insinuating" to Tansley "the greatness of man's intellect, even in its decay, the subjection of all wives . . . to their husband's labours." This insinuation makes Tansley "feel better pleased with himself than he had done yet, and he would have liked, had they taken a cab, for example, to have paid the fare" (pp. 22–23). Like Katharine Hilbery and Clarissa Dalloway, Lily seeks a new way of relating to men, one which will allow her to maintain her own dignity and individuality. At the same time she knows Mrs. Ramsay has something which she lacks: her life seems "so little, so virginal, against the other" (p. 81). Intolerant of her attitude, society has forced her to pay for the independence she has gained.

William Bankes, another guest of the Ramsays, similarly admires and criticizes Mr. Ramsay. Marriage has destroyed something in Mr. Ramsay; his "eccentricities, weaknesses" seem to have increased; he now depends so much "upon people's praise" (p. 40). Nor is his mind as good as it had been before he had married (p. 41). Both Lily and William prefer the life of the single person devoted to his work. Yet watching the Ramsays with their children sometimes makes them envious. On one occasion, for instance, William Bankes could not "clear himself in his own mind from the imputation of having dried and shrunk" (p. 38). In short, each character is seen in different ways at different moments, and, as in life, the resulting contradictions are not resolved. Thus, the evanescent, chaotic quality of life is preserved.

Yet, like Lily Briscoe, Virginia Woolf combined the "shifting" with the "solid." The "shape" of *To the Lighthouse* is more sharply defined than it is in *Mrs. Dalloway*. First of all, unlike *Mrs. Dalloway,* it is actually divided into three main parts: "The Window," "Time Passes," and "The Lighthouse." As already mentioned, the setting—the Ramsays' summer house on the Isle of Skye—is the same throughout (p. 17). The first section, "The Window," describes an afternoon and evening in mid-September, 1910, as lived by Mr. and Mrs. Ramsay, their eight children, and five guests. The third section, "The Lighthouse," describes a morning ten years later as lived by Mr. Ramsay, two of his children, and two of the same guests (the artist, Lily Briscoe, and a poet, Augustus Carmichael). In the short, middle section the reader learns, in retrospect as Mrs. NcNab and Mrs. Bast clean the Ramsays' long-empty summer home, what has happened during the intervening years. The overall time pattern is established by these three divisions.

Throughout, the progression of clock-time is paralleled with the characters' inner sense of time, which permits an intermingling of thoughts about the past, present, and future. However, there is a difference in tonal stress in each section.

In "The Window" the emphasis is upon the present, in "Time Passes" the emphasis is upon the future when the house will be reoccupied, and in "The Lighthouse" the emphasis is upon the past—the morning's activities are haunted by the memory of Mrs. Ramsay, whose death was announced in Part II. Because of repeated references in Part III to the beginning section of the book, a circular movement and a sense of wholeness is suggested by the novel's structure. Virginia Woolf made this comment about the book in her diary: "I feel as if it fetched its circle pretty completely this time" (p. 100). The time pattern is held together as a unit by the existence of the lighthouse, the slow realization of Lily's aesthetic vision, and the influence of Mrs. Ramsay.

In Part I of the novel Mrs. Ramsay is knitting a "reddish-brown stocking" which is to be taken to the son of the lighthouse keeper the next day. Her six-year-old son, James, is excitedly looking forward to the trip. But then Mr. Ramsay appears and unmercifully insists in front of James that the weather "won't be fine" tomorrow; therefore, they won't be able to go to the lighthouse. James's disappointment is so great that Mrs. Ramsay is sure that "he will remember that all his life" (p. 99). In "Time Passes" the reader is not permitted to forget the presence of the lighthouse, for its light continues to flash across the now-deserted rooms. In Part III Mr. Ramsay plans a trip to the lighthouse and forces his children, James and Cam, to accompany him. Disliking his domineering personality, the two teenagers vow "to resist tyranny to the death" (p. 252). However, as they progress across the green sea water (the color green and the sea image are both associated with Mrs. Ramsay and her talent for dissolving human differences), Cam's feminine senses are aroused and she begins to find her father "most lovable" and "wise" (p. 291). Even James begins to feel a kinship with his father—a kinship of loneliness. Finally, Mr. Ramsay changes, at least momentarily; instead of seeking sympathy from others, as he usually

does, he tries to make Cam happy and he remembers to praise
James. Their relationships having improved, they reach the
lighthouse.

In Virginia Woolf's novels the sea is at once consoling and
terrifying. Mrs. Ramsay usually regards it as consoling, for
she identifies it with an underlying unity; Mr. Ramsay usually
regards it as terrifying, for he associates it primarily with the
void. Both Mrs. and Mr. Ramsay are fascinated by the sea.

Mr. Ramsay's interest in fishermen, whose work forces
them to confront courageously the threat of being swallowed
by the sea, is set up in Part I, when he weeps over Steenie's
drowning in Scott's novel *The Antiquary* (p. 185). In Part III
Mr. Ramsay and the children go to the lighthouse in the sailboat of a fisherman named Macalister. Throughout Part III
Macalister is telling a story about eleven ships caught in a
storm; three sank, causing three men to drown (pp. 254, 315).
A storm at sea and a drowning are also the subject of the lines
from "The Castaway" which Mr. Ramsay quotes periodically
during the voyage to the lighthouse. Implicit in all of this is
not only Mr. Ramsay's concern with the void but also the
grief he feels on his wife's death. At the end, however, he succeeds somewhat in coming to terms with death: when Macalister mentions that their sailboat has arrived at the spot where
the three men were drowned, James and Cam expect their father to burst out again with the line, "But I beneath a rougher
sea"; instead he simply says " 'Ah' as if he thought to himself,
But why make a fuss about that? Naturally men are drowned
in a storm, but it is a perfectly straightforward affair, and the
depths of the sea . . . are only water after all" (p. 316). In a
sense, like Lily, he finds a certain equilibrium between the
masculine and feminine visions. The expression of his vision is
basically masculine, however, just as the expression of Lily's
vision, like that of Mrs. Ramsay, is basically feminine: that is,
he utilizes facts, she essences.

Like Mr. Ramsay, Cam and James move towards an androgynous vision. Both children had heretofore accepted their mother's vision and rejected their father's. In "The Window," for instance, James had sided with his mother against his father's certainty that rain would make the next day's trip to the lighthouse impossible (pp. 12–13), and Cam had willingly been persuaded by Mrs. Ramsay that a sheep's skull (symbolizing death, a "masculine" fact) could be transformed by a shawl into "a mountain, a bird's nest, a garden" (p. 177). In the course of the voyage, however, both adopt for the first time a sympathetic attitude towards their father. Responding to him as a female, Cam is the first to identify with Mr. Ramsay's point of view. Her vision of the island on which they live echoes his vision of it in Part I. There we read:

> he thought, looking at the land dwindling away, the little island seemed pathetically small, half swallowed up in the sea.
> "Poor little place," he murmured with a sigh. (P. 110)

and in Part III:

> It was like that then, the island, thought Cam, once more drawing her fingers through the waves. She had never seen it from out at sea before. It lay like that on the sea, did it, with a dent in the middle and two sharp crags, and the sea swept in there, and spread away for miles and miles on either side of the island. It was very small; shaped something like a leaf stood on end. (P. 289)

Cam's use of the leaf image to describe the island recalls Lily's use of "leaves shaking" as an example of the "eternal passing and flowing" (p. 249). Whereas Lily uses the leaves to symbolize evanescence, she regards the tree as symbolizing "stability": the line she draws in the center of her painting represents a tree (p. 228). The tree and leaf images are also prominent in lines quoted by Mr. and Mrs. Ramsay; "And all the lives we ever lived and all the lives to be / Are full of trees and changing leaves" (pp. 171, 183).

Cam's vision of the evanescent quality of life as symbolized by the leaf-shaped island is further emphasized by the way in which this leaf seems gradually to be swallowed up by the sea (Mr. Ramsay's symbol for the void). As their sailboat moves further over the sea, Cam becomes increasingly conscious of the void:

> She gazed back over the sea, at the island. But the leaf was losing its sharpness. It was very small; it was very distant. The sea was more important now than the shore. Waves were all round them, tossing and sinking . . . About here, she thought, dabbling her fingers in the water, a ship had sunk, and she murmured, dreamily, half asleep, how we perished, each alone. (P. 293)

Further on during the voyage,

> She gazed at the immense expanse of the sea. The island had grown so small that it scarcely looked like a leaf any longer. It looked like the top of a rock which some big wave would cover. (P. 313)

When they are about to land at the lighthouse, Cam notices her father "looking back at the island." She wonders whether "with his long-sighted eyes perhaps he could see the dwindled leaf-like shape standing on end on a plate of gold quite clearly." But, perhaps because she is near-sighted like her mother, "It was all a blur to her" (p. 317).

Although they have arrived, Mr. Ramsay still

> sat and looked at the island and he might be thinking, We perished, each alone, or he might be thinking I have

reached it [the lighthouse]. I have found it, but he said nothing. (P. 318)

While Mr. Ramsay is looking back towards the island where Lily is trying to finish the painting of his wife, Lily looks at the almost invisible lighthouse and says, "He must have reached it" (p. 318). As earlier in Part III, when she answers Mr. Ramsay's need for feminine sympathy by praising his boots, she accepts once more the female role formerly ascribed to Mrs. Ramsay:

the effort of thinking of him landing there, which both seemed to be one and the same effort, had stretched her body and mind to the utmost. Ah, but she was relieved. Whatever she had wanted to give him, when he left her that morning, she had given him at last. (Pp. 318–319)

This symbolic union of male and female recalls the two most important scenes between Mr. and Mrs. Ramsay in Part I (pp. 61–64, 188–191); indeed, to complete her painting, Lily has to experience this union. When Lily declares "It is finished," she is referring to both the trip to the lighthouse and her vision. Lily's remark, "It is finished," contrasts with Mrs. Ramsay's remark in reference to the "reddish-brown stocking" at the end of Part I: "I shan't finish it" (pp. 319, 189).

As I pointed out in Chapter II, the line which Lily proceeds to make on her painting is the lighthouse as well as the tree, both androgynous symbols. The androgynous quality of the lighthouse is made clear when James has his vision. When he sees that the lighthouse is not only that which his mother saw ("a silvery, misty-looking tower with a yellow eye that opened suddenly and softly in the evening") but that which his father saw ("the tower, stark and straight"), he lessens his hostility for his father by becoming conscious of the reasons for it. He recalls little by little two incidents which occurred in "The Window": his father saying they couldn't go to the lighthouse and his father taking away his mother's attention and leaving him "impotent, ridiculous, sitting on the floor grasping a pair of scissors" (pp. 261, 286–287). James is not ready to give love and sympathy to his father, however, until Mr. Ramsay praises him for steering "like a born sailor" (p. 316). To receive praise from his father represents a victory for James, for it signifies that he is no longer "impotent" or "ridiculous." Indeed, whereas he lost the battle with his father for his mother's attention ten years earlier, he has just won the battle with his father for Cam's sympathy. He had feared Cam would desert him as his mother had but then noticed that "Cam dabbled her fingers in the water and stared at the shore and said nothing. No, she won't give way, he thought; she's different, he thought" (p. 261). As Josephine Schaefer says in *The Threefold Nature of Reality*, James, in coercing Cam to submit to him, has "beaten his father at his own game, and in doing so he has laid the ghost of his old hatred" (p. 133).

Thus, in the final section of the novel Mr. Ramsay's vision of the sea, Cam's vision of the island, Lily's vision of Mrs. Ramsay, and James' vision of the lighthouse, all become androgynous or complete. A fusion occurs in their views of "reality" as well as in their personal relationships. Paradoxically, it is the threat of the void (their consciousness of "how we perish, each alone") that makes each forget himself and extend sympathy towards the others. Both literally and symbolically, the trip to the lighthouse is a success, because the characters have unconsciously adopted Mrs. Ramsay's philosophy: in light of the senselessness and suffering inherent in the human condition and therefore common to us all, we must try to create individual happiness and group harmony as often as possible. They succeed in identifying with her point of view just as Mrs. Dalloway identified with and therefore understood Septimus'. Significantly, at this final moment of harmony, vision, and identification, Augustus Carmichael reminds Lily of Neptune: "Mr. Carmichael stood beside her, looking like an old pagan God, shaggy, with weeds in his hair and the trident (it was only a French novel) in his hand" (p. 319). As a poet, he is, like Lily and Mrs. Ramsay, a unifier.

Parts I and III are similar in that each treats in detail a short period of time, whereas the linking section covers in an abbreviated form a long period. Moreover, the central events in Parts I and III (the dinner party, the trip to the lighthouse) involve situations in which a sense of oneness is achieved by a group of disparate individuals. Likewise, as Lily is painting in Part III, she slips into the "waters of annihilation" (a state of impersonality) just as Mrs. Ramsay does while sitting alone in Part I (pp. 278, 100). For Lily, like Mrs. Ramsay, "the world seemed to dissolve into a pool of thought, a deep basin of reality" (p. 275). Also, scenes from "The Window" are re-called by James and Lily in Part III; and, of course, in "The Lighthouse" Lily completes her painting of the scene which dominates Part I—that of Mrs. Ramsay and James framed by the window. Indeed, the characters' thoughts, for the most part, continue in the third section to focus upon Mrs. Ramsay much as they did in the first; this is true also in the linking section, but the characters whose thoughts we follow there are not the same as in parts I and III. Finally, the trip and the painting provide the focus for much of the thinking in "The Window" and "The Lighthouse"; yet they play no role in "Time Passes."

However, "Time Passes" is an important part of the overall rhythm and theme of the novel. Its very existence at once un-dermines and enhances the semimystical experiences of one-ness (products of the "feminine" vision) which dominate the first section of the book. For in "Time Passes" Mr. Ramsay's view of life comes to the fore. In it the emphasis falls on time not timelessness, death not life, flux not permanence; suddenly there is separateness not unity, chaos not order, facts not vi-sions. The unused house has deteriorated; the garden has grown wild; war has broken out; and the deaths of Mrs. Ramsay and two Ramsay children, Prue and Andrew, are announced. In Part I Mrs. Ramsay's belief that human beings should establish and preserve harmony despite the facts is sanctioned while Mr. Ramsay's insistence upon facts is ridiculed. But Part II shows that the "facts" cannot be ignored for long: eventually even a visionary like Mrs. Ramsay and the dreams she had for her children are affected by them. By showing that the masculine approach to truth is valid, just as the feminine is valid, the way is prepared for the balancing of the two in the final section of the novel.

Virginia Woolf regarded *To the Lighthouse* as the end towards which she had.been moving in *Jacob's Room* and *Mrs. Dalloway* (AWD, p. 99). In it she was perfecting her "method" (AWD, p. 102); her vision of life and the novel was on the whole the same as in *Mrs. Dalloway*. Perhaps because of this and because she knew the subject matter well (since it is basically autobiographical), she was able to write in her diary on February 23, 1926: "after that battle *Jacob's Room,* that agony—all agony but the end—*Mrs. Dalloway,* I am now writing as fast and freely as I have written in the whole of my life; more so—20 times more so—than any novel yet" (p. 85). Writing her next novel was not easy, however, for both her personal and aesthetic vision had changed: on March 28, 1930, she spoke of *The Waves* as "the most complex and difficult of all my books" (AWD, p. 156).

In *A Room of One's Own* Virginia Woolf revealed the shift in emphasis which accounts for the difference between *To the Lighthouse* (1927) and *The Waves* (1931). She claimed that to write well one must recognize "that there is no arm to cling to, but that we go alone and that our relation is to the world of reality and not only to the world of men and women." Whereas in *To the Lighthouse* we see human beings primarily "in their relation to each other," in *The Waves* the emphasis falls upon human beings "in relation to reality" (AROO, pp. 171–172). What Virginia Woolf meant by "reality" is symbolized by the sea: it is both the all-absorbing one and the inescapable void.

The *Waves,* then, is a novel of "silence" in a much deeper sense of the word than her other two stream-of-consciousness novels, *Mrs. Dalloway* and *To the Lighthouse.* The "outer life" infringes even less than before upon Virginia Woolf's primary subject matter—that which is "eternal," "the spirit we live by, life itself." For instance, there is no dialogue and no injection of the author's comments or descriptions. Virginia Woolf seems to have prepared herself to work on *The Waves* by writing her fantasy-biography *Orlando.* For in *Orlando,* she mocks by comical exaggeration what she minimizes in *The Waves*—for instance, the physical description of characters and their activities. Whereas Orlando is described in great detail ("the down on the lips was only a little thicker than the down on the cheeks"), we are not asked to consider the appearance of the six main personages in *The Waves.* Furthermore, Orlando's adventurous life contrasts with the uneventful lives of Bernard, Louis, Neville, Susan, Jinny, and Rhoda. It is as if in writing *Orlando* ("a Defoe narrative for fun") Virginia Woolf relieved her mind of and laughed out of existence the externalities she wished to exclude from *The Waves* ("my first work in my own style") (AWD, pp. 105, 176). In *The Waves,* the lives of the six main characters are suggested entirely through their interior monologues. Moreover, the poetic and symbolic nature of their soliloquies enables the author to transfer our attention from the inner life to what she called the "common life" (AROO, p. 171), that is, the essence of all inner lives. As Jean Guiguet notes in *Virginia Woolf and Her Works:* "*The Waves* is less an expression of the inner life than an attempt to formulate Being" (p. 378).

Indeed, as noted in Chapter II, *The Waves* is a verbalization of a mystical vision which Virginia Woolf had as she was finish-

Virginia Woolf in 1928, the year she published *Orlando,* a fantasy-biography inspired by her belief in androgyny.

ing *To the Lighthouse*. Writing in her diary, Virginia Woolf referred to *The Waves* as "that fin in the waste of water which appeared to me over the marshes out of my window at Rodmell" (p. 169). The fin represents a feeling or intuition about reality which cannot be described but rather must be, in Virginia Woolf's words, "suggested and brought slowly by repeated images before us until it stays, in all its complexity, complete" (CE IV, 2). It is this mystical awareness of reality or being that Virginia Woolf tried to evoke through the lives of the six "characters" in *The Waves*.

Bernard, the most interesting of the six characters, is an aspiring writer who all his life has diligently accumulated phrases in a notebook in the hope that someday he will be able to provide "a meaning for all [his] observations—a line that runs from one to another, a summing up that completes" (p. 83). Like Virginia Woolf's friend, Desmond MacCarthy, Bernard, stimulated by society, begins many stories, but, unable to carry on in solitude, fails to finish them.[2] Unable to find "the true story, the one story to which all [his] phrases refer," he begins to tire of stories and neat designs of life on half-sheets of paper: "I begin to long for some little language such as lovers use, broken words, inarticulate words, like the shuffling of feet on the pavement. I begin to seek some design more in accordance with those moments of humiliation and triumph that come now and then undeniably" (pp. 133, 169). What Bernard experiences is comparable to what T. S. Eliot expresses in these lines from "Little Gidding": "For last year's words belong to last year's language / And next year's words await another voice." As he grows older, he becomes more and more often a disinterested observer of life. He does not aspire to capture, as Virginia Woolf did in *To the Lighthouse,* what life is like to a few individuals, but the very nature of human existence as epitomized by his own life. However, he finds it difficult to give "the effect of the whole" (p. 182). The whole must include himself as distinct from the others, himself as an embodiment of the people and places that made up his life, himself as defined both by his many selves and the selves he might have been but wasn't.

This is the vision, but can he transform it into a work of art? His psychological response to the challenge passes through three stages, which must be understood in terms of the sea-wave image central to both the form and meaning of the book. The rhythm of his states of mind parallels the rhythm of the waves: despair (the crash), renewal of strength (the calm), desire for confrontation (the re-formation). The despair is often caused by a sense of the void; the renewal of strength, by a sense of oneness, the desire for confrontation, by the sense of a rebirth. His experience, therefore, is archetypal: sometimes he falls into despair (life is a "dust dance"; all is "mutable, vain," p. 202; life is disgusting, disorderly, p. 208; phrases are useless, false; "I have done with phrases," p. 209); sometimes he experiences a renewal of strength (my being is "immeasurably receptive, holding everything, trembling with fullness, yet clear, contained. . . . It lies deep, tideless, immune," p. 206); and sometimes he courageously prepares himself for the inevitable confrontation ("there is a gradual coming together, running into one, acceleration and unification. . . . I regain the sense of the complexity and the reality and the struggle," p. 208; "in me too the wave rises. It swells; it arches its back. I am aware once more of a new desire, something rising beneath me like the proud horse whose rider first spurs and then pulls him back," p. 211). Until the end of the novel, the confrontation is with the machinery of life, which demands that human beings act and commit themselves in order to survive. Just when Bernard's grasp of life might have enabled him to write the unwritten novel, he is confronted not by life but by death. What he leaves undone, however, Virginia Woolf accomplished; *The Waves* is the book Bernard might have written. Indeed, Bernard functions very much as Lily Briscoe does in *To the Lighthouse:* he clarifies the aesthetics of the novel in which he appears.

Bernard is reminiscent of the despairing author (who is spoken of but never seen) in Luigi Pirandello's play *Six Characters in Search of an Author* (1921). This author refuses to struggle further to press his six characters into the frame of the conventional drama. His six created characters are too alive; they refuse to have various aspects of their personality suppressed in order to fit properly into the whole. As is true of Bernard, his vision of reality has outgrown the known forms and techniques. Bernard wonders, for example: "But why impose my arbitrary design? Why stress this and shape that and twist up little figures like the toys men sell in trays in the street? Why select this, out of all that—one detail?" (p. 134). Pirandello's author, like Bernard, failed to create new methods for representing reality as he saw it. Virginia Woolf and Luigi Pirandello gave a fictional embodiment to their own struggle; and while spelling out for their audience the precise nature of their problem, they simultaneously resolved it.

Furthermore, like Pirandello, Virginia Woolf was obsessed with the question of identity. She would have sympathized with the father in Pirandello's play who refuses to be summed up as the man he was at a particular moment, involved in a particular relationship (with his stepdaughter in Madame Lapace's shop): what one is at one moment often contradicts what one is at another. Virginia Woolf's sensitivity to the complex, ambiguous, contradictory nature of man was similar to the Cubist's concept of the total reality of an object or set of objects. Like the Cubist painter, she wanted to increase the number of possible perspectives and thus, in that sense, make her characters more lifelike. Bernard, for instance, is a composite of what he seems not only to himself but also to his five friends and not just at one particular moment but at many moments throughout his life. We have seen the origin of this way of portraying character in both *Mrs. Dalloway* and *To the Lighthouse.*

Virginia Woolf's portrayal of character undoubtedly origi-nated with her own intuitions and observations regarding the human personality; however, this approach was probably rein-forced by her contact with Cubist ideas and paintings. She certainly must have gone to Roger Fry's "Second Post-Impres-sionist Exhibit," held at the Grafton Galleries from October 5 to December 31, 1912, since her husband, whom she married in August of 1912, was the secretary for it. In Werner Haft-mann's description of the 1912 show in *Painting in the Twen-tieth Century,* he indicates the extent to which Cubism was represented: "Fauvism and Cubism were the centres of attrac-tion. The two leading masters—Matisse and Picasso—were amply and significantly represented."[3] In addition, she un-doubtedly heard some of the heated discussions evoked by the exhibit; in her essay "Roger Fry" she recalled that Picasso was among the painters "hotly debated" at that time (CE IV, 88).

Another aspect of Virginia Woolf's approach to character (seen also in the relationship between Mr. and Mrs. Ramsay) is summed up in *Six Characters in Search of an Author.* Within the play, the manager is speaking to his leading man about his role in a play by Pirandello: "You stand for reason, your wife is instinct. It's a mixing up of the parts, according to which you who act your own part become a puppet of yourself."[4] In order to depict a human personality in all its ambiguity and complexity, Virginia Woolf used several characters. Each be-comes somewhat more like a puppet than a human being, be-cause each, while remaining credible as an individual, symbol-izes one aspect of that personality. Seen in this way, the six characters in *The Waves* are, without contradiction, both many (that is, concrete, individual) and one (the whole, which is necessarily an abstraction).

Therefore, *The Waves* is at once a group biography and both Bernard's and Virginia Woolf's autobiography. It is a group biography in that it simultaneously traces in excerpt form the lives of Bernard, Neville, and Louis, Rhoda, Jinny, and Susan. It is Bernard's autobiography in the sense that, as a writer, the "moments" which he is trying to record and sum up are those which are recorded in the first eight sections of the book and summed up by Bernard in the ninth. His experiences from childhood through middle age are necessarily interlaced with those of his close friends; therefore, his autobiography necessarily envelops the group biography. In another sense, however, Bernard the creative writer may be viewed abstractly as a representation of one element—the most important one—in Virginia Woolf's own personality. In 1929 when *The Waves* was still little more than an "angular shape" in her mind, she commented in her diary: "Autobiography it might be called" (AWD, pp. 142–143). Jean Guiguet specifically identifies Virginia Woolf with her six protagonists:

> She is in love with words, like Bernard: in love with books, like Neville: a lover of action, like Louis: like Susan feminine, earthy, nature-loving: like Jinny sensual and sociable; like Rhoda hypersensitive and solitary—must one anticipate and say that like Rhoda she was to kill herself? She is all this, and now one aspect, now another predominates.[5]

However, in a still deeper sense, the six protagonists represent not just aspects of Virginia Woolf's personality but aspects of the human personality. C. B. Cox, in his book *The Free Spirit* describes the six aspects as follows: "the imaginative impulse [Bernard], the desire to impose order upon material things [Louis], delight in personal relationships [Neville], pleasure of the body [Jinny], joy in motherhood [Susan], and the life of solitude [Rhoda]."[6] This interpretation of *The Waves* clarifies Virginia Woolf's remark on October 5, 1931, about a review of the book: "Odd, that they (*The Times*) should praise my characters when I meant to have none" (AWD, p. 175). Indeed, her aim in this, the least representational of her novels, was to capture what she referred to in *A Room of One's Own* as "the common life which is the real life and not . . . the little separate lives which we live as individuals" (p. 171).

Virginia Woolf's original vision of *The Waves,* a "fin in the waste of waters," develops into a series of "fins" or waves; hence, the "spatial form" of the novel may be envisioned as a series of "angular" shapes (AWD, pp. 169, 142). So, too, Bernard describes his original vision of his *magnum opus* in these terms:

> Leaning over this parapet I see far out a waste of water. A fin turns. This bare visual impression is unattached to any line of reason, it springs up as one might see the fin of a porpoise on the horizon. Visual impressions often communicate thus briefly statements that we shall in time to come uncover and coax into words. (P. 134)

Bernard has difficulties, however, in seizing that fin, for sometimes it is not there: "Nothing, nothing, nothing broke with its fin that leaden waste of waters" (p. 174) and again: "No fin breaks the waste of this immeasurable sea" (p. 201); and sometimes it appears ("a fin rose in the wastes of silence") only to disappear ("the fin, the thought, sinks back into the depths") (p. 194). But finally, although somewhat late, he too evokes from his unconscious his vision of the "common life" as symbolized by the angular shapes of the waves: "Yes, this is the eternal renewal, the incessant rise and fall and fall and rise again" (pp. 210–211).

When Virginia Woolf spoke of *Anon* (the book she planned to write after *Between the Acts*), the "fin" became a "mountain top": "I think of taking my mountain top—that persistent vision—as a starting point."[7] "Anon" is derived from the Anglo-Saxon *on an* meaning "in one" or "together"; it is also, of course, the abbreviation for anonymous. I suspect that, like the crest of the wave, the top of the mountain (her "starting point") represents what T. S. Eliot called "The point of intersection of the timeless / With time."

The rhythm of the waves permeates both Bernard's vision of the continuity of life and the thought-processes of the six characters in their soliloquies. This undulating movement is particularly obvious in section nine, for there in contrast to the first eight sections, in which the soliloquies of one personality are interwoven with those of several others, we follow only Bernard's stream of consciousness. However, throughout the novel Bernard especially and to some extent the others (Louis, Neville, Jinny, Susan, and Rhoda) alternate between moments characterized by integration, order, and inner satisfaction (reached at the crest of the wave) and moments characterized by disintegration, chaos, and dissatisfaction (the crash from illusion to reality as one hits the surface of the sea). Here is an example from Bernard's experience:

I, who had been thinking myself so vast, a temple, a church, a whole universe, unconfined and capable of being verywhere . . . am now nothing but what you see—an elderly man, rather heavy, grey above the ears, who (I see myself in the glass) leans one elbow on the table, and holds in his left hand a glass of old brandy. That is the blow you have dealt me. I have walked bang into the pillar-box. I reel from side to side. I put my hands to my head. My hat is off—I have dropped my stick. I have made an awful ass of myself and am justly laughed at by any passer-by.

Lord, how unutterably disgusting life is! What dirty tricks it plays us, one moment free; the next, this. Here we are among the breadcrumbs and the stained napkins again. That knife is already congealing with grease. Disorder, sordidity and corruption surround us. We have been taking into our mouths the bodies of dead birds. It is with these greasy crumbs, slobbered over napkins, and little corpses that we have to build. Always it begins again; always there is the enemy; eyes meeting ours; fingers twitching ours; the effort waiting. Call the waiter. Pay the bill. We must pull ourselves up out of our chairs. We must find our coats. We must go. Must, must, must—detestable word. Once more, I who had thought myself immune, who had said, "Now I am rid of all that," find that the wave has tumbled me over, head over heels, scattering my possessions, leaving me to collect, to assemble, to heap together, summon my forces, rise and confront the enemy. (Pp. 207–208)

The rhythm of the waves permeates the novel in still another sense. An intricate network of similarities and differences among the characters exists; however, the overall movement is between integration (into a group personality through a mystical experience of oneness) and disintegration (into separate identities). Normally, each character is extremely aware of how different or separate he or she is from the others. Rhoda notes, for instance,

I have no face. Other people have faces; Susan and Jinny have faces; they are here. Their world is the real world. The things they lift are heavy. They say Yes, they say No; whereas I shift and change and am seen through in a second. (Pp. 30–31)

Or Louis thinks upon seeing the five others:

We differ, it may be too profoundly . . . for explanation. But let us attempt it. I smoothed my hair when I came in, hoping to look like the rest of you. But I cannot, for I am not single and entire as you are. I have lived a thousand lives already. (P. 91)

This sense of being unique and alien to others is usually disturbing; for instance, Louis notes, "They laugh at my neat-

ness, at my Australian accent" (p. 14), and in Neville's presence Bernard feels like "an untidy, an impulsive human being
whose bandanna handkerchief is for ever stained with the
grease of crumpets" (p. 60). Sometimes, however, solitude
permits them to escape the burden of their uniqueness. When
Neville leaves Bernard alone in a room, Bernard comments:

> He is gone; I stand here, holding his poem. Between us is
> this line. But now, how comfortable, how reassuring to feel
> that alien presence removed, that scrutiny darkened and
> hooded over! How grateful to draw the blinds, and admit
> no other presence . . . For I am more selves than Neville
> thinks. We are not simple as our friends would have us to
> meet their needs. (Pp. 64–65)

It is a sense of oneness, however, not solitude, which actually eliminates the characters' consciousness of their separate identities. There are three major scenes in the novel, all
of which take place in restaurants. Symbolically speaking, in
each scene the separate waves merge again with the sea. In the
first two a reunion, both physical and spiritual, of the six actually occurs; in the third, the reunions occur only within Bernard's memory.

Living together as children, in the beginning of the book
the six have not yet suffered the pain of separation; their personalities are individualized, but they share a common existence. Bernard says later: "We suffered terribly as we became
separate bodies" (p. 171). As adolescents, the group is divided
according to sex, for they go away to school. Each of the
groups splits again when as young adults Neville and Bernard
go to the university while Louis works in an office and Rhoda
and Jinny participate in London social life while Susan returns to the country. The six are first reunited at a farewell
dinner for Percival, a friend who is spoken of but never
speaks in the novel. Louis compares Percival's "magnificence"
to "that of some mediaeval commander" (p. 26). Indeed, his

physical prowess and spiritual leadership suggest his kinship with the knight Percival, who figures in Malory's *Morte d'Arthur* (especially Books 13–17) and Tennyson's idyll, "The Holy Grail." Percival's lack of self-consciousness makes him irresistibly attractive to the others. They refer to him as a leader, a hero, and a god (pp. 109, 88, 97). Percival is a "god" just as Mrs. Ramsay is a goddess, and he, too, is a unifier. His attitude creates an atmosphere which draws each of the other six from a conscious to an unconscious state of mind. They then can experience unity and harmony. When he enters the restaurant, Neville thinks, "My heart rises. . . . The reign of chaos is over. He has imposed order. Knives cut again." Bernard observes that under his influence,

> we who have been separated by our youth (the oldest is not yet twenty-five), who have sung like eager birds each his own song and tapped with the remorseless and savage egotism of the young our own snail-shell till it cracked . . . now come nearer; and shuffling closer on our perch in this restaurant where everybody's interests are at variance, and the incessant passage of traffic chafes us with distractions, and the door opening . . . solicits us with myriad temptations . . . sitting together here we love each other and believe in our own endurance. (P. 88)

Louis and Neville are similarly sensitive to the reintegration of the group:

> "Now let us issue from the darkness of solitude," said Louis.
> "Now let us say, brutally and directly, what is in our minds," said Neville. "Our isolation, our preparation, is over. The furtive days of secrecy and hiding, the revelations on staircases, moments of terror and ecstasy." (Pp. 88–89)

They have come together "to make one thing, not enduring —for what endures?—but seen by many eyes simultaneously. There is a red carnation in that vase. A single flower as we sat here waiting, but now a seven-sided flower, many-petalled, red, puce, purple-shaded, stiff with silver-tinted leaves—a whole flower to which every eye brings its own contribution" (p. 91).

Like Mrs. Ramsay, Percival has made of the moment a work of art which they will always remember. Reluctant to abandon the sense of wholeness, Jinny thinks, "Let us hold it for one moment . . . this globe whose walls are made of Percival, of youth and beauty, and something so deep sunk within us that we shall perhaps never make this moment out of one man again" (p. 104). Under the spell of "the swelling and splendid moment created by us from Percival," Bernard feels,

> We have proved, sitting eating, sitting talking, that we can add to the treasury of moments. We are not slaves bound to suffer incessantly unrecorded petty blows on our bent backs. We are not sheep either, following a master. We are creators. We too have made something that will join the innumerable congregations of past time. We too, as we put on our hats and push open the door, stride not into chaos, but into a world that our own force can subjugate and make part of the illumined and everlasting road. (Pp. 104–105)

Enriched by their moment of harmony, they experience a rebirth, a renewed sense of energy.

But the crash of the wave is inevitable. Percival "galloped in India" but only until "his horse tripped" and "he was thrown" (pp. 211, 107). Reacting to Percival's untimely and senseless death, Neville says, "The sails of the world have swung round and caught me on the head. . . . From this moment I am solitary" (pp. 107–108). "I need silence, and to be alone," says Bernard; "I am alone in a hostile world," says

Rhoda (pp. 109, 113). They no longer experience oneness but loneliness; their vision of life is no longer feminine but masculine. The wholeness which they felt in the presence of their god (Percival) is shattered by his death. Momentarily, at least, his death has made the threat of the void a reality.

Thereafter, the more each develops his individual personality and finds satisfaction in his or her own way (for instance, through sex or motherhood or business), the more divided the group is. But as the six protagonists reach middle-age, they begin to question the choices they have made. At this point, therefore, a spiritual reunion again becomes possible. They come together to dine at Hampton Court. Bernard chooses Hampton Court as the site, because he recalls that once Percival had asked him to go there and he had refused (p. 113). As Josephine Schaefer points out, "Now, years later, through the power of memory he and the others bring Percival there. Like the trip in *To the Lighthouse,* this banquet becomes a kind of fulfillment."[8]

The spirit of Percival reigns over the banquet just as the spirit of Mrs. Ramsay reigns over Part III of *To the Lighthouse.* As if compelled by Percival, the six again attain a state of unconsciousness and oneness. As Aileen Pippett writes in her biography of Virginia Woolf, Percival represents the "ideal figure, the Whole Man, the Ordinary Man made perfect, the all-containing, incomprehensible Norm, the great Unifier, the Beloved, made safe by death from time's corruption."[9] All that he could have been remains intact, sealed by his premature death; he remains whole, silent, godlike. He is like the legendary Sir Percivale "Whom Arthur and his knighthood call'd The Pure."[10] As the dinner at Hampton Court progresses, the six "characters" gradually experience again the unity which he represents. Bernard notes:

> We have dined well. The fish, the veal cutlets, the wine have blunted the sharp tooth of egotism. Anxiety is at rest. The

vainest of us, Louis perhaps, does not care what people think. Neville's tortures are at rest. Let others prosper— that is what he thinks. Susan hears the breathing of all her children safe asleep. Sleep, sleep, she murmurs. Rhoda has rocked her ships to shore. Whether they have foundered, whether they have anchored, she cares no longer. (P. 159)

Implicit in this is the appeal of death as a symbol of eternal rest and absolute silence. Little by little, however, they are called back into life:

"we are extinct, lost in the abysses of time, in the darkness."

"Silence falls; silence falls," said Bernard. "But now listen; tick, tick; hoot, hoot; the world has hailed us back to it. I heard for one moment the howling winds of darkness as we passed beyond life. Then tick, tick (the clock); then hoot, hoot (the cars). We are landed; we are on shore; we are sitting, six of us, at a table. It is the memory of my nose that recalls me. I rise; 'Fight,' I cry, 'fight!' remembering the shape of my own nose, and strike with this spoon upon this table pugnaciously."

"Oppose ourselves to this illimitable chaos," said Neville, "this formless imbecility. Making love to a nursemaid behind a tree, that soldier is more admirable than all the stars." (P. 160)

Again, however, they cling to the moment, knowing, as Rhoda reminds us, "how short a time silence lasts" (p. 160). Again "the red carnation that stood in the vase on the table of the restaurant when [they] dined together with Percival, is become a six-sided flower; made of six lives."

"A mysterious illumination," said Louis . . .

"Built up with much pain, many strokes," said Jinny.

. . . said Bernard ". . . a many-sided substance cut out
of this dark; a many-faceted flower. Let us stop for a moment; let us behold what we have made. . . . One life.
There. It is over. Gone out." (P. 162)

Once more they begin to hear the "Knock, knock, knock.
Must, must, must. Must go, must sleep, must wake, must get up
—sober, merciful word which we pretend to revile, which we
press tight to our hearts, without which we should be undone"
(p. 166). They must arouse themselves from passivity to activity; they must reassume the burden of responsibilities and
appointments. This time, however, being older, Bernard
notices a change in his outlook which leads him to wonder:
"Was this, then, this streaming away mixed with Susan, Jinny,
Neville, Rhoda, Louis, a sort of death? A new assembly of
elements? Some hint of what was to come?" (p. 198). Nor
is he sure now whether he is "man or woman, Bernard or Neville, Louis, Susan, Jinny, or Rhoda—so strange is the contact of one with another" (p. 199). Indeed, he no longer knows
whether he is "all of them" or "one and distinct" (p. 205). Involved in his attitude is a preparation for death, for the moment when he will become one not just with "all of them" but
with the all. Once more, however, the wave "swells" within
him, and despite this preparation he declares defiantly that
"Death is the enemy. . . . Against you I will fling myself, unvanquished and unyielding, O Death!" (p. 211).

The wave image controls the structure of the book in yet
another way: it exists not just as a rhythm inherent in human
thought and human existence but also as an inescapable moving force which marks time as relentlessly in *The Waves* as Big
Ben does in *Mrs. Dalloway*. The interludes which precede
each of the nine soliloquy-sections of *The Waves* abruptly
bring us out of the world of unspoken thoughts up to the
physical, external world visibly subject to the changes
wrought by time. The interludes depict "the majestic march of

day across the sky" (p. 193). Nothing the characters think or imagine can stop this march of time over their lives. They can fight against it, but they cannot win. The interludes serve to remind us that a lifetime is brief (like a solar day) and, consequently, rather insignificant when seen in perspective. Thus, each time we come to an interlude, we are forced to readjust our angle of vision. We feel somewhat as Bernard did one day sitting with Neville in his room:

> Yes, but suddenly one hears a clock tick. We who had been immersed in this world became aware of another. It is painful. It was Neville who changed our time. He, who had been thinking with the unlimited time of the mind, which stretches in a flash from Shakespeare to ourselves, poked the fire and began to live by that other clock which marks the approach of a particular person. The wide and dignified sweep of his mind contracted. He became on the alert. (P. 194)

We too become aware of the particular details of a representational reality. We note the changes which have taken place during our absence. The light falls differently upon the sea and upon the land; the birds sing in a different way; and once more we hear the waves upon the shore. They fall again and again "like the thud of a great beast stamping" (p. 107). Finally, the sun sinks and darkness covers everything like "waves of water" (p. 168). Despite Bernard's valiant battle against death, as the novel ends, again "the waves broke on the shore" (p. 211). As A. D. Moody says in *Virginia Woolf,* the wave image expresses "the relations of the transient individual to the continuing force of life. It [has] the advantage of suggesting the successive and continuous nature of life, as well as the way in which the individual being forms within, is carried upon, and finally merges back into its elemental source."[11]

While differing in form (direct description rather than interior monologues), each interlude is closely linked in its images (for instance, the handling of the birds) and in its general concept (changes wrought by the advancement of time), to the content of the soliloquies it precedes. Also, we discover in the soliloquies echoes of phrases read in the interludes (pp. 207–210). Such devices help to make the novel an organic whole. Unity is also established through the relationship of both the interludes and soliloquies to the wave image. As Winifred Holtby points out, the sea functions differently in *The Waves* than it does in Virginia Woolf's earlier novels:

> That sea over which Rachel Vinrace sailed to Santa Marina, over which Tim Durrant and Jacob sailed to Cornwall, over which Cam and James and Mr. Ramsay sailed to the lighthouse, has now overflowed from its geographical significance. It has passed into time; it has passed into the swing and surge of Mrs. Woolf's deliberate prose; it has passed into the hearts and minds of men and women, until the characters themselves are tossed upon its restless waters, carried by the tide which is time to meet the final challenge of death. From cover to cover the novel is saturated in the sea.[12]

The novel is further unified by the abnormal density and intensity of emotion, of symbolic meaning, and of stylistic expression in both the interludes and the soliloquies. Because the author's aim was to write "an abstract mystical eyeless book: a playpoem," not a representational novel, the entire book is written in the same compressed, poetic style, as if all six characters, even as children, had Virginia Woolf's command of the English language (AWD, p. 137). With a simple sentence her characters have the power to penetrate to the core of a personality; for example, Bernard says of Louis, "His heroes wore bowler-hats and talked about selling pianos for tenners" (p. 179). Jinny wraps up the experience of having lost the sex-

ual appeal of one's youth, "I shall look into faces, and I shall
see them seek some other face" (p. 138). Although gifted with
the same power of expression, the characters are differentiated
by what they observe either about nature or about themselves
and each other. They each grow and change somewhat, but
when old, as Dorothy Brewster points out, "they still have
within them the children they once were."[13] For instance, as
a child Jinny kisses Louis on the nape of the neck; Susan is
jealous; Bernard comforts her and is inspired to write a poem;
Neville sees Bernard's decision to leave to follow Susan as a
breach in their relationship; and Louis and Rhoda feel themselves to be lonely outsiders. *The Waves,* therefore, is made
into an organic whole not only by the wave image but also by
the sameness of texture (its intensity, its density), substance
(well-defined youth-to-age pattern), and tone (due to the uni-
formity of the prose style) as well as by the consistency and
integrity which characterize the portraits of the six speakers.
Also, in the last of the three restaurant scenes, Bernard looks
back upon his life and in so doing sums up the content of the
novel, thereby helping us to see the whole.

Another unifying device used by the author is the repetition
and variation of certain themes, images, and phrases. The
themes include the question of individual identity, the pressure
upon an individual created by the presence of other people,
the quest for the consolations of order and meaning, and the
constant threat of cruelty and annihilation. Images like the
globe, the "swing-door," the virginal white wax, the opening
door, and the willow tree, lend continuity to the development
of these and other themes. Variations of certain phrases like
"the door opens and the tiger leaps," "I heard songs by the
Nile and the chained beast stamping," "the swallow dipped
her wings in dark pools," "the drip falls," "to gather flowers
and present them—oh, to whom?" and "the immitigable tree"
expand in meaning as they are recalled and reapplied in vary-
ing circumstances. This rhythmic echoing of significant

themes, images, and phrases helps to establish the form of the novel.

The form of the whole is seen to be infinitely complex when one adds to what has already been mentioned the network of relationships among the six characters. Similarities and differences are set up between them even in their initial observations:

> "I see a ring," said Bernard, "hanging above me. It quivers and hangs in a loop of light."
>
> "I see a slab of pale yellow," said Susan, "spreading away until it meets a purple stripe."
>
> "I hear a sound," said Rhoda, "Cheep, chirp; cheep, chirp; going up and down."
>
> "I see a globe," said Neville, "hanging down in a drop against the enormous flanks of some hill."
>
> "I see a crimson tassel," said Jinny, "twisted with gold threads."
>
> "I hear something stamping," said Louis, "a great beast's foot is chained. It stamps, and stamps, and stamps." (P. 6)

As Josephine Schaefer points out,

> Bernard and Neville see a round shape; one is interested in the movement and luminosity of this shape, the other in its proportions and relation to something else. Susan and Jinny see colors; Susan's are gentle and soft, Jinny's are intense. Rhoda and Louis experience life differently, from a more removed angle. Before opening their eyes in the morning, they listen to the awakening world. Rhoda hears a tiny bird sound; Louis hears a great beast stamp. Throughout the novel the children's conceptions of life grow along the lines laid down in these early responses to life.[14]

The way in which the characters are paired here is further reinforced by the facts that Bernard and Neville are the most intellectual, although one is untidy in his habits and the other neat; Susan and Jinny are the most animal in their desires, although one seeks the quiet security of family and land while the other seeks the excitement of the city and innumerable lovers; Rhoda and Louis are linked by their loneliness and timidity although one wanders in her dreams to a spatial infinity beyond time whereas the other wanders in time and feels he has lived thousands of years; one seeks privacy and annihilation while the other seeks community and a secure place in the existing world. But the subject easily shifts and the characters pair off differently. Louis and Neville both love neatness and order, but one imposes it through business upon the contemporary world while the other seeks to discover it through his scholarship about the past. Ironically, it is Louis who loves the past in terms of tradition and Neville, the scholar, who hates it. Louis and Neville are also alike in having clear, strong intellects, in their desire to write poetry, in their desire to be loved, and in their uncertainty about how to make themselves appealing. Neville and Susan are similar in their strong desire for one person, and they contrast with Bernard and Jinny, who need the stimulation of many people to be happy. In contrast to all four, Rhoda prefers solitude. Yet Bernard and Susan are alike in their desire for children, and as artist and mother, both are creators. Neville and Jinny share an interest in the existentialist enjoyment of the moment at hand, and they are alike in being primarily interested in sex; Neville, however, is attracted to his own sex, Jinny to the opposite sex. For her part, Rhoda quotes Shelley, whom Virginia Woolf described in *A Room of One's Own* as "sexless." Rhoda and Neville are linked, because each is "in love" with Percival. Rhoda and Susan are both unhappy at school but Rhoda because she is rootless, Susan because she is rooted elsewhere. As homemaker and businessman, respectively, Susan and Louis choose the ways of life most conventionally acceptable according to one's sex, whereas in their ways of life, Jinny and Neville "embody the two enemies of traditional society: individualism and promiscuity."[15] Bernard has an interesting relationship with Susan, for she, of the three girls, is the only one who becomes "wholly woman, purely feminine" (p. 175). Thus, "she was born to be the adored of poets, since poets require safety; someone who sits sewing, who says, 'I hate, I love,' who is neither comfortable nor prosperous, but has some quality in accordance with the high but unemphatic beauty of pure style which those who create poetry so particularly admire" (p. 176). But his relationship with Rhoda is perhaps the most interesting, for Bernard and Rhoda represent the life-death duality inherent in Virginia Woolf's vision of life.

Rhoda is unable to accept the conditions and limitations imposed upon human beings by the physical nature of their existence. She is irritated by the consequent self-centeredness which emphasizes differences and, out of jealousy or indifference, withholds sympathy due to others. She has so little self-confidence that she fails to create an identity of her own. "I have no face," she says (pp. 93, 158); moreover, she refuses to have a face because "the human face is hideous" (p. 113). Neville says, "She has no body as the others have" (p. 16). She refuses the separation from others imposed by physical being ("I hate all details of the individual life," p. 76), and she wants no part of the compromise and imperfection which characterize physical love. She leaves Louis, because she fears embraces (p. 146). She prefers to love Percival who is absent, and she is able to give her complete love to him only after he is dead (p. 117).

Rhoda in her dreams has visions of a white shape. In life she discovers such purity only once as she listens to music. Listening, she sees the "thing"—a square placed "accurately" upon an oblong, leaving "very little" outside. Discovering aesthetic purity so created by man ("This is our triumph; this is our consolation," p. 116), she is reconciled momentarily with life and, immersing herself in it, discovers she is no longer "injured" or "outraged" by contact with it. But the purity of annihilation, of nothingness, is still more tempting, for the creation or perception of aesthetic purity is the exception rather than the rule in life. Therefore, she again turns against it.

> "Oh, life, how I have dreaded you," said Rhoda, "oh, human beings, how I have hated you! How you have nudged, how you have interrupted, how hideous you have looked in Oxford Street, how squalid sitting opposite each other staring in the Tube! . . . I have been stained by you and corrupted. You smelt so unpleasant too. . . . What dissolution of the soul you demanded in order to get through one day, what lies, bowings, scrapings, fluency and servility! How you chained me to one spot, one hour, one chair, and sat yourselves down opposite! How you snatched from me the white spaces that lie between hour and hour and rolled them into dirty pellets and tossed them into the wastepaper basket with your greasy paws. Yet those were my life." (P. 145)

Previously, she had yielded to life and remained on the fringe of nothingness, but now she refuses even this compromise. Like Septimus Smith, she chooses death.

Rhoda wishes "to spread in wider and wider circles of understanding that may at last . . . embrace the entire world." Having to "go through the antics of the individual" prevents her from grasping the "circumference" of life, the vast bubble which can "be cast off and escape from the here and now" (pp. 158–159). Bernard would also like "to indulge impossible desires to embrace the whole world with the arms of understanding—the impossible to those who act." Whereas she wants to sacrifice herself, to be consumed in the sea of nothingness, he wishes to absorb, to consume all of life into his being. She closes herself off from life; he opens himself to all impressions and sensations. He too experiences moments of peace and happiness in the "sunless territory of non-identity":

"Am I not, as I walk, trembling with strange oscillations and vibrations of sympathy, which, unmoored as I am from a private being, bid me embrace these engrossed flocks; these starers and trippers; these errand-boys and furtive and fugitive girls who, ignoring their doom, look in at shop-windows?" (pp. 82–83). Yet, despite such moments, he is not satisfied with only the circumference of life; he also seeks the core of life, "a meaning for all my observations," and he knows that the core can be reached, if at all, only by an active study of the particulars. Therefore, replenished by his solitude and passive absorption of life, he chooses to rise again on the wave to mix again with his surroundings:

> Oh, to . . . be active! Anybody will do. . . . The crossing sweeper will do; the postman; the waiter in this French restaurant . . . Images breed instantly. I am embarrassed by my own fertility. I could describe every chair, table, luncher here copiously, freely. My mind hums hither and thither with its veil of words for everything. To speak, about wine even to the waiter, is to bring about an explosion. Up goes the rocket. Its golden grain falls, fertilising, upon the rich soil of my imagination. The entirely unexpected nature of this explosion—that is the joy of intercourse. I, mixed with an unknown Italian waiter—what am I? There is no stability in this world. Who is to say what meaning there is in anything? Who is to foretell the flight of a word? It is a balloon that sails over tree-tops. To speak of knowledge is futile. All is experiment and adventure. We are for ever mixing ourselves with unknown quantities. What is to come? I know not. (P. 84)

Mixing with life teaches him again that there seems to be no one meaning for all his observations. But the pursuit itself is exciting and rewarding.

Paralleling Rhoda's experience with music after Percival's death is Bernard's experience with paintings in the National

Gallery. Percival was a hero, because, being "naturally truthful," he saw everything in its proper relationship to the whole; nothing was exaggerated beyond its importance, hence his stability and calm, his mastery of "the art of living" (p. 111). Bernard recognizes that he fails to perceive the overall pattern, because he takes an exaggerated interest in one thing after another. Beneath the gardens and madonnas in the paintings, for instance, one must find something nonrepresentational, "unvisual"—the significant form or pattern created by the lines and colors themselves. To see this, one must have, like Percival, "indifference one might almost say . . . save that he had also compassion" (p. 111). Aesthetic detachment, of which Rhoda was capable, is insufficient alone; the artist must begin with keen and sympathetic sensitivity towards his subject matter—life. Bernard looks at paintings as if Roger Fry (or perhaps Clive Bell) had taught him how to do so. In "Roger Fry" Virginia Woolf claims that Fry did "more than anyone" to make people "enjoy looking at pictures." She adds that that, at least, was her experience (CE IV, 88). Indeed, Bernard's experience in the National Gallery expands his consciousness of Percival and helps him master the art of life. He gains a certain control and perspective upon life; he is no longer willing to vacillate weakly from one thing to another; moreover, he finally realizes that it is the rhythm of life and of prose which matters, not the story or the isolated phrase.

Thus, he increases his understanding of what he discovered at the farewell dinner for Percival: "We are not slaves. . . . We are not sheep. . . . We are creators" (p. 104). As A. D. Moody says in *Virginia Woolf,* death "is made acceptable by virtue of the creative will which raises a human continuity and civilisation above the brute process of nature" (p. 61). The value is not in the individual accomplishment, which too is subject to the life-death process, but in the continuity of man's creative will. We are not "raindrops, soon dried by the wind" because "we come up differently, for ever and ever" (p. 82). This is the form which lies beneath life's complexity; it is the unity amidst the multiplicity which, having supplemented his sensitivity with Percival's detached sense of the whole, Bernard seizes in his vision of "the eternal renewal" just before he dies.

Despite Bernard's affirmation of life, which at the end wins out over Rhoda's point of view, the overall vision of human existence in *The Waves* is that of Mr., not Mrs., Ramsay. The threat of the void, the sense of isolation are almost always there; the moments of oneness are rare. Also, the final passage of the novel, in which Bernard rises to defy death, is reminiscent of the lines from Tennyson's poem, "The Charge of the Light Brigade," quoted by Mr. Ramsay in *To the Lighthouse*.[16] Like the attack of the Light Brigade and Percival's final charge, Bernard's assault on death is courageous but useless: "It is death against whom I ride with my spear couched and my hair flying back like a young man's, like Percival's, when he galloped in India. I strike spurs into my horse. Against you I will fling myself, unvanquished and unyielding, O Death!" (p. 211). Indeed, this final passage provides the moment of vision which illuminates the rest of the novel. It emphasizes the absurd nature of man's existence: like the wave, he rises only to fall. His continuous efforts, like those of Sisyphus, are admirable; but seen from a detached point of view, they are ridiculous.

Yet, however absurd their efforts, Percival and Bernard still prefer, like the Light Brigade, "to do and die." Virginia Woolf contrasts this Western attitude to that of the Oriental, who is less inclined "to do." Bernard's word choice reflects the values of his colonialist society when he imagines this scene in India:

The cart sways *incompetently* from side to side. Now one wheel sticks in the rut, and at once *innumerable natives* in loin-cloths *swarm* round it, *chattering* excitedly. But they do nothing. Time seems endless, ambition vain. Over all broods a sense of the uselessness of human exertion. [Italics mine]

But Percival comes along, and "by applying the standards of the West, by using the violent language that is natural to him, the bullock-cart is righted in less than five minutes. The oriental problem is solved. He rides on" (p. 97). Ironically, however, what he rides toward is his death.

The fact that Bernard never translates his vision into a work of art seems indicative of Virginia Woolf's increasingly pessimistic view of life. In her first novel Terence Hewet wants to write a "novel of silence," and there is hope that someday he will. In *To the Lighthouse* Lily Briscoe has her vision and completes her painting. In *The Waves* Bernard is so overwhelmed by the meaningless, chaotic nature of life that his vision of the whole comes too late in his life for him to transform it into a work of art. His vision of the "fin," his dislike of stories, his interest in the moment, his search for an adequate "design," all suggest a strong similarity between his attitudes and problems and those of Virginia Woolf. The fact that he has more difficulty than Lily did in achieving the kind of equilibrium which will enable him to function successfully as an artist suggests that, at least psychologically if not aesthetically, Virginia Woolf was likewise finding it more and more difficult to balance the "shifting" with the "solid." Bernard's words could have been hers when he says that others seemed to have found "something that stood them in stead."

> Thus I visited each of my friends in turn, trying, with fumbling fingers, to prise open their locked caskets. I went from one to the other holding my sorrow—no, not my sorrow but the incomprehensible nature of this our life—for their inspection. Some people go to priests; others to poetry; I to my friends, I to my own heart, I to seek among phrases and fragments something unbroken— (P. 189)

Her despair of being able to find "something unbroken" is still more evident, as we shall see, in her last two novels.

CHAPTER VI

The Years and *Between the Acts*

In *A Room of One's Own* Virginia Woolf speaks of the male and female "powers" that "preside" in the soul: "in the man's brain the man predominates over the woman, and in the woman's brain the woman predominates over the man. The normal and comfortable state of being [exists] . . . when the two live in harmony together, spiritually co-operating." When the male and female powers are fused (as in the androgynous mind), then "the mind is fully fertilised and uses all its faculties" (pp. 147–148). Virginia Woolf's male and female "powers" are traditionally designated as the male and female principles, what the Chinese refer to as yang (male) and yin (female). As Linda Thurston points out in an excellent article, "On Male and Female Principle," "Male and Female, as cosmic principles, should not be confused to mean men or women." These terms provide us with a useful metaphor based upon the reproductive process; unfortunately, the terms seem confusing to us at first because "what our society has been doing is defining the total person by [his or her] reproductive process when we are, in fact, much more than this function." Indeed, whereas in biology "neither Male nor Female is productive by itself,"[1] likewise, each human being must embody both the male and the female powers. The androgynous mind utilizes rational (like Mr. Ramsay, A to Z) as well as intuitive (like Mrs. Ramsay, straight to Z) faculties; it strives not only to dissect but to connect. In terms of Virginia

Woolf's aesthetic, the androgynous mind perceives both the multiplicity and the underlying unity.

In *The Years* and *Three Guineas,* we witness the expansion of this concept to apply not just to souls but to societies. In societies as in individuals the active must be balanced with the contemplative, the productive with the receptive, the competitive with the co-operative. Virginia Woolf realized that she lived in a patriarchal society and saw that in a male-dominated society not only are the women oppressed but also that which is considered female is suppressed. The male rulers repress the female or yin within themselves and, in turn, create social and political structures which likewise exclude or minimize the feminine, for instance, the contemplative, the receptive, the co-operative. As Thurston explains,

> Male processes are those which, like an ejaculation, come from a single powerful source and move in multiple directions. . . . Male social processes are characterized by a one way flow (of power, knowledge, whatever) from a single source (an individual or elite group) to people who are isolated and divided from each other.
>
> Female processes are those which, like the womb, provide a nourishing environment for growth. There are no distinctions among the people.[2]

Unchecked, the male social structure is authoritarian, as in fascist or military organizations. Unchecked, the female social structure is chaotic and unable to function. A balance between the two must be found. In a society as in an individual, when either the male or the female "power" dominates the other, the dominating power becomes destructive rather than creative.

In *The Years* (1937), as in Part II of *To the Lighthouse,* the masculine "facts" have come to the fore. The disruptive masculine power has taken over, and the feminine power, which might re-establish harmony, is simply absent. There is not even the memory of a unifying figure (like Mrs. Ramsay or Percival) to restore a sense of oneness. As Bernard Blackstone says, *The Years* depicts a world in which "coherence" has "vanished,"[3] Although some hope is expressed in *The Years* that man will change so that the future will be different, these occasional professions of faith are undermined by the overall tone of the novel.

On November 2, 1932, Virginia Woolf described her concept of *The Years* in her diary: "It's to be an Essay-Novel called *The Pargiters*—and it's to take in everything, sex, education, life etc.: and come, with the most powerful and agile leaps, like a chamois, across precipices from 1880 to here and now" (AWD, p. 189). The novel may be divided into two parts, the first consisting of ten chapters, the second consisting of a long section entitled "Present Day." The ten chapters present excerpts from the lives of two families, Colonel Abel Pargiter's and Sir Digby Pargiter's, in selected years from 1880 through 1918. Those who are children in Part I are old enough to have adult children of their own in Part II. We see the characters in the "Present Day" (about 1935) as products of the patriarchal society described in Part I; for by portraying the 1880–1918 period, Virginia Woolf prepares her reader to see and understand the "Present Day" in terms of this past.

In order to understand how Virginia Woolf saw the "present day" in terms of the past it is helpful to refer to *Three Guineas*, for this book was in her mind while she was working on *The Years*. In fact, the idea of writing "a sequel to *A Room of One's Own*" came to her before she had finished *The Waves* (AWD, p. 165). On May 21, 1935, she noted in her diary: "Oddities of the human brain: woke early and again considered dashing off my book on Professions [*Three Guineas*], to which I had not given a single thought these 7 or 8 days. Why? This vacillates with my novel—how are they both to come out simultaneously" (AWD, p. 249). On the day *Three*

Guineas was published, she spoke of "lumping the *Years* and *Three Guineas* together as one book—as indeed they are" (AWD, p. 295). Thus, to see the relationship between the two books—the one an essay, the other an "Essay-Novel"—is important.

In *Three Guineas* Virginia Woolf stated "that the public and the private worlds are inseparably connected; that the tyrannies and servilities of the one are the tyrannies and servilities of the other" (p. 258). She criticized the tyrannical rule of the father in the English household and pointed out the relationship between this and the tyrannical rule of men over women within the whole of society. Moreover, she drew a parallel between the patriarchal structure in the home and state and fascism abroad (TG, pp. 186, 236 ff.). She attributed the threat of war both to fascism and the patriarchal power structure. In accordance with the male and female principle, she regarded warmongering (which separates) as "masculine" and peace-making (which unifies) as "feminine." Theoretically, masculine or feminine behavior may be found in either sex; however, she noted that

> to fight has always been the man's habit, not the woman's. Law and practice have developed that difference, whether innate or accidental. Scarcely a human being in the course of history has fallen to a woman's rifle; the vast majority of birds and beasts have been killed by you [men], not by us . . . (TG, pp. 13–14)

She suggested that it is largely due to the repression of women, and hence the feminine "power," that warmongering has been allowed to go on unchecked (p. 153). Because the feminine "power" has not been cultivated, men's minds tend to be purely "masculine" rather than androgynous.[4] Moreover, peace and freedom may be preserved only in an androgynous society (pp. 260–261). Therefore, Virginia Woolf gave

Only in an adrogynous society will there be peace and freedom.

only one of her three guineas to the antiwar movement, for the other two guineas had to be contributed to projects which would help correct the imbalance in England by rebuilding a woman's college and opening professions to women (pp. 72, 152).

As a woman in a patriarchal society, Virginia Woolf considered herself an "outsider" (p. 193). Even as one of the "daughters of educated men," she was part of a powerless segment of society (pp. 24, 96). Therefore, she would "take no share in patriotic demonstrations" (p. 198). In *Three Guineas* the daughter of an educated man says,

> " 'Our' country still ceases to be mine if I marry a foreigner. 'Our' country denies me the means of protecting myself, forces me to pay others a very large sum annually to protect me, and is so little able, even so, to protect me that Air Raid precautions are written on the wall. Therefore if you [men] insist upon fighting to protect me, or 'our' country, let it be understood, soberly and rationally between us, that you are fighting to gratify a sex instinct which I cannot share; to procure benefits which I have not shared and probably will not share; but not to gratify my instincts, or to protect either myself or my country." (P. 197)

In short, it is because women have been "outsiders" to whom their brothers have said, "You shall not learn; you shall not earn; you shall not own" (p. 190), that feminine values have been repressed in England (p. 133).

This notion, developed in *Three Guineas,* helps to explain Virginia Woolf's vision of both society and the individual in *The Years*. There is a lack of wholeness, a lack of harmony in the world presented in *The Years*. It is not characterized by unity (feminine) but by separateness (masculine). For instance, it is significant that in Colonel Abel Pargiter's family the mother, the person who in earlier novels would normally function as the peacemaker and unifier, lies dying upstairs. Milly looks to Eleanor, the eldest daughter, to fulfill the function of "the soother, the maker-up of quarrels," but Eleanor does not in fact seem to play this role (pp. 13 ff.). Certainly, jealousy and tension mar the relationships among the Pargiter children. To cite the two most obvious examples, Milly and Delia react to each other with hostility; Martin and Rose "always" quarrel (pp. 10, 14, 449). Also, throughout *The Years* various characters long to communicate with each other (Colonel Pargiter with Eugénie, Kitty with Eleanor, Martin with Sally), but their conversations are abortive; their important feelings are never spoken (pp. 136, 194, 249). After such conversations, the characters feel isolated and unsatisfied. Martin Pargiter feels similarly unsatisfied after a party at Kitty's. Like Peter Walsh in *Mrs. Dalloway,* Martin goes to the party hoping to talk with the hostess. Like Martin, Peter never finds the opportunity to speak privately with his hostess, but Mrs. Dalloway at least provides Peter with a moment of vision (and, hence, a sense of wholeness) before he leaves. In *The Years,* however, Kitty dismisses Martin without any such "gift":

> "Sit down, Martin, and let us talk," said Kitty. He sat down: but he had a feeling that she wanted him to go. He had seen her glance at the clock. They chatted for a moment. Now the old lady came back; she was proving, beyond a doubt, from her unexampled store of anecdotes, that it must be Uncle William on the cob; not Grandpapa. She was going. But she took her time. Martin waited till she was fairly in the doorway, leaning on her nephew's arm. He hesitated; they were alone now; should he stay, or should he go? But Kitty was standing up. She was holding out her hand.
>
> "Come again soon and see me alone," she said. She had dismissed him, he felt. (P. 286)

Martin and Kitty's abortive relationship is typical in *The Years*. It is symbolic of a society which has failed to unite the "masculine" with the "feminine" in order to achieve a state of equilibrium and wholeness.

Like *Three Guineas, The Years* is an indictment of the English patriarchal society. For example, Eleanor Pargiter never marries, because she has to live with her father until his death. In *Three Guineas* Virginia Woolf used facts from the lives of Elizabeth Barrett Browning, Charlotte Brontë, and Sophie Jex-Blake to illustrate how fathers, because of the " 'Oedipus complex,' " try to keep their daughters dependent upon them (pp. 235 ff.). Also, Rose Pargiter, a feminist, is imprisoned for her political activities (p. 453). Significantly, several references to the story of *Antigone* are made both in *The Years* and in *Three Guineas*. In *Three Guineas* Creon's statement is quoted, "While I live, no woman shall rule me" (p. 303). Kitty Malone, a cousin of the Pargiters, is likewise a victim of masculine tyranny. She wanted to be a farmer but, as a woman, she was not trained to earn her living in that or any other way. Indeed, she has been so repressed by society's image of what she must be as the "daughter of an educated man" that she welcomes old age:

> "And how I hated it [dancing when young]!" said Kitty, looking at her fingers, which were short and pricked. "How nice it is," she said, "not to be young! How nice not to mind what people think! Now one can live as one likes," she added, ". . . now that one's seventy." (P. 454)

All the characters who were children in the 1880s hate the memory of their youth, for the males as well as the females suffered from the lack of harmony and wholeness which characterized the Victorian society. Their hatred is summed up in the "Present Day" section of the novel, when Delia refers to her life at Abercorn Terrace:

"It was Hell!" she exclaimed. "It was Hell!" she repeated. . . .

"D'you know," she said, looking at Eleanor, "when I go to Paddington, I always say to the man, 'Drive the other way round!' "

"That's enough . . ." Martin stopped her; his glass was full. "I hated it too . . ." he began. (P. 450, *cf.* p. 239)

Indeed, in a patriarchal society it is not only the victims of the "tyranny" who suffer, for, as North Pargiter concludes in Part II, "we are all deformed" (pp. 409–410).

We see the characters (both the old and the young) in the "Present Day" as products of this past and, hence, of this repressive society. They do not feel free and whole but frustrated and fragmented. For instance, Peggy Pargiter feels during the party at Delia's: "Directly something got together, it broke. She had a feeling of desolation" (p. 423). Through the characters it is suggested that the "present" of the 1930s is a transitional period—a period of uncertainty in which an old way of life has been rejected but a new way of life has not been found.

If tyranny is to be eliminated in the home, the professions, the university, the church, and the government, Virginia Woolf believed that human beings must change. She referred in *Three Guineas* to a picture of a dictator:

And behind him lie ruined houses and dead bodies—men, women and children. But we have not laid that picture before you in order to excite once more the sterile emotion of hate. On the contrary it is in order to release other emotions such as the human figure, even thus crudely in a coloured photograph, arouses in us who are human beings. . . . It [the image of the dictator] suggests that we cannot dissociate ourselves from that figure but are ourselves that figure. It suggests that we are not passive spectators doomed to unresisting obedience but by our thoughts and actions can ourselves change that figure. (P. 258)

The hope that human beings can improve is likewise expressed in *The Years*. For example, Nicholas at the end of the party drinks to "the human race . . . which is now in its infancy, may it grow to maturity!" (pp. 459–460). Eleanor Pargiter states the nature of the problem: "We know nothing, even about ourselves. We're only just beginning, she thought, to understand here and there" (p. 461).

Virginia Woolf indicated that the ultimate aim is a state of oneness. Even in *Three Guineas* she was haunted by her longing for it:

> Even here, even now your letter tempts us to shut our ears to these little facts, these trivial details, to listen not to the bark of the guns and the bray of the gramophones but to the voices of the poets, answering each other, assuring us of a unity that rubs out divisions as if they were chalk marks only; to discuss with you the capacity of the human spirit to overflow boundaries and make unity out of multiplicity. But that would be to dream— (P. 259)

As suggested earlier, the dream will not become reality until the feminine "power" is liberated so it can be united with the masculine. In *The Years* North Pargiter voices a similar desire for both unity (feminine) and multiplicity (masculine), for a balance between the inner and the outer:

> Why not down barriers and simplify? But a world, he thought, that was all one jelly, one mass, would be a rice pudding world, a white counterpane world. To keep the emblems and tokens of North Pargiter—the man Maggie laughs at; . . . but at the same time spread out, make a new ripple in human consciousness, be the bubble and the

stream, the stream and the bubble—myself and the world together— (Pp. 442–443)

Likewise, at the end of *The Years* Eleanor has a symbolic vision of this binding together of the masculine and the feminine. From Delia's window she watches a girl and a young man get out of a taxi and go up to a neighboring house: " 'There,' Eleanor murmured, as he opened the door and they stood for a moment on the threshold. 'There!' she repeated, as the door shut with a little thud behind them" (p. 469). At the beginning of *The Years* Delia and Milly watch a young man arrive in a taxi to call on a neighbor (p. 18). The girls would have liked him to stop at their house. When in the "Present Day" Peggy asks Eleanor if she was "suppressed" in her youth, Eleanor recalls this scene. Thus, her final vision of the married couple suggests a future that will not demand the sacrifice she made to care for her aging father. Significantly, in *A Room of One's Own* Virginia Woolf uses the sight of a girl and a young man getting into a taxi together to symbolize the harmonious union of the masculine and feminine powers in the androgynous mind (pp. 145–148).

The possibility of attaining such a state of harmony or equilibrium seems remote in *The Years,* however, for this novel is not only an indictment of society (like *Three Guineas*) but also an indictment of human beings. The view of humankind presented in *The Years* is summed up by Sara Pargiter's exclamation, "Pah! They stink!" (p. 203). This is an echo of Hamlet's remark in the grave-digging scene: "And smelt so? Pah!" The shift in Virginia Woolf's outlook since *Night and Day* is pointed out by Josephine Schaefer:

Like her own creation Septimus, she has turned from the lyrical, romantic Shakespeare whose spirit imbued *Night and Day* to the Shakespeare who "loathed humanity." In a way the chronicle [of the Pargiter family] relates what Septimus thought: that "the secret signal which one generation passes under disguise to the next is loathing, hatred, and despair."[5]

Innumerable details throughout *The Years* serve to convey Virginia Woolf's "loathing, hatred, and despair." The pictures presented are more than depressing; they are grotesque. For example, Colonel Pargiter, while his wife lies dying, continues to see and think about his mistress Mira, although repulsed by her lack of taste and the cheap, sordid atmosphere in which she lives. Later, his young daughter Rose has an upsetting experience when she passes a man by a lamppost. "As she passed he sucked his lips in and out. He made a mewing noise. But he did not stretch his hands out at her; they were unbuttoning his clothes" (p. 29). In Part II North Pargiter goes to dine with his cousin Sara and thinks: "What a dirty . . . sordid . . . low-down street to live in" (p. 334). The girl who brings up their dinner breathes hard and is clumsy around the table. They eat "underdone" mutton, "a slabbed-down mass of cabbage," "hard" yellow potatoes, and "fly-blown fruit" on a gravy-stained tablecloth (pp. 338 ff.). The shift in Virginia Woolf's vision since she wrote *To the Lighthouse* may be illustrated by comparing Sara's dinner with Mrs. Ramsay's. After dinner North recites poetry to Sara but is interrupted by noises in the room opposite hers. She explains:

"The Jew having a bath," she said.

"The Jew having a bath?" he repeated.

"And tomorrow there'll be a line of grease round the bath," she said.

"Damn the Jew!" he exclaimed. The thought of a line of grease from a strange man's body on the bath next door disgusted him. . . .

They listened to the water running. The man was coughing and clearing his throat as he sponged.

"Who is this Jew?" he asked.

"Abrahamson, in the tallow trade," she said.

They listened.

"Engaged to a pretty girl in a tailor's shop," she added. . . .

"But he leaves hairs in the bath," she concluded.

North felt a shiver run through him. Hairs in food, hairs on basins, other people's hairs made him feel physically sick.

"D'you share a bath with him?" he asked.

She nodded.

He made a noise like "Pah!"

" 'Pah.' That's what I said," she laughed. " 'Pah!'—when I went into the bathroom on a cold winter's morning. . . .

"And then—?" he asked.

"And then . . . I came back into the sitting-room. . . . Fried eggs and a bit of toast. Lydia with her blouse torn and her hair down. The unemployed singing hymns under the window. And I said to myself—" she flung her hand out, " 'Polluted city, unbelieving city, city of dead fish and worn-out frying pans'—thinking of a river's bank, when the tide's out," she explained. (pp. 365–367)

Sara's remarks may have been inspired by the passage in T. S. Eliot's *The Waste Land* (ll. 60 ff.) which begins with "Unreal City" and speaks of a crowd flowing over London Bridge. In her talk with North, Sara goes on to mention a bridge and many people passing. Also, the reference here to "the Jew" possibly echoes Eliot's reference to "the jew" in "Gerontion."

The attitude towards human beings conveyed by *The Years* is one of mental and physical repulsion. In depression John Custance experienced a heightened sense of repulsion; in mania, on the contrary, he felt an attraction even to that which he would normally find repulsive.[6] Thus, the sense of repulsion displayed in *The Years* may be symptomatic of Virginia Woolf's depressed state of mind. Just as Septimus Smith could not be happy because "brutality blared out on placards; men were trapped in mines; women burnt alive,"[7] Peggy (North's sister) cannot be happy while "on every placard at every street corner was Death; or worse—tyranny; brutality; torture; the fall of civilisation; the end of freedom" (p. 418). The world's misery torments her; yet paradoxically, she does not love her kind. Nor did Virginia Woolf always love her kind. In 1932 she wrote to Vita Sackville-West: "My God, Vita, I wish one hadn't picked this age to live in: I hate my kind." This statement was inspired by plans for the construction of three "vast galvanized iron sheds" on the down near her country home at Rodmell.[8] In *The Years* Peggy has a mental picture of "faces mobbed at the door of a picture palace; apathetic, passive faces; the faces of people drugged with cheap pleasures; who had not even the courage to be themselves, but must dress up, imitate, pretend" (p. 419).

North's feeling of repulsion focused upon his aunt, Milly, and her husband, Hugh Gibbs. Milly (one of Eleanor's sisters) "had grown very stout. In order to disguise her figure, veils with beads on them hung down over her arms. They were so fat that they reminded North of asparagus; pale asparagus tapering to a point." As she gives him "her fat little hand," he notes "how the rings were sunk in her fingers, as if the flesh had grown over them. Flesh grown over diamonds disgusted him" (p. 402). As her equally fat husband sits down "cautiously" in an overstuffed chair, North hears him say, "Chew, chew, chew," and Milly say "Tut-tut-tut":

> That was what it came to—thirty years of being husband and wife—tut-tut-tut—and chew-chew-chew. It sounded like the half-inarticulate munchings of animals in a stall. Tut-tut-tut, and chew-chew-chew—as they trod out the soft steamy straw in the stable; as they wallowed in the primeval swamp, prolific, profuse, half-conscious . . . (P. 404)

As Hugh and Milly Gibbs begin to converse with Maggie Digby, North continues his observations. He is disappointed to note that Maggie is as bad as the Gibbses. "They're not interested in other people's children, he observed. Only in their own; their own property; their own flesh and blood . . . How then can we be civilised, he asked himself?" (pp. 407–408). He likes Maggie's fine, strong hands, "but if it were a question, he thought, watching the fingers curl slightly, of 'my' children, of 'my' possessions, it would be one rip down the belly; or teeth in the soft fur of the throat" (p. 409). In North's eyes human beings seem even more than "deformed"; they are despicable.

Whether or not it was part of Virginia Woolf's conscious intention, the impact made by this novel upon the reader arises from the tone of horror which coexists with but prevails over the tone of naive optimism. The reader is left with the impression that every time a bit of rose appears, it is instantly smeared over or encircled in a threatening manner by darker colors. For instance, one scene ends with Eleanor's statement that life seems to her a "perpetual discovery," "a miracle," and the next begins with Peggy's opening a book at random and discovering there an expression of what she has been thinking:

> *"La médiocrité de l'univers m'étonne et me révolte,"* she read. That was it. Precisely. She read on. *". . . la petitesse de toutes choses m'emplit de dégoût. . ."* She lifted her eyes. They [the dancers] were treading on her toes. *". . . la pauvreté des êtres humains m'anéantit."* (P. 413)

A little later in the novel Eleanor's optimism is again effectively undermined by her niece Peggy:

> "What I mean is, we've changed in ourselves," Eleanor was saying. "We're happier—we're freer. . . ."

What does she mean by "happiness," by "freedom"? Peggy asked herself, lapsing against the wall again. (Pp. 416–417)

Therefore, in a somewhat similar manner, the phrase "extraordinary beauty, simplicity and peace" rings false when used at the end of the novel to describe the dawn; for the occasional optimistic statements made in the course of the novel have been continually undermined by the accumulation of details which convey horror, bitterness, and despair.

Virginia Woolf's view of humankind in *The Years* strongly resembles that of the only two characters in her earlier novels who commit suicide, namely, Septimus and Rhoda. Significantly, the writing of *The Years* (1932–1936) was punctuated by periods of illness, and Leonard Woolf wrote that after completing this novel "she was much nearer a complete breakdown than she had ever been since 1913."[9] On July 10, 1933, she spoke of "stamping along the road, with gloom and pain constricting my heart: and the desire for death, in the old way, all for two I daresay careless words"; and on August 12, 1933, she spoke of a "collapse": "I went to bed for two days and slept I daresay 7 hours, visiting the silent realms again" (AWD, p. 209). Towards the end of January 1934, her work was interrupted for three weeks by her "headache." After completing her first draft of the book, she again experienced depression. She revised her work a second time and then a third. As Jean Guiguet points out, "physical and mental lassitude are apparent in every reference to her book throughout this third revision,"[10] and towards the end of this revision she was again plagued with headaches (AWD, p. 265). She subsequently suffered what she described as an "almost catastrophic illness" during a period of two months (AWD, p. 268). On June 11, 1936, she began her final revision but soon collapsed again, this time for a period of four months (AWD, p. 270). Encouraged by her husband, she subsequently went on to revise *The Years* "in the most ruthless and drastic way" until it was finished.[11] Looking back, she commented in her diary: "I wonder if anyone has ever suffered so much from a book as I have from *The Years*. . . . Think of that summer, every morning a headache, and forcing myself into that room in my nightgown; and lying down after a page: and always with the certainty of failure" (AWD, p. 273).

Writing *The Years* evidently contributed to Virginia Woolf's mental instability during this time; in turn, however, her periods of depression undoubtedly helped to determine the state of mind conveyed through the novel. Both in her illnesses and in her novel she was probably reacting to certain facts which were threatening the stability of her world. For instance, the deaths of several friends and acquaintances during the 1930s (Arnold Bennett, 1931; G. Lowes Dickinson, 1932; John Galsworthy, 1933; Stella Benson, 1933; Francis Birrell, 1935) made her keenly aware of the evanescent quality of life and "the inane pointlessness of all this existence" (AWD, p. 180). When Lytton Strachey died in 1932, she felt deserted: "I wake in the night with the sense of being in an empty hall" (AWD, p. 179). The subsequent suicide of Dora Carrington (who had loved Lytton) added to her sense of "things generally wrong in the universe" (AWD, p. 180). She wrote at the time:

A saying of Leonard's comes into my head in this season of complete inanity and boredom. "Things have gone wrong somehow." It was the night C. killed herself. We were walking along that silent blue street with the scaffolding. I saw all the violence and unreason crossing in the air: ourselves small; a tumult outside: something terrifying: unreason— (AWD, p. 181)

In 1934 she wrote that Roger Fry's death had upset her even more than Lytton's: "Why I wonder? Such a blank wall. Such a silence: such a poverty" (AWD, p. 230). His death made her feel "the poverty of life" and "the substance gone out of everything" (AWD, p. 223). As Josephine Schaefer points out,

> These deaths and the sense of impoverishment they created in Virginia Woolf seem to cast a shadow over *The Years*. Death punctuates the novel. Almost every chapter up to 1914 can be remembered in terms of who died that year: 1880, Mrs. Pargiter finally dies; 1891, Parnell dies; 1908, Eugénie and Digby die; 1910, the King dies; 1911, Abel Pargiter dies; 1913, Crosby's dog, her last tie with her old life as a servant in the Pargiter home, dies. The years that follow 1913 lead to the Great War, to the destruction of a generation. (Pp. 176–177)

Virginia Woolf's emotional stability was certainly undermined during the 1930s by the increasing threat of war. On August 7, 1934, she referred in her diary to the German financial situation and the exodus of the Jews. That same year her husband wrote an anti-fascist book entitled *Quack, Quack!* and on February 26, 1935, she expressed her own desire "to write an anti-fascist pamphlet." In May of 1935, she and Leonard traveled in both Germany and Italy. At the German customs she observed that a passing car had a swastika on it, that the windows of the customs building were barred, that a little boy said "Heil Hitler" as he opened his small bag at the barrier. She also noted, "We become obsequious—delighted that is when the officer smiles at [our marmoset] Mitzi—the first stoop in our back" (AWD, p. 248). On March 13, 1936, with Hitler's army on the Rhine, she wrote in her diary: "it's odd, how near the guns have got to our private life again. I can quite distinctly see them and hear a roar, even though I go on, like a doomed mouse, nibbling at my daily page."

In *The Years* there are few direct references to the oncoming war, but the mood of the 1930s prevails throughout the "Present Day." First of all, there are several references to World War I, characterized by the bitterness and disappointment of those who saw that it had brought neither a "new world" nor a prolonged peace. Eleanor, for instance, feels frustrated as she recalls the night of an air raid in 1917:

> They had sat in a cellar; and Nicholas—it was the first time she had met him—had said that the war was of no importance. "We are children playing with fireworks in the back garden"... she remembered his phrase; and how, sitting round a wooden packing-case, they had drunk to a new world. "A new world—a new world!" Sally had cried, drumming with her spoon on top of the packing case. She [Eleanor] turned to her writing table, tore up a letter and threw it away. (Pp. 354–355)

Eleanor also notes the bitterness of her niece Peggy, who lost her brother Charles in the first world war (pp. 362, 363). When Eleanor reads the words on a pedestal and comments, "The only fine thing that was said in the war," we read: " 'It didn't come to much,' said Peggy sharply" (p. 362). Eleanor reacts angrily to an image of the new threat, that of "a fat man gesticulating" (probably Mussolini): " 'Damned—' Eleanor shot out suddenly, 'bully!' She tore the paper across with one sweep of her hand and flung it on the floor" (p. 356). She subsequently explains her anger to her niece:

> "it means the end of everything we cared for."
> "Freedom?" said Peggy perfunctorily.
> "Yes," said Eleanor. "Freedom and justice." (P. 357)

These references to World War I and to the threat of World War II are of prime importance in *The Years,* because they serve to explain and justify the pessimistic tone not only of the "Present Day" but of the entire novel. The view of the

1880–1918 period is colored by subsequent political events, for, as was mentioned earlier, in *The Years* as in *Three Guineas* Virginia Woolf tried to show the movement towards war in the 1930s to be due to the past and present patriarchal nature of the English (as well as the fascist) society. By demonstrating the inadequate and destructive nature of a predominantly masculine society, she indicated the need to create a "new world," one which includes the feminine and is therefore androgynous.

Although Virginia Woolf's basic concept of the novel did not change, *The Years* differs from her previous novels not only in tone but also in "angle of vision." Her sensitivity to the threatening political situation seemingly influenced her shift in both. In "The Artist and Politics" (1936) she explained how the situation affected the novelist:

> the novelist turns from the private lives of his characters to their social surroundings and their political opinions. Obviously the writer is in such close touch with human life that any agitation in his subject matter must change his angle of vision. Either he focuses his sight upon the immediate problem; or he brings his subject matter into relation with the present; or in some cases, so paralysed is he by the agitations of the moment that he remains silent. (CE II, 230)

Virginia Woolf's primary concern in *The Years* is still the inner life—in this case, the state of mind predominant in the 1930s; however, in order to project the "present" state of mind as she perceived it, she evidently felt obliged to shift her angle of vision to focus upon the outer rather than the inner lives of her characters. Therefore, in *The Years* she did not use the stream-of-consciousness technique as she had done in *Mrs. Dalloway, To the Lighthouse,* and *The Waves.* Moreover, she did not emphasize personal relationships as she had done, for instance, in *Night and Day* or *Mrs. Dalloway,* nor the individual's relationship to being as in *The Waves,* but rather the relationship between the individual and his society, a theme that is prominent only in her other war-related novels, *Jacob's Room* and *Between the Acts.*

Virginia Woolf's perspective in *The Years* seems to be, to use her own terms, more like Defoe's than Emily Brontë's,[12] for she relied heavily upon what she referred to in her diary as "facts" or "externality" (AWD, p. 190). However, she employed these "facts" (that is, the visible as opposed to the invisible) more as a means than as an end. The reader of *The Years,* like the observer of Vanessa Bell's paintings, is supposed to "tunnel" behind the particulars of this "outer" aspect of reality to the "feeling" (or state of mind) which cannot be described directly but must be, as Virginia Woolf wrote in one of her essays, "suggested and brought slowly by repeated images before us until it stays, in all its complexity, complete" (CE IV, 2). Thus, as I have said, the "facts" included in *The Years* were carefully selected to build up in the course of the novel an impression of horror, bitterness, and despair—the mood of the 1930s.

Moreover, Virginia Woolf conceived of this seemingly "representational" novel in a "nonrepresentational" way. In writing *The Years,* as in writing her earlier novels, she thought in terms of rhythms and patterns, for she was influenced by both music and painting. Thus, she spoke in her diary of "keeping a kind of swing and rhythm" through all the scenes (AWD, p. 234). At one point she considered *Music* a possible title for the book and planned to end *The Years* with "a chorus, a general statement, a song for four voices" (AWD, pp. 221, 222). Influenced by painting, she spoke of the novel's "design" and of being able to "see" the book "as a whole" (AWD, pp. 227, 270). Also, composing a scene, she spoke of using "different layers by bringing in music and painting together with certain groupings of human beings" (AWD, p. 257).

In accordance with this continuing interest in rhythm and pattern, Virginia Woolf employed in *The Years* many of the unifying devices used in her earlier novels: the repetition and variation of rhythmic phrases such as, "Take two coos, Taffy; take two coos, Taffy; tak . . ." (pp. 123, 202, 467) and the repeated appearance of certain objects (the chair with the gilt claws, the walrus with a brush on its back); themes (freedom and justice, intimacy interrupted); and symbols (falling leaves, the kettle that won't boil). In particular, the reappearance of these phrases, objects, themes, and symbols in Part II serves to evoke the past within the "Present Day." Similarly, as Sara is awakened at the end of Delia's party, we have a feeling it has happened before; for her remarks echo those made in Part I when Maggie and Martin awakened her in the Kensington Gardens. At the party

> Maggie looked at her. Then she took a flower from the table and tossed it at her. She half-opened her eyes. "It's time," said Maggie, touching her on the shoulder. "Time, is it?" she sighed. She yawned and stretched herself. She fixed her eyes on Nicholas as if she were bringing him back to the field of vision. Then she laughed.
> "Nicholas!" she exclaimed.
> "Sara!" he replied. They smiled at each other. Then he helped her up and she balanced herself uncertainly against her sister, and rubbed her eyes.
> "How strange," she murmured, looking round her, ". . . how strange. . . ." (P. 466)

In the park

> Sara was still asleep. . . . Martin stooped and threw a twig at her. She opened her eyes but shut them again. . . .
> "It's time," said Maggie. She pulled herself up. "Time is it?" she sighed. "How strange. . .!" she murmured. She sat up and rubbed her eyes.

"Martin!" she exclaimed. . . . She looked at him as if she were bringing him back to the field of vision.
"Martin!" she said again. (P. 266)

Likewise, Nicholas has the same discussion with North in 1935 as he had with Eleanor in 1917. The same remarks are well known to Sara (p. 339). As in the previous novels, Virginia Woolf uses this repetition and variation to try to suggest that aesthetically and philosophically a unifying pattern exists beneath the multiplicity of detail—one such as Eleanor senses sitting next to Nicholas at Delia's party:

He was looking at the lady. She seemed upheld by their gaze; vibrating under it. And suddenly it seemed to Eleanor that it had all happened before. So a girl had come in that night in the restaurant: had stood, vibrating, in the door. She knew exactly what he was going to say. He had said it before, in the restaurant. He is going to say, She is like a ball on the top of a fishmonger's fountain. As she thought it, he said it. Does everything then come over again a little differently? she thought. If so, is there a pattern; a theme, recurring, *like music*) half remembered, half foreseen?. . . a gigantic pattern, momentarily perceptible? The thought gave her extreme pleasure: that there was a pattern. (P. 398, italics mine)

In *The Years* as in *The Waves* the meetings among various combinations of characters suggest a pattern. For example, there is one minor reunion (a political meeting in Part I) and one major reunion (Delia's party in Part II). In addition, Virginia Woolf gave some form and unity to *The Years* by beginning each section of the novel with a passage on the season and weather. These introductory passages suggest symbolically the content and general mood of the scenes which follow;[13] the device is reminiscent of the poetic interludes in *The Waves.*

However, this suggestion of a mysterious underlying pattern or unity is too weak to offset the novel's disturbing picture of fragmented, essentially meaningless lives. Hence, momentary glimpses of an underlying pattern seem less pertinent here than in Virginia Woolf's earlier novels, where her vision of life was less "masculine." With its philosophical basis undermined in this way, the aesthetic pattern suggested by the novel's structure is likewise, if compared with previous novels, less effective in *The Years.*

Indeed, the structure of *The Years* is much looser than that of her stream-of-consciousness novels: the multiplicity of characters and incidents seems to outbalance any sense of formal structure which the reader derives from the novel. Moreover, there is no central character like Jacob Flanders to hold the novel together; and our attention is even more dispersed than usual because we do not know any of the characters in *The Years* as well as we know the main characters in *The Voyage Out, Night and Day, Mrs. Dalloway, To the Lighthouse,* or *The Waves.*

In contrast with her earlier novels, Virginia Woolf attains her "nonrepresentational" goal—in this case, the evocation of a state of mind—not so much through structure as through tone. In making her indictment of society and of man, she presents a world in which there is little harmony. This vision of life is projected not only, as we have seen, through her selection of repulsive situations but also, as we shall see, through her choice of words. Children in *The Years* do not simply play hopscotch; they skip "in and out of their chalk cages" (p. 8). When Crosby serves tea, she puts down the tray "with an exasperating little clink." She goes out "creaking in her cheap shoes" (p. 19). The funeral flowers for Mrs. Pargiter are not attractively arranged but "clubbed together, head to head, in circles, in ovals, in crosses so that they scarcely looked like flowers" (p. 88). Certainly, the flower-woman in *The Years* is unlike the one seen by Peter Walsh in *Mrs. Dalloway:* this one "had no nose; her face was seamed with white patches; there were red rims for nostrils. She had no nose—she had pulled her hat down to hide that fact" (p. 253). In one short scene Delia speaks "irritably," Rose "grumpily," Delia again, "gloomily" and "severely," and Martin "sharply" (pp. 9–10). The dominant tone of *The Years* is built up through an accumulation of such details. It is this tone which provides the book with its unity and the reader with his moment of vision (a perception of the mood of the 1930s "in all its complexity, complete") as he closes the book.[14]

The Years differs from Virginia Woolf's earlier novels in another significant way. Previously she utilized a character's final moment of vision to synthesize her novel and thus to provide a model for the reader's own moment of vision at the end of the book. This device was used most effectively in her three stream-of-consciousness novels, *Mrs. Dalloway, To the Lighthouse,* and *The Waves.* For instance, the reader experiences "the effect of the book as a whole on his mind"[15] when he shares Peter's final vision of Mrs. Dalloway, Lily's final vision of Mr. and Mrs. Ramsay, or Bernard's final vision of the nature of human existence. The reader of *The Years,* however, does not share Eleanor's final vision; for it is not related to but contrasted with the disturbing picture of life presented in the novel. To perceive an androgynous whole Eleanor seems compelled to turn away from the past as it was depicted in Part I and the "present day" as it was depicted in Part II to look out at an unknown couple who cross a symbolic threshold into an unknown future. Because the masculine vision of life in *The Years* denies her the possibility of finding what in *The Waves* Bernard called "something unbroken," Eleanor's vision of the couple is divorced from life as it is portrayed in the novel. The reader's moment of vision, on the contrary, is limited to the horror, bitterness, and despair expressed in *The Years.*

Therefore, unlike her stream-of-consciousness works, *The Years* neither ends with nor evokes an androgynous vision. On the one hand, Eleanor's vision of wholeness—a union of the masculine and feminine—is not in itself androgynous, for it remains a dream unrelated to life. On the other hand, the reader's vision of the mood of the 1930s cannot be androgynous, for Virginia Woolf's vision of life in *The Years* is predominantly masculine. In short, Eleanor's vision is essentially feminine, the reader's masculine.

Moreover, at the close of the novel the two visions are, in effect, not reconciled but contrasted. Indeed, the reader's masculine vision is heightened by this contrast with its opposite and vice versa. By using this device of contrasting the two visions, Virginia Woolf emphasizes that the realities of the political situation ("the bark of the guns and the bray of the gramophones") in the 1930s have made it increasingly difficult, if not impossible, to find the point of equilibrium between the masculine and the feminine (TG, p. 259). She thereby conveys through *The Years* what she concludes in *Three Guineas,* that to speak now of "the capacity of the human spirit to overflow boundaries and make unity out of multiplicity . . . would be to dream—to dream the recurring dream that has haunted the human mind since the beginning of time; the dream of peace, the dream of freedom" (TG, p. 259).

In Virginia Woolf's words, *Between the Acts* was to represent, " 'We'. . .the composed of many things. . .we all life, all art, all waifs and strays—a rambling capricious but somehow unified whole—the present state of my mind" (AWD, pp. 289–290). Thus, in 1938, despite her loss of faith in the capacity of her generation to make "unity" out of the many contradictory details of their daily lives, Virginia Woolf still envisioned reality and art in terms of multiplicity and unity.

Basically, in terms of this duality, her vision of life and art had not changed since she wrote her first novel. As we know, she conceived of *The Voyage Out* as a combination of "tumult" and "pattern." Similarly, as she intended, *Between the Acts* (1941) contains all the contradictory aspects of "we" (her generation) and yet conveys a unified impression of a "state of mind"; hence, the novel is "rambling" and "capricious" but still a "unified whole." Furthermore, we find in *Between the Acts* the same impatience with the difficult task of creating within life an androgynous whole—a workable marriage of the male and female—that we found in *The Voyage Out;* we see in Isa Oliver, the main character of *Between the Acts,* the same longing for oneness and timelessness that we saw in Rachel Vinrace.

Yet, as we know from our discussion of *The Years* and *Three Guineas,* Virginia Woolf's vision of life was not exactly the same in 1937 and 1938 as it had been even in 1931 when *The Waves* was published. Nor was her method of presenting her dual vision of reality the same in *The Years* as it had been in any of her previous novels. In turn, *Between the Acts* is in structure and tone a very different book from *The Years.* Therefore, it is important not only to perceive the relationship between this final work and her other novels but also to see *Between the Acts* as an experiment indicating a new direction in her development. As Josephine Schaefer points out, "There is . . . much to be said for a comparison between the position *Jacob's Room* occupies in relation to *Mrs. Dalloway, To the Lighthouse,* and *The Waves* and the position *Between the Acts* might have occupied in relation to the works Virginia Woolf would have written had she lived."[16]

As we shall see, *Between the Acts* is similar to *The Years* in that the vision of life which it presents is predominantly "masculine." However, the structure through which this vision is conveyed is quite different. Instead of leaping "like a chamois, across precipices from 1880 to here and now" (AWD,

p. 189), Virginia Woolf chose to adhere strictly to the unities of time, place, and action. *Between the Acts* begins and ends on a "summer's night" and covers a period of only twenty-four hours in June 1939 (AWD, p. 288; *Acts,* pp. 23, 26). The action takes place before, during, and after a village pageant. The setting is restricted to the garden (where the pageant is presented) and the interior of Pointz Hall, the Olivers' country home. Also, in contrast with the many characters whom the author created for *The Years,* there are only seven major characters in *Between the Acts:* Giles Oliver; his wife Isa; his father; his aunt Lucy Swithin; the Olivers' guests, William Dodge and Mrs. Manresa; and, finally, Miss La Trobe, the author and director of the pageant given at the Olivers' home. The name Pointz Hall is significant; it is the "point" to which all these characters have been drawn this June day in 1939.

There are three dramas going on simultaneously in *Between the Acts.* One revolves around the strained relationship between Isa and Giles Oliver; another revolves around the pageant—its production and the audience's reactions to it. The backdrop for these two dramas is a third, the least alluded to but, in effect, the most important, namely, the emotional drama created by the impending war. This drama is the most important, for in *Between the Acts* as in *The Years* references to it serve to explain and justify the state of mind evoked in the course of the novel. The title, *Between the Acts,* alludes to all three dramas. It refers, of course, to the fact that the novel takes place between the wars. It also refers to what occurs between the acts of the pageant. Finally, as the last line of the novel indicates ("Then the curtain rose. They spoke."), the story takes place between those moments when, alone, Giles and Isa really interact as male and female (p. 256).

To understand the prewar drama to which Virginia Woolf alluded in *Between the Acts,* it is helpful to find out through her diary how she herself reacted to it. When she began her final novel in April 1938, war seemed imminent. On August

17, she voiced the feeling of apprehension and the sense of helplessness and frustration that we find expressed in the novel later:

> Hitler has his million men now under arms. Is it only summer manoeuvres or—? Harold broadcasting in his man of the world manner hints it may be war. That is the complete ruin not only of civilisation in Europe, but of our last lap. Quentin [Bell, her nephew] conscripted etc. One ceases to think about it—that's all. Goes on discussing the new room, new chair, new books. What else can a gnat on a blade of grass do? (AWD, p. 300)

Then on September 5, 1938, she contrasted her present life with what life would be like during the war. This contrast is implicit in *Between the Acts,* written concurrently with *Roger Fry* (1940), to which she refers in this entry:

> It's odd to be sitting here, looking up little facts about Roger and the M.M. [Metropolitan Museum] in New York, with a sparrow tapping on my roof this fine September morning when it may be 3rd August 1914 . . . What would war mean? Darkness, strain: I suppose conceivably death. And all the horror of friends: and Quentin: . . . All that lies over the water in the brain of that ridiculous little man. Why ridiculous? Because none of it fits: encloses no reality. Death and war and darkness representing nothing that any human being from the pork butcher to the Prime Minister cares one straw about. Not liberty, not life. (AWD, pp. 301–302)

Five days later she blessed Roger for giving her something to think about in this "welter of unreality." The international situation referred to in *Between the Acts* seemed to her irrational and therefore absurd; moreover, she felt trapped by it:

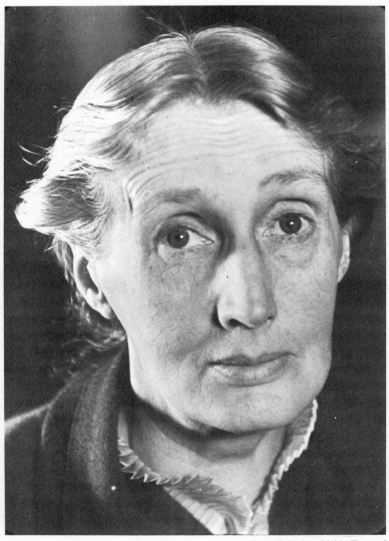

Between the Acts was to present "the present state of my mind."

> All these grim men appear to me like grown ups staring in-
> credulously at a child's sand castle which for some
> inexplicable reason has become a real vast castle, needing
> gunpowder and dynamite to destroy it. Nobody in their
> senses can believe in it. Yet nobody must tell the truth. So
> one forgets. Meanwhile the aeroplanes are on the prowl,
> crossing the downs. Every preparation is made. (AWD, p.
> 303)

The war had still not begun when, on April 15, 1939, Virginia Woolf spoke of "the community feeling: all England
thinking the same thing—this horror of war—at the same
moment" (AWD, p. 313). It is this prewar community feeling
of horror and its ramifications, helplessness, frustration, and a
sense of being trapped within an absurd situation, that we find
depicted in *Between the Acts.*

Virginia Woolf did not convey the "state of mind" of the
late 1930s in the same straightforward manner that she conveyed the "state of mind" of the mid-1930s in *The Years.* In
Between the Acts she is much more subtle. She purposely
makes the threat of war seem as incredible and absurd as it
had seemed to her. By distracting the reader's attention from
the actual situation, she intensifies the horror which he feels
when he becomes fully aware of it. That is, the pastoral setting and the ordinary quality of the characters' conversations
and activities (centering on the pageant) seem to belie the reality of the threat. Why would any sane individual plan the destruction of this countryside and these people? However, brief
but persistent references to the international situation serve to
build up the reader's consciousness of the political context
within which he must see everything that is thought, said, or
done in the novel.

For instance, several references to the impending war may
be found among the remarks made in the audience between

the acts and after the pageant. As if we too were among the spectators, we overhear bits of conversation; for instance,

> "And what about the Jews? The refugees. . .the Jews . . .People like ourselves, beginning life again. . .But it's always been the same. . . . My old mother, who's over eighty, can remember. . .Yes, she still reads without glasses. (P. 145)

And again,

> I agree—things look worse than ever on the continent. And what's the channel, come to think of it, if they mean to invade us? The aeroplanes, I didn't like to say it, made one think. . . . No, I thought it much too scrappy. (P. 232; *cf.* pp. 177, 231)

Another reference may be gleaned from Lucy Swithin's imaginative view of the leaves floating on the lily pond:

> Now the jagged leaf at the corner suggested, by its contours, Europe. There were other leaves. She fluttered her eye over the surface, naming leaves India, Africa, America. Islands of security, glossy and thick. (P. 239)

By turning her eyes away from the Europe-shaped leaf to look for "islands of security," Lucy reveals that she is fearful of the future. Virginia Woolf also refers indirectly to the threat by evoking another feeling prevalent in this prewar period—a feeling of being not only helpless but also trapped. For example, Giles Oliver anticipates the beginning of the pageant in the same way that she had anticipated the beginning of the war: "manacled to a rock he was, and forced passively to behold indescribable horror" (p. 74). Her description of the manner in which the characters await the pageant's final scenes entitled "Present time. Ourselves" likewise evokes this sense of being trapped: "They were all caught and caged; prisoners; watching a spectacle. Nothing happened. The tick of the machine was maddening" (p. 205). A similar feeling is conveyed by William Dodge's response to an incidental allusion to the future: " 'The doom of sudden death hanging over us,' he said. 'There's no retreating and advancing . . . for us as for them' " (p. 136).

There are two other references to the oncoming war, both made by Giles. Although they seem superficially to function as an explanation for his ill-humor, they are, in fact, much more than this. Like all the references to the war, they undermine the importance of everything else that is thought, said, or done. They echo the awareness of incongruity which Virginia Woolf voiced in her diary when she felt "odd" looking up facts about Roger Fry, whereas that very day might mark the beginning of another war. Here is the way Giles feels, continuing his conventional pattern of behavior despite what he has learned that morning:

> And he came into the dining-room looking like a cricketer, in flannels, wearing a blue coat with brass buttons; though he was enraged. Had he not read, in the morning paper, in the train, that sixteen men had been shot, others imprisoned, just over there, across the gulf, in the flat land which divided them from the continent? Yet he changed. It was Aunt Lucy, waving her hand at him as he came in, who made him change. (P. 58)

Again, after lunch with his family and guests, he is struck by the absurdity of continuing their usual activities when both they and the countryside may soon be destroyed:

> Giles nicked his chair into position with a jerk. Thus only could he show his irritation, his rage with old fogies who

sat and looked at views over coffee and cream when the whole of Europe—over there—was bristling like. . . . He had no command of metaphor. Only the ineffective word "hedgehog" illustrated his vision of Europe, bristling with guns, poised with planes. At any moment guns would rake that land into furrows; planes splinter Bolney Minster into smithereens and blast the Folly. He, too, loved the view. And blamed Aunt Lucy, looking at views, instead of—doing what? (Pp. 66–67)

As indicated in *A Writer's Diary,* Virginia Woolf felt the war would mean "the complete ruin" of civilization (p. 300). Thus, to emphasize what would be lost she injected the concept of English civilization into the novel. She achieved this mainly through Miss La Trobe's pageant, which evokes in its scenes the literature and mood of each century—what each generation had passed on to the others. Moreover, civilization is symbolized in the "Present time. Ourselves" section of the pageant by a wall. By conveying the notion that the wall was in ruins after World War I, Miss La Trobe suggests what another world war will mean (pp. 211–212).

Also implicit in the pageant is the belief that World War I not only left civilization in ruins but also left man in fragments. Before men can rebuild the wall of civilization, they must reestablish within themselves the wholeness (or unity) which has been lost. Otherwise, as an anonymous voice warns near the end of the pageant, the wall may never be repaired:

Look at ourselves, ladies and gentlemen! Then at the wall; and ask how's this wall, the great wall, which we call, perhaps miscall, civilization, to be built by (here the mirrors flicked and flashed) *orts, scraps and fragments like ourselves? (P. 219)*

The pageant conveys the dual nature of man in terms of multiplicity and unity. The audience sees itself as "orts, scraps and fragments" (multiplicity) in this scene: the actors and actresses come out carrying

> Anything that's bright enough to reflect, presumably, ourselves?
>   Ourselves! Ourselves!
>   Out they leapt, jerked, skipped. Flashing, dazzling, dancing, jumping. Now old Bart . . . he was caught. Now Manresa. Here a nose . . . there a skirt . . . then trousers only . . . Now perhaps a face. . . . Ourselves? But that's cruel. To snap us as we are, before we've had time to assume . . . And only, too, in parts. . . . That's what's so distorting and upsetting and utterly unfair. (P. 214)

Finally,

> hand glasses, tin cans, scraps of scullery glass, harness room glass, and heavily embossed silver mirrors—all stopped. And the audience saw themselves, *not whole by any means,* but at any rate sitting still. (P. 216, italics mine)

Later, however, the audience is shown its unrealized potential for unity. With the aid of music (which "makes us see the hidden, join the broken," p. 143) Miss La Trobe creates for a moment a state of harmony:

> Like quicksilver sliding, filings magnetized, the distracted united. The tune began; the first note meant a second; the second a third. Then down beneath a force was born in opposition; then another. On different levels they diverged. On different levels ourselves went forward; flower gathering some on the surface; others descending to wrestle with the meaning; but all comprehending; all enlisted. The whole population of the mind's immeasurable profundity came flocking; . . . but not the melody of surface sound alone

controlled it; but also the warring battle-plumed warriors straining asunder: To part? No. Compelled from the ends of the horizon; recalled from the edge of appalling crevasses; they crashed, solved; united. And some relaxed their fingers; and others uncrossed their legs.

Was that voice ourselves? Scraps, orts and fragments, are we, also, that? (Pp. 220–221)

Through the pageant Miss La Trobe has revealed to the spectators the masculine and feminine poles of the human personality. The difficulty, of course, is to reconcile these opposites, to find the point of equilibrium between the fragments and the whole, between the evanescent masculine and the eternal feminine. Only if men become balanced (and, therefore, androgynous) can civilization be saved.

The need for man to become androgynous is illustrated by the fragmented nature of the characters in *Between the Acts*. Like Christians who have lost touch with God, they seem to have lost touch with the one, for which so many of Virginia Woolf's characters have longed. Each seems to be merely a fragment of his potential self. This is symbolized by the fact that the personalities of the different characters seem to complete each other. For example, Giles is complemented by Rupert Haines and William Dodge, Isa by Mrs. Manresa, and Bart Oliver by his sister Lucy Swithin.

Like Percival in *The Waves,* Miss La Trobe is related to each of the six other major characters but only in her role as unifier. Like Percival, she makes possible the moment of harmony which the others experience. He achieves this sense of oneness through the power of his androgynous personality. However, as symbolized by the fact that Miss La Trobe is a lesbian (pp. 72, 246), her personality is not androgynous and, therefore, she must rely upon the power of art. But even as an artist, she seems limited by her lack of wholeness. Whereas Percival creates several moments of unity, she creates only one.

Of the seven main characters in *Between the Acts* Isa and Giles are the most important. The strain in their conjugal relationship throughout the novel symbolizes the lack of harmony between the masculine and feminine in 1939; the reasons given for this strain support Miss La Trobe's vision of her contemporaries as "orts, scraps and fragments." Each of the two is only a fragment of the whole (or androgynous) person the other thought he (or she) had married. In Isa's opinion, Giles has become too conventional. Here is the way she reacts to him that summer's night after the pageant: "Giles now wore the black coat and white tie of the professional classes, which needed—Isa looked down at his feet—patent leather pumps. 'Our representative, our spokesman,' she sneered" (pp. 251–252). Giles, a "dapper city gent" (p. 60), has failed to become the whole, natural man, the farmer, whom Isa would like him to be. Even Aunt Lucy has no respect for the way in which Giles spends his time in London every weekday:

> Aunt Lucy, foolish, free; always, since he had chosen, after leaving college, to take a job in the city, expressing her amazement, her amusement, at men who spent their lives, buying and selling—ploughs? glass beads was it? or stocks and shares?—to savages who wished most oddly—for were they not beautiful naked?—to dress and live like the English? A frivolous, a malignant statement hers was of a problem which, for he had no special gift, no capital, and had been furiously in love with his wife—he nodded to her across the table—had afflicted him for ten years. Given his choice, he would have chosen to farm. But he was not given his choice. So one thing led to another; and the conglomeration of things pressed you flat; held you fast, like a fish in water. So he came for the week-end, and changed. (P. 59)

Thus, Isa desires the gentleman farmer, Rupert Haines, who seems to have (she can't really know, for they are barely acquainted) what Giles has lost: "She had met him at a Bazaar; and at a tennis party. He had handed her a cup and a racquet —that was all. But in his ravaged face she always felt mystery; and in his silence, passion" (p. 9).

Yet Isa feels for her husband not only hate but love (p. 252). She loves him because he is handsome and the father of her children (p. 252). She is frustrated because what she really wants is a combination of Rupert Haines and her husband.

> Inside the glass, in her eyes, she saw what she had felt overnight for the ravaged, the silent, the romantic gentleman farmer. "In love," was in her eyes. But outside, on the washstand, on the dressing-table, among the silver boxes and tooth-brushes, was the other love; love for her husband, the stockbroker—"The father of my children," she added, slipping into the cliché conveniently provided by fiction. Inner love was in her eyes; outer love on the dressingtable. (Pp. 19–20)

The problem is to reconcile the opposites—the inner love with the outer, the love with the hate.

The presence of William Dodge at the Olivers' home points out another way in which Giles is not a "whole," androgynous man. Giles is not only less masculine than Rupert Haines, he is less feminine than William Dodge. Giles lacks the artistic or feminine sensibility that Isa finds attractive in William. Because of her own poetic, romantic temperament, she immediately feels an affinity with William that would be impossible with Giles:

> "I'm William," he said, taking the furry leaf and pressing it between thumb and finger.
> "I'm Isa," she answered. Then they talked as if they had known each other all their lives; which was odd, she said, as they always did, considering she'd known him perhaps

one hour. Weren't they, though, conspirators, seekers after hidden faces? (P. 136)

Giles, the practical, conventional man, has little in common with Isa, the poet and dreamer. Therefore, she hides her writings in an account book, and he never guesses her secret (p. 62). He is blind to an aspect of his wife that the strangers, Mrs. Manresa and William Dodge, recognize in her almost immediately. William questions the origin of the poetry she mumbles, and Mrs. Manresa assumes that she is the author of the pageant (pp. 64, 75).

In turn, however, Isa is not a whole person. She is not even feminine in the fullest sense of the word. Like Giles, she is overcivilized; both have lost touch with what is earthy and, in that sense, real. Therefore, Giles finds in Mrs. Manresa, a natural, frankly sensual woman, what he misses in his wife. Mrs. Manresa is referred to as "a wild child of nature" (pp. 63, 69), and both Giles and his father are sensitive to the fact that "the air around her became threaded with sensation" (p. 70). Moreover, she is the antithesis of the self-conscious writer. First of all, she is not self-conscious; during the "Present time. Ourselves" section of the pageant she is the only one who can face her own reflection in the mirrors. In fact, she uses one of the mirrors to powder her nose: " 'Magnificent!' cried old Bartholomew [Giles' father]. Alone she preserved unashamed her identity, and faced without blinking herself" (p. 217). Secondly, she is not a writer:

> "For myself," Mrs. Manresa continued, "speaking plainly, I can't put two words together. I don't know how it is—such a chatterbox as I am with my tongue, once I hold a pen—" She made a face, screwed her fingers as if she held a pen in them. But the pen she held thus on the little table absolutely refused to move. (Pp. 75–76)

Thus, Mrs. Manresa is what Isa is not; but conversely, she is not what Isa is. In short, she too is no more than a fragment of the feminine.

In *Between the Acts* the fragmented nature of "ourselves" is further symbolized by two older characters, Bart Oliver and his sister, Lucy Swithin. Like the Hilberys and the Ramsays, these two represent Virginia Woolf's concept of the masculine and feminine personalities. For instance, Mr. Oliver states quite plainly that "she belonged to the unifiers; he to the separatists" (p. 140). Moreover, we are told that "what she saw he didn't; what he saw she didn't—and so on, *ad infinitum*" (p. 33). The difference in the way these siblings approach life is summed up in this passage:

> "It's very unsettled. It'll rain, I'm afraid. We can only pray," she added, and fingered her crucifix.
> "And provide umbrellas," said her brother.
> Lucy flushed. He had struck her faith. When she said "pray," he added "umbrellas." She half covered the cross with her fingers. She shrank; she cowered; but next moment she exclaimed:
> "Oh there they are—the darlings!" (P. 31)

As the unifier, Lucy is much more lovable than her insensitive though rational brother, who, even without wanting to, hurts her feelings and, when he wants to play, makes his grandson cry. Indeed, "he would carry the torch of reason till it went out in the darkness of the cave" (p. 240). Therefore, Isa sides with her:

> What an angel she was—the old woman! Thus to salute the children; to beat up against those immensities and the old man's irreverences her skinny hands, her laughing eyes! How courageous to defy Bart and the weather! (P. 31)

Yet Lucy is impractical and a little ridiculous (pp. 65, 35). Furthermore, she is not quite of this world:

> The door trembled and stood half open. That was Lucy's way of coming in—as if she did not know what she would find. Really! It was her brother! And his dog! She seemed to see them for the first time. Was it that she had no body? Up in the clouds, like an air ball, her mind touched ground now and then with a shock of surprise. (Pp. 138–139).

In short, Bart belongs too much to the realm of time and Lucy too much to the realm of the timeless.

Thus, Virginia Woolf depicts in *Between the Acts* the threat which the oncoming war poses to civilization and the fragmented nature of those whose duty it is to save it. The final scene between Giles and Isa symbolizes the hoped-for union of the masculine and the feminine within the individual. The creation of an androgynous human being is seemingly envisaged for some future time when humankind will also have found the point of equilibrium between love and hate:

> Left alone together for the first time that day, they [Giles and Isa] were silent. Alone, enmity was bared; also love. Before they slept, they must fight; after they had fought, they would embrace. From that embrace *another life might be born*. But first they must fight, as the dog fox fights with the vixen, in the heart of darkness, in the fields of night. (Pp. 255–256, italics mine)

Alone in the night, they are no longer Giles and Isa—what they are for society—but male and female:

> Isa let her sewing drop. The great hooded chairs had become enormous. And Giles too. And Isa too against the window. The window was all sky without colour. The

house had lost its shelter. It was night before roads were made, or houses. It was the night that dwellers in caves had watched from some high place among rocks.
Then the curtain rose. They spoke. (P. 256)

The union of the eternal male and the eternal female makes possible the eternal renewal. However, the story that follows always seems to be the same: reintegration is always followed by disintegration. As Isa suggests earlier, "Surely it was time someone invented a new plot" (p. 252). For only if the plot changes so that human beings become and remain whole can civilization survive.

In *Between the Acts* Virginia Woolf wavers between a concern for the salvation of man and civilization and the temptation to forget the problems involved by escaping to another realm. Throughout the novel Isa voices her longing for this other realm—that of timelessness, not time, of wholeness, not fragmentation. She imagines this world to be

In some harvestless dim field where no evening lets fall her mantle; nor sun rises. All's equal there. Unblowing, ungrowing are the roses there. Change is not; nor the mutable and lovable; nor greetings nor partings; nor furtive findings and feelings, where hand seeks hand and eye seeks shelter from the eye." (Pp. 181–182)

And during the pageant she muses "What do I ask? To fly away, from night and day, and issue where—no partings are —but eye meets eye" (p. 101). She seeks the oneness not found in life. As we shall see, a desire for death is implicit in these passages.

Miss La Trobe also contemplates suicide: "One of these days she would break—which of the village laws?" (pp. 246–247). The description of her departure from the pageant grounds links the idea of drowning with her desire for a drink at the inn:

She strode off across the lawn. . . . It was strange that the earth, with all those flowers incandescent . . . should be hard. From the earth green waters seemed to rise over her. She took her voyage away from the shore, and, raising her hand, fumbled for the latch of the iron entrance gate.

She would drop her suit case in at the kitchen window, and then go on up to the Inn. Since the row with the actress who had shared her bed and her purse the need of drink had grown on her. And the horror and terror of being alone. (P. 246)

Miss La Trobe seeks "oblivion" not only to escape from the problems of life but also to experience a rebirth. In *Between the Acts* a sense of rebirth, as well as oblivion, is associated with mud, water, and drinking: "What she [Miss La Trobe] wanted, like that carp (something moved in the water) was darkness in the mud; a whisky and soda at the pub; and coarse words descending like maggots through the waters (pp. 237–238). At the inn, for instance, Miss La Trobe's mind once again becomes fertilized so that she can write a new play:

voices; oblivion. . . . She raised her glass to her lips. And drank. And listened. Words of one syllable sank down into the mud. She drowsed; she nodded. The mud became fertile. Words rose above the intolerably laden dumb oxen plodding through the mud. Words without meaning— wonderful words. (Pp. 247–248)

Just as the experience of oneness via mania often fertilized Virginia Woolf's mind, the experience of oneness via oblivion fertilizes Miss La Trobe's. Both here and elsewhere in her novels Virginia Woolf associates a reunion with the one (whether in life or through death) with the possibility of a rebirth. This is conveyed in *The Waves* through the wave image:

the wave falls into the sea only to rise again (pp. 104–105, 206, 211).

Like Miss La Trobe, Isa is thirsty. She, too, wishes to return to a state of wholeness; she too longs to experience a renewal. What happened to Isa when she fell in love with Giles is symbolized by the salmon he caught at that moment and pulled out of the water. Since then, she has longed to escape from his love and his hate back into the water. His annoyance with her the day of the pageant makes her feel imprisoned as she sits among the others awaiting the next act.

Through the bars of the prison . . . blunt arrows bruised her; of love, then of hate. Through other people's bodies she felt—she had drunk sweet wine at luncheon—a desire for water. "A beaker of cold water, a beaker of cold for water. "A beaker of cold water, a beaker of cold water," she repeated, and saw water surrounded by walls of shining glass. (P. 82)

Later her thirst is satisfied by a cup of tea. Her drink, which was first associated with a rebirth, is now associated with oblivion.

"Dispersed are we," she murmured. And held her cup out to be filled. She took it. "Let me turn away," she murmured, turning, "from the array"—she looked desolately round her—"of china faces, glazed and hard. Down the ride, that leads under the nut tree and the may tree, away, till I come to the wishing well, where the washer-woman's little boy—" she dropped sugar, two lumps, into her tea, "dropped a pin. He got his horse, so they say. But what wish should I drop into the well?" She looked round. She could not see the man in grey, the gentleman farmer; nor anyone known to her. "That the waters should cover me," she added, "of the wishing well." . . .

"That's what I wished," Isa added, "when I dropped my pin. Water. Water. . ." . . .

"There," Isa mused, "would the dead leaf fall, when the leaves fall, on the water. Should I mind not again to see may tree or nut tree? Not again to hear on the trembling spray the thrush sing, or to see, dipping and diving as if he skimmed waves in the air, the yellow woodpecker?" (Pp. 123–125)

Isa's question, "Should I mind not again to see may tree or nut tree?" is an allusion to a Mother Goose game entitled "Nuts an' May." Isa's longing to be taken away by Rupert Haines reminds her of the game. The game is played with two groups of children advancing towards each other as they sing until the girl who is chosen to be taken away and the boy who is to take her away have a tug of war. The child who wins takes the loser to join his group. The words sung are an appropriate parallel for Isa's thoughts. The first four stanzas, sung alternately by the two groups of children, begin with the following lines: "Here we come gathering nuts an' may"; "Pray who will you gather for nuts an' may"; "We'll gather [Isa] for nuts an' may"; and "Who'll you send to take her away?" And the final stanza reads:

> We'll send [Rupert] to take her away,
> To take her away, to take her away;
> We'll send [Rupert] to take her away,
> On a fine and frosty morning.[17]

Isa regards both death and Rupert Haines as means of escape from her present way of life with Giles.

Why Isa does not actually commit suicide is explained: "above all things, she desired cold water, a beaker of cold water; but desire petered out, suppressed by the leaden duty

she owed to others" (p. 83). What is true of her desire for the
cold water is also true of her desire for Rupert Haines, whose
silence attracts her. As she herself admits, " 'Abortive,' was
the word that expressed her" (p. 21). By the use of symbols,
she explains her state in terms of her position in history. She
grew up as a donkey whose baskets were burdened with the
fruits of the past. The past had told her, " 'Rise up donkey.
Go your way till your heels blister and your hoofs crack' " (p.
182). Then suddenly

> "comes the lightening . . . from the stone blue sky. The
> thongs are burst that the dead tied. Loosed are our
> possessions." . . .
> "It's a good day, some say, the day we are stripped
> naked. Others, it's the end of the day. They see the Inn and
> the Inn's keeper. But none speaks with a single voice. None
> with a voice free from the old vibrations. Always I hear
> corrupt murmurs; the chink of gold and metal. Mad
> music. . . ."
> . . . "On little donkey, patiently stumble." (P. 183)

Unable to speak with a single voice, she exists suspended between life (in its fullest sense) and death. She is neither wholly
alive nor wholly dead. Isa's (and her generation's) seeming inability to make a final choice of one or the other is summed
up by Mrs. Manresa's recitation after lunch of Hamlet's "To
be or not to be, that is the question. Whether 'tis nobler . . ."
(p. 68). As Virginia Woolf implies in the case of Septimus
Smith in *Mrs. Dalloway,* if it is not possible "to be"—whole
and uncorrupted by the "lies" and "chatter"—perhaps it is
nobler "not to be" (p. 202).

  "To be or not to be" was a major theme even in her first
novel and again in *Mrs. Dalloway* (1925) and *The Waves*
(1931). However, in *Between the Acts,* because of the plight

of both the individual and society in 1939, the theme assumes an added significance. It is no longer just a personal question but a question for a whole generation to answer.

Echoed in *Between the Acts* is another theme that is important in *The Voyage Out*—that of "words" versus "silence" (meaning "thoughts without words," p. 68). Just as Rachel tells Terence she prefers music to novels because music "says all there is to say at once," whereas with writing " 'there's so much . . . scratching on the match-box' " (p. 251), Bart Oliver criticizes the English for preferring literature to painting (p. 67). Here, as elsewhere in Virginia Woolf's writings, words are associated with multiplicity and evanescence, wordlessness with unity and the eternal. Therefore, of the two paintings in the Olivers' dining room Bart prefers the "silent" one:

> He was a talk producer, that ancestor. But the lady was a picture. In her yellow robe, leaning, with a pillar to support her, a silver arrow in her hand, and a feather in her hair, she led the eye up, down, from the curve to the straight, through glades of greenery and shades of silver, dun and rose into silence. (P. 46; *cf.* pp. 57, 62)

Like the works of Vanessa Bell, the latter is a "silent painting" which invites the spectator to tunnel through its representational (or descriptive) reality to a nonrepresentational one. Beneath its multiplicity of detail he can perceive, if he tries, an underlying shape or unity.

By these renewed references to her aesthetic concept of silence, Virginia Woolf indicated that she was still concerned with uniting within the novel the evanescent masculine and the eternal feminine, the representational and the nonrepresentational. She invites the reader of *Between the Acts* to tunnel beneath the representational aspect of reality (the setting, the characters, the day's activities) to its nonrepresentational counterpart—the state of mind—which it evokes. Yet, in this final book Virginia Woolf combined old approaches and techniques in such a way as to create a new type of novel. She seemingly hoped to accomplish in prose something similar to what her friend T. S. Eliot had achieved, for instance, in *The Waste Land* (1922).

The friendship between the Woolfs and T. S. Eliot is described by Leonard Woolf in *Downhill All the Way* (pp. 107–111). Leonard and Virginia published T. S. Eliot's *Poems* (which includes "Gerontion") in 1919 (p. 16). *The Waste Land* was published in 1922, and T. S. Eliot stayed with them in Rodmell several times in the years 1920 to 1923. Referring to a visit with them in 1920, Leonard Woolf writes:

> About literature, even about his own writing, even in those early days of knowing him, he was easy and unreticent— and always very interesting. During this visit Virginia one evening tackled him about his poetry and told him that 'he wilfully concealed his transitions.' He admitted this, but said that it was unnecessary to explain; explanation diluted facts. (P. 109)

Virginia Woolf's remarks about Eliot in her diary suggest that she respected him (p. 28) and was envious of his success as a writer (pp. 14, 361). A remark made in her diary on December 29, 1940, about a month after she had completed her draft of *Between the Acts,* suggests that occasionally she had been tempted to "copy" him: "When Desmond [MacCarthy] praises *East Coker,* and I am jealous, I walk over the marsh saying, I am I: and must follow that furrow, not copy another" (p. 361). *Between the Acts* is certainly not a copy of any of Eliot's poems, and the form of the novel is clearly rooted in the techniques she developed and utilized in earlier works. However, her concept of what she aimed to do in *Between the Acts* may have been influenced, consciously or unconsciously, by her familiarity with his works.

The world presented in *Between the Acts* is, in a sense, a waste land. Civilization is "in ruins," men are mere "orts, scraps and fragments," and the books in the Olivers' library, mirror "a tarnished, a spotted soul":

> For as the train took over three hours to reach this remote village in the very heart of England, no one ventured so long a journey, without staving off possible mind-hunger, without buying a book on a bookstall. Thus the mirror that reflected the soul sublime, reflected also the soul bored. Nobody could pretend, as they looked at the shuffle of shilling shockers that week-enders had dropped, that the looking-glass always reflected the anguish of a Queen or the heroism of King Harry. (Pp. 22–23)

Moreover, for what is wrong with Isa's generation there is no remedy to be found in books. Isa looks over the titles in the library in search of a cure, but "none of them stopped her toothache. For her generation the newspaper was a book" (p. 26). Books do not hold her interest, perhaps because the modern books, products of a fragmented world, have no real cure to offer and the classical books, written for a different age, no longer seem relevant. However, newspaper reports, which do not pretend to offer any cures, only facts, do satisfy her curiosity about the present day. When she reads of rape and violence in the *Times*, "That was real; so real that on the mahogany door panels [in the Olivers' library] she saw the Arch in Whitehall; through the Arch the barrack room; in the barrack room the bed, and on the bed the girl was screaming and hitting him about the face" (p. 27). In this between-the-wars' world of "shilling shockers" and newspaper stories of violence, as we have seen, Isa longs for water. Her thirst represents her longing for death and renewal—for a return to the mystical one, which unites within it the masculine and feminine. According to both T. S. Eliot and Virginia Woolf, the only hope for Isa's generation lies in such a spiritual rebirth. Virginia Woolf often used allusions to classic literary works to enrich the meaning of her previous novels. We may recall, for example, her use of *Comus* and "Adonais" in *The Voyage Out,* her references to *The Idiot* in *Night and Day* and to *The Antiquary* in *To the Lighthouse.* However, this technique assumes a much more important role and serves a new purpose in her final novel. Here, as in *The Waste Land,* it sets up a contrast between the spiritual richness of the past and the spiritual poverty of the present.

Like Eliot, Virginia Woolf alluded to Spenser's "Prothalamion" and suggested, as he did, this difference between the past and the present. Whereas Spenser's "nymphs" throw flowers into the Thames, Eliot's modern "nymphs" throw debris: "empty bottles, sandwich papers, / Silk handkerchiefs, cardboard boxes, cigarette ends" (ll. 177–178). In *Between the Acts* Woolf evokes the two swans in stanza three of Spenser's poem:

> So purely white they were,
> That euen the gentle streame, the
>   which them bare,
> Seem'd foule to them, and bad his
>   billowes spare
> To wet their silken feathers, least
>   they might
> Soyle their fayre plumes with water
>   not so fayre
> And marre their beauties bright,
> That shone as heauens light,
> Against their Brydale day, which was
>   not long:

Sweete *Themmes* runne softly,
till I end my Song.

Quite different in tone is the description of Virginia Woolf's "two swans," Isa Oliver and Rupert Haines. For them there will be no "Brydale day":

> The words made two rings, perfect rings, that floated them, herself and Haines, like two swans down stream. But his snow-white breast was circled with a tangle of dirty duckweed; and she too, in her webbed feet was entangled, by her husband, the stockbroker. (Pp. 9–10)

Virginia Woolf made the two swans male and female; in Spenser's poem, of course, they are both brides.

Virginia Woolf also referred to the Philomela myth just as T. S. Eliot did in *The Waste Land*. In each case, the nightingale's unforgettable sorrow is related to the contemporary scene. The "nightingale" in *Between the Acts* is Bart Oliver, who cannot forget that his son Giles is unhappy. He is the counterpart of Philomela, who was transformed by the gods into a nightingale and condemned to mourn eternally her son Itylus (Itys). Philomela had murdered Itylus and served him as food to her husband Tereus, because Tereus had dishonored her sister Procne. The gods subsequently turned Procne into a swallow. In the novel Bart's sister Lucy Swithin is the "swallow." Bart reproaches her because, like Procne in Swinburne's version of the myth, she forgets what he cannot. Happiness is more important to Lucy than the "facts." In some accounts of the myth the roles of Philomela and Procne are reversed. Like Matthew Arnold in his poem "Philomela," Virginia Woolf makes Itylus the son of the nightingale, not the swallow; in Swinburne's "Itylus" he is the son of the swallow. In both poems, however, it is the nightingale who cannot forget. Bart identifies Lucy with lines which he quotes from Swinburne's "Itylus": "Swallow, my sister, O sister swallow, / How can thy heart be full of the spring?" (pp. 131, 137–139). The final lines of Swinburne's poem are: "Thou has forgotten, O summer swallow, / But the world shall end when I forget." As long as his son Giles is unhappy (because he senses his lack of wholeness), Bart cannot forget the masculine "facts" (the effects of war, the fragmented nature of man) which make it impossible for him to share his sister's faith and feminine vision. Only his son matters:

> Arms akimbo, he stood in front of his country gentleman's library. Garibaldi; Wellington; Irrigation Officers' Reports; and Hibbert on the Diseases of the Horse. A great harvest the mind had reaped; but for all this, compared with his son, he did not care one damn. (P. 138)

His sadness and his preoccupation with his son may have been inspired, moreover, by a sense of guilt. By naming Bart's Afghan hound Sohrab, Virginia Woolf evokes the story of Rustum, who unknowingly killed his son Sohrab in Arnold's poem "Sohrab and Rustum." Paralleling this, Bart may feel responsible for his son's living death (Giles' wasteland existence). After all, the father helped create the world which the son inherited.

Along with these allusions to Spenser, Byron, Swinburne, and Arnold (among others), the pageant is used to evoke the richness of English literary history. Included within its medley of quotations are street calls (pp. 184–185), proverbs (p. 149), old songs (pp. 140, 220), and nursery rhymes (pp. 139, 211–212). These, too, are part of the English civilization, which is menaced again by a world war.

The use of nursery rhymes may have been inspired by T. S. Eliot's works. For example, in *The Waste Land* we find the line, "London Bridge is falling down falling down falling down" (1. 427), and in "The Hollow Men" we read,

> *Here we go round the prickly pear*
> *Prickly pear prickly pear*
> *Here we go round the prickly pear*
> *At five o'clock in the morning.*

Virginia Woolf not only quoted from nursery rhymes, she also alluded to them. For example, Lucy's and Bart's conversation (p. 29) about whether it will be "wet" or "fine" for the pageant is seemingly based upon the nursery rhyme "St. Swithin's Day." Lucy Swithin is obviously named for that saint, and Giles' first name and his desire to be a farmer are perhaps meant to evoke the nursery rhyme, "Old Farmer Giles." We have already discussed the use of the game "Nuts an' May."

Evoking all of English civilization was one way of evoking in this final novel "all life, all art, all waifs and strays." As already suggested, this desire to be all-inclusive is not new. For instance, in *Jacob's Room* she wanted to "enclose everything, everything," in *Mrs. Dalloway* to "pour everything in," in *The Years* to "take in everything, sex, education, life etc." (AWD, pp. 23, 62, 189). However, throughout her work this desire for everything (multiplicity) was counterbalanced by a desire for oneness (unity). Thus, in *Between the Acts* she evokes "all life" and "all art" from one village pageant and the activities of one small group of characters during one day at one place.

According to what Virginia Woolf said about the silent painting in her foreword to *Recent Paintings by Vanessa Bell* (1930), *Between the Acts* is a silent novel, not only because the reader is invited to tunnel beneath the representational aspect of reality to the nonrepresentational, but also because, in her role as author, Virginia Woolf is more silent than she was in her other works. That is, the reader now receives less guidance from her than he previously did (for example, there is no principal spokesman for the author like Bernard or Lily Briscoe); therefore, the reader must seek more actively than before to find out what the novel is about. Like the reader of *The Waste Land,* he is presented with many fragments (of everything—"all life," "all art") which he must interrelate in order to see the whole. For instance, the pageant is not merely referred to, it is played out before him as if he were a member of its audience. Along with the characters who try to figure out what Miss La Trobe means to say, he too must make his interpretation. Virginia Woolf suggests that Miss La Trobe likewise prefers to be a "silent" author. When Isa wonders, " 'What did she mean?' " Mrs. Swithin says, " 'When Mr. Streatfield [the clergyman] asked her to explain, she wouldn't' " (p. 249).

Virginia Woolf requires the reader's co-operation also in the task of evoking all art. Since she quotes from or alludes to many literary works, he must bring to the novel a knowledge of English literature. The meaning of the novel is enriched in proportion to the amount of knowledge he can provide. Similarly, when she cites lines from songs, nursery rhymes, and street calls, she undoubtedly expects the reader to supply, as he reads, the music or rhythmic pattern associated with them. The pageant is intended to be a visual as well as a musical or literary experience; for often the villagers fail to recite or sing the words loudly or clearly enough (pp. 96, 108–109, 148), yet usually "It didn't matter what the words were; or who sang what. Round and round they whirled, intoxicated by the music" (p. 113). Thus, the reader can "see" the pageant much as he would see a "silent painting," that is, in terms of colors and patterns. How he is to see it is suggested by the way in which "the silent guest," William Dodge, sees it:

It was a mellay; a medley; an entrancing spectacle (to William) of dappled light and shade on half clothed, fantastically coloured, leaping, jerking, swinging legs and arms. He clapped till his palms stung. (p. 112)

Like Virginia Woolf, Miss La Trobe evidently conceived of her plays in visual terms. For instance, just as *The Waves* originated with a vision of a "fin in a waste of water," Miss La Trobe's idea for a new play originates with a visual experience:

> The clothes were strewn on the grass. Cardboard crowns, swords made of silver paper, turbans that were sixpenny dish cloths, lay on the grass or were flung on the bushes. There were pools of red and purple in the shade; flashes of silver in the sun. The dresses attracted the butterflies. Red and silver, blue and yellow gave off warmth and sweetness. Red Admirals gluttonously absorbed richness from dish cloths, cabbage whites drank icy coolness from silver paper. Flitting, tasting, returning, they sampled the colours.
>
> Miss La Trobe stopped her pacing and surveyed the scene. "It has the makings . . ." she murmured. For another play always lay behind the play she had just written. Shading her eyes, she looked. The butterflies circling; the light changing; the children leaping; the mothers laughing— (Pp. 77–78)

In this vision, as in her pageant, the pattern is not stable as in a painting but constantly changing as in a film. The emphasis in either case is the same; it falls not upon the representational but upon the nonrepresentational aspect of reality, that is, upon pattern, rhythm, and color. Certainly, in order to reconstruct Miss La Trobe's vision of what she wanted the pageant to be, the reader must see the pageant in these terms. In short, he does not merely hear about the pageant as he heard about Rachel Vinrace's music or Lily Briscoe's painting. Rather he is asked to see it, to listen to it, and to interpret it. In this sense, Virginia Woolf is silent while the reader is constantly re-acting to and contributing to the content of the novel.

Virginia Woolf felt she was doing something new in *Between the Acts*. Having just completed it, she wrote in her diary on November 23, 1940: "I am a little triumphant about the book. I think it's an interesting attempt in a new method. I think it's more quintessential than the others. More milk skimmed off. A richer pat" (AWD, p. 359). Indeed, it is a "richer" novel than her previous works in that it is more evoc-ative. It evokes a wealth of material from the reader's memo-ries (of nursery rhymes, songs, street calls, traditions), knowl-edge (of music, art, and literature, including poetry, drama, and prose), and feelings (about the past, the present age, and the future). Because it is highly evocative and because the reader is called upon to supply the transitions and interrela-tionships himself, this final novel is both highly complex and extremely compact. Virginia Woolf did not provide footnotes to help the reader of *Between the Acts* recognize her many al-lusions as T. S. Eliot did for the reader of *The Waste Land,* but one feels that she was moving in this direction.

Thus, her concern with the "present day" had led her, in terms of her art, to experience a kind of rebirth. Despite the fact that the Battle of Britain was well under way before she finished her draft of *Between the Acts* in 1940, she found joy in her work, for she was busy developing this "new method" for handling her new material (AWD, p. 359). As Jean Guiguet points out:

> Of all the books whose genesis the Diary enables us to follow, this one seems to have been written with the great-est ease: . . . If sometimes she cannot write for more than an hour, or if excess of concentration makes her head ache, she shows neither irritation nor despondency. The most fre-quent note is that of satisfaction and pleasure.[18]

Leonard Woolf prefaced *Between the Acts* with this "Note":

> The MS. of this book had been completed, but had not
> been finally revised for the printer, at the time of Virginia
> Woolf's death. She would not, I believe, have made any
> large or material alterations in it, though she would proba-
> bly have made a good many small corrections or revisions
> before passing the final proofs.

The job of revising the book was evidently not sufficiently interesting to protect her mind from the outer "welter of unreality." On January 26, 1941, she was fighting a "battle against
depression," and she noted in her diary:

> There's a lull in the war. Six nights without raids. But
> Garvin says the greatest struggle is about to come—say in
> three weeks—and every man, woman, dog, cat, even weevil
> must girt their arms, their faith—and so on. It's the cold
> hour, this: before the lights go up. A few snowdrops in the
> garden. Yes, I was thinking: we live without a future.
> That's what's queer: with our noses pressed to a closed
> door. (P. 364)

Living "without a future," she could no longer hope that
someday both human beings and societies would become androgynous. In the final volume of Leonard Woolf's autobiography, we learn that by March 26, 1941, "desperate depression
had settled upon Virginia; her thoughts raced beyond her control; she was terrified of madness." Then, on March 28, 1941,
convinced that she was "going mad" and that this time she
would not recover, she drowned herself in the river Ouse.[19]
Seen in terms of what we know of her from her novels, her suicide represents both an act of despair and an act of faith—
despair that the androgynous whole would ever be established
on earth but faith in the existence (in the timeless realm of
death) of its mystical equivalent—oneness.

Notes

CHAPTER I: A Quest for Equilibrium

1. *Apropos of "Lady Chatterley's Lover"* (London, 1931), p. 88.
2. See Eliot's essay "The Metaphysical Poets" and Jung's *The Undiscovered Self*, trans. R. F. C. Hull (Boston, 1958), p. 74.
3. C. G. Jung, *Two Essays on Analytical Psychology*, trans. R. F. C. Hull. Collected Works of C. G. Jung, VII (New York, 1953), p. 219.
4. Aileen Pippett, *The Moth and the Star: A Biography of Virginia Woolf* (Boston and Toronto, 1955), p. 11.
5. Noel Annan, *Leslie Stephen: His Thought and Character in Relation to His Time* (London, 1951), pp. 98–99.
6. Pippett, *Moth*, p. 48.
7. *Ibid.*, p. 54.
8. As editor of the Hogarth Press, he published works by Helene Deutsch, Karl Abraham, and Sigmund Freud (including the standard edition of Freud). In 1924 the Institute of Psycho-Analysis asked him to become the publisher of the International Psycho-Analytical Library. In the next forty years he published seventy volumes in it. For further details see Leonard Woolf, *Downhill All the Way: An Autobiography of the Years 1919–1939* (London, 1967), pp. 163–168.
9. Leonard Woolf, *Beginning Again: An Autobiography of the Years 1911–1918* (New York, 1964), p. 76. On manic-depression, see, for instance, Robert W. White, *The Abnormal Personality* (New York, 1956), pp. 513–529; Leopold Bellak, *et al.*, *Manic-Depressive Psychosis and Allied Conditions* (New York, 1952); John D. Campbell, *Manic-Depressive Disease* (Philadelphia, 1953); Hassan Azima and Bernard C. Glueck, eds., *Psychiatric Research Reports of the American Psychiatric Association*, No. 17 (November, 1963), 73–83, 91–97; and William A. White, *et al.*, eds., *Manic-Depressive Psy-*

chosis, Association for Research in Nervous and Mental Disease, XI (Baltimore, 1931).

10. *Wisdom, Madness and Folly* (New York, 1952), p. 88. *Adventures into the Unconscious* was published in London. For another inside account of manic-depressive psychosis, see C. W. Beers, *A Mind That Found Itself* (New York, 1908).

11. Robert W. Gibson ("Psychotherapy of Manic-Depressive States," *Psychiatric Research Reports* . . . , No. 17, p. 92) and others say there is a high incidence of manic-depression in the same family. In *The Abnormal Personality* Robert W. White states: "For about 20 to 25 per cent of manic-depressive patients the history shows that one parent or the other had a mental illness, generally manic-depressive illness" (p. 532).

12. F. W. Maitland, *Life and Letters of Leslie Stephen* (London, 1906), p. 433.

13. Annan, *Leslie Stephen,* pp. 12, 97.

14. White (*Abnormal Personality,* p. 527) discusses Sandor Rado's belief that the behavior of a depressed person may be explained in part "as a cry for love: a display of helplessness and a direct appeal for the affection and security that have been lost." Compare Virginia Woolf's portrait of her father (Mr. Ramsay) in *To the Lighthouse,* especially p. 63. Stephen wrote in 1900 that he was often depressed; in 1875 he mentioned that sometime earlier he had had a "nervous depression" (Maitland, *Life and Letters,* pp. 455, 434). Furthermore, Stephen's irrational fear of bankruptcy (described by Annan, *Leslie Stephen,* p. 71) characterizes most manic-depressives when in a state of depression. Whereas the manic eats and acts as if his bank account were unlimited, the depressive refuses to eat, fearing bankruptcy and starvation (White, *Abnormal Personality,* p. 530).

15. Pippett, *Moth,* p. 20. Laura, daughter of Leslie Stephen and his first wife, Minny Thackeray, was retarded (Annan, *Leslie Stephen,* p. 92). Her condition may also have been related to what seems to have been a hereditary weakness in the Stephen family.

16. White, *Abnormal Personality,* p. 535.

17. See *ibid.,* p. 523. Leopold Bellak and Robert W. Gibson take a similar position. Others tend to emphasize either the somatogenic or the psychogenic position. John D. Campbell, for instance, espouses the former. Accounts of psychoanalytic contributions may be found in O. Fenichel, *The Psychoanalytic Theory of Neurosis* (New York, 1945), ch. 17, and Phyllis Greenacre, ed., *Affective Disorders* (New York, 1953).

18. Leonard Woolf, *The Journey Not the Arrival Matters: An Autobiography of the Years 1939–1969* (New York, 1970), pp. 79–80.

19. Published in *An Agnostic's Apology and Other Essays* (London, 1890). Some of the material in his unpublished journal is discussed by Annan (*Leslie Stephen*, p. 99).

20. Freud discusses female development in these terms in "The Psychology of Women," *New Introductory Lectures on Psycho-analysis*, trans. W. J. H. Sprott (New York, 1933), pp. 161–185.

21. Pippett, *Moth*, p. 14.

22. Maitland, *Life and Letters*, pp. 475–476.

23. *The Ethics of Belief and Other Essays* (London, 1947), p. 124.

24. See, for example, pages 27, 49–50, 279. For a comparison of her attributes with those of certain female figures in pagan mythology, see Joseph L. Blotner's interesting article, "Mythic Patterns in *To the Lighthouse*," *PMLA*, 71 (1956), 547–562.

25. Maitland, *Life and Letters*, pp. 224, 337.

26. Letter to Katherine Mansfield, written in December, 1918 (*Letters of D. H. Lawrence*, ed. Aldous Huxley [New York, 1932], p. 462).

27. *An Agnostic's Apology*, p. 3.

28. *Life and Letters*, p. 436.

29. Annan, *Leslie Stephen*, pp. 100–101. Also, see Maitland, *Life and Letters*, p. 323.

30. *Wisdom*, pp. 55, 46.

31. Leonard Woolf, *Downhill All the Way*, p. 153.

32. Since this book was written, more unpublished material has been made available in the Berg Collection at the New York Public Library. Scholars may now read hundreds of Virginia Woolf's letters as well as the thirty-three volumes of her diaries. Thus far, John Hulcoop is the only person besides Quentin Bell and Leonard Woolf to have read all the diaries. However, in his report on the diaries in the *New York Public Library Bulletin* (September 1971), Mr. Hulcoop states that the theories presented in this chapter will "find confirmation" (p. 302).

Of the seven diaries written during the years 1899–1919, pages 149–156 of Diary No. 2 (Hyde Park Gate, June 30, 1903–October 1, 1903 [?]) support what I have said of the connection between her relationship to her parents and her psychosis. This connection is further supported by an autobiographical fragment, "The tea table was the centre of Victorian family life," in her "Articles, essays, fiction and re-

226   *Virginia Woolf and the Androgynous Vision*

views," Vol. 9, dated January 28, 1940, Part I of 1940, pp. 55–69; see in particular, pp. 57, 65–69.

33. *Cf.* Virginia Woolf's *Three Guineas* (1938).

34. In *Wisdom*, pp. 31–81. In *Mysticism: Sacred and Profane* (London, 1957), R. C. Zaehner draws a parallel between the manic and depressive experiences described by Custance and the expansion-contraction experiences described by mystics. See the chapter in his book entitled "Madness."

35. The words are Custance's (*Wisdom*, p. 37). *Cf. Lighthouse*, p. 100.

36. Similarly, in *Mrs. Dalloway*, Septimus Smith feels he is the recipient of an ineffable revelation which should be conveyed immediately (pp. 28, 109); for if the Establishment had this information, everything would be different. White describes this aspect of manic behavior in *The Abnormal Personality*, p. 520.

37. C. A. Bonner, "Psychogenic Factors as Causative Agents in Manic-Depressive Psychosis," in *Manic-Depressive Psychosis*, ed. William A. White, *et al.*, p. 547.

38. White, *Abnormal Personality*, p. 544.

39. Pippett, *Moth*, p. 368.

40. See Leonard Woolf's remarks about this in *Beginning Again*, p. 81, and in *Downhill All the Way*, p. 149.

41. *Beginning Again*, p. 81.

CHAPTER II: The Spherical Vision

1. *The Archetypes and the Collective Unconscious*, trans. R. F. C. Hull. Collected Works of C. G. Jung, Vol. IX, Part I (New York, 1959), pp. 20–21.

2. See AWD, p. 138. *Cf.* her reference to life as a "luminous halo" (CE II, 106). Also, many characters in her novels refer to the "globe" of life. For a number of examples, see Dorothy Brewster, *Virginia Woolf* (London, 1963), pp. 79–80.

3. CE II, 106–107, and VO, p. 262. See also CE I, 153, and CE III, 19.

4. *Mrs. Dalloway* was published in 1925. Freud first presented his concept of the life instinct (Eros) and death instinct (Thanatos) in *Beyond the Pleasure Principle* (1920). Leonard Woolf writes in *Downhill All the Way:* "In the decade before 1924 in the so-called Bloomsbury circle there was great interest in Freud and psycho-analysis, and the interest was extremely serious." For instance, Adrian Stephen (Vir-

ginia Woolf's brother), James Strachey (Lytton Strachey's brother), and their wives became professional psychoanalysts. The Hogarth Press began publishing English translations of Freud's works in 1924 (London, 1967, pp. 164, 166). Hence, Virginia Woolf was undoubtedly aware of Freud's ideas while writing *Mrs. Dalloway*. However, she did not mention reading Freud until 1939 (AWD, pp. 321, 326), and on the basis of what we know about the way her mind worked, we may assume that Freud's terminology merely helped to illuminate, for her, feelings which she herself had experienced and wanted to express.

5. See her remarks about E. M. Forster's failure to convey the real and the symbolical simultaneously in CE I, 346–347.

6. "Pictures," *The Moment and Other Essays* (London, 1952), p. 141. This essay is not included in the *Collected Essays* I–IV.

7. Boston, 1957, p. 130.

8. *Downhill All the Way: An Autobiography of the Years 1919–1939* (London, 1967), pp. 205, 206. In "A Letter to a Young Poet" she wrote, "for my part I do not believe in poets dying" (CE II, 190).

9. Aileen Pippett, *The Moth and the Star: A Biography of Virginia Woolf* (Boston, Toronto, 1955), p. 4.

10. F. W. Maitland, *The Life and Letters of Leslie Stephen* (London, 1906), pp. 317, 323.

11. "Foreword," *Recent Paintings by Vanessa Bell* (London, 1930), p. 1.

12. *Virginia Woolf and Lytton Strachey: Letters,* ed. Leonard Woolf and James Strachey (London, 1956), p. 75.

13. Joseph Frank, "Spatial Form in Modern Literature," *Criticism: The Foundation of Modern Literary Judgment,* ed. Mark Schorer *et al.* (New York, 1948), p. 381. Frank is using "image" as Ezra Pound defines it in "A Few Don'ts": "An 'Image' is that which presents an intellectual and emotional complex in an instant of time" (*The Literary Essays of Ezra Pound*, ed. T. S. Eliot [London, 1954]).

14. *Cf.* also CE II, 77, where she speaks of "spectral architecture."

15. Whereas I place the primary emphasis on Virginia Woolf's psychology, other critics stress the influence of Roger Fry; see John Hawley Roberts, "Vision and Design in Virginia Woolf," *PMLA,* LXI (September 1946), 835–847, and Josephine O'Brien Schaefer, *The Three-Fold Nature of Reality* (London, The Hague, Paris, 1965), esp. pp. 16–19. For similarities between Virginia Woolf and others in the "Bloomsbury Group" (including Fry), see J. K. Johnstone, *The*

Bloomsbury Group: A Study of E. M. Forster, Lytton Strachey, Virginia Woolf, and Their Circle (New York, 1954).

16. Pippett, *Moth*, p. 74, and Virginia Woolf, *Roger Fry* (London, 1940), pp. 149, 152–153. In the 1910–1914 period this group included eight people who lived in Bloomsbury—Adrian Stephen, Virginia and Leonard Woolf (who married in 1912), Clive and Vanessa Bell, Duncan Grant, Maynard Keynes, Saxon Sidney Turner—and five people who lived outside of Bloomsbury—Lytton Strachey, Roger Fry, E. M. Forster, Desmond and Molly MacCarthy. These are the thirteen intimate friends whom Leonard Woolf refers to as "Old Bloomsbury." They were separated during the war but began to meet regularly again when in March of 1920 they formed a Memoir Club. See Leonard Woolf's accounts of Bloomsbury in *Beginning Again*, pp. 21–26, and in *Downhill All the Way*, pp. 114–117.

17. Werner Haftmann, *Painting in the Twentieth Century* (New York and Washington, 1966), I, 150.

18. For further details on the reactions to this exhibit, see *Roger Fry*, pp. 153–159. In 1966 Quentin Bell wrote of the effect of this exhibit in 1910: "There was an outcry such as has never been heard since then in this country" (Quentin Bell, *et al.*, *Vision and Design, The Life, Work and Influence of Roger Fry, 1866–1934*. Exhibition arranged by the Arts Council and the University of Nottingham [1966], p. 8). Werner Haftmann claims that as a consequence of the postimpressionist exhibits in 1910 and 1912 "English art underwent a decisive change" (p. 155).

19. Arnold Bennett, "Neo-Impressionism and Literature," *Books and Persons: Being Comments on a Past Epoch 1908–1911* (New York, 1917), p. 284. Virginia Woolf referred to this passage in "Books and Persons," *Contemporary Writers*, ed. Jean Guiguet (London, 1965), p. 62. Katherine Mansfield was also impressed by this exhibit; she said that Van Gogh's paintings taught her something about writing which was "a kind of freedom, or rather a striking force." (Quoted by J. Isaacs, *An Assessment of Twentieth-Century Literature* [London, 1951], p. 9. *Cf.* the influence of the Futurist painters on D. H. Lawrence. See Jack Lindsay, "The Impact of Modernism on Lawrence," *Paintings of D. H. Lawrence*, ed. Mervyn Levy [London, 1964], pp. 35–53.)

20. Virginia Woolf, *Roger Fry*, pp. 164, 172.

21. Monroe C. Beardsley speaks of the "extraordinarily valuable educational work" of Fry and Bell, which "consisted in helping people to look at paintings without predispositions and preconceptions, and without being distracted by irrelevant associations with the representa-

tional subject-matter" (*Aesthetics from Classical Greece to the Present: A Short History* [New York and London, 1966], p. 364). Probably the best known of Fry's works are *Vision and Design* (1920), *Transformations* (1926), *Cézanne* (1927), and *Last Lectures* (1939). In his day Fry was perhaps even more influential as a lecturer than as a writer. Although Roger Fry was the greater art critic of the two, I have found that Clive Bell's name is as frequently and often more frequently mentioned by aestheticians; for his book *Art* (1913) and his term "significant form" sum up in an oversimplified way what in 1910–1913 was a new approach to painting. Aestheticians who speak more of Bell than of Fry include: Rolf Ekman, *Problems and Theories in Modern Aesthetics* (Malmo, 1960); Edward G. Ballard, *Art and Analysis* (The Hague, 1957); W. E. Kennick, "Does Traditional Aesthetics Rest on a Mistake?" *Collected Papers on Aesthetics,* ed. S. J. C. Barrett (New York, 1966). For references to others who have dealt with the concept of "significant form," see Monroe Beardsley, *Aesthetics: Problems in the Philosophy of Criticism* (New York, 1958), p. 315.

22. Haftmann, *Painting in the Twentieth Century*, I, 34.

23. "Pictures," *The Moment*, p. 142.

24. See [Autobiographical Fragment], "The tea table . . . ," unpublished, in "Articles, essays, fiction and reviews," Vol. 9, dated January 28, 1940, Part I of 1940, pp. 55–69, esp. p. 67. Located in the Berg Collection, the New York Public Library.

25. Diary No. 2, Hyde Park Gate, June 30-October 1, 1903(?), unpublished manuscript in the Berg Collection, the New York Public Library, pp. 149–156. See her remark about work, p. 154.

26. See, for example, VO, p. 452, and JR, p. 30.

27. See the Autobiographical Fragment, pp. 57, 65–67. She speaks of the two sides of herself and her room (also a chrysalis).

In *Psychology of the Unconscious* (New York, 1916), C. G. Jung has a chapter entitled "The Song of the Moth," in which he quotes a song written by a Miss Miller. This song helps to illuminate why Virginia Woolf chose the moth and chrysalis image and how it was related to her intensity as an artist. Suggested, too, is the fact that the wholeness she sought is a projection of that which was rooted in her unconscious.

The Moth to the Sun
I longed for thee when first I crawled to consciousness.
My dreams were all of thee when in the chrysalis I lay.
Oft myriads of my kind beat out their lives

Against some feeble spark once caught from thee.
And one hour more—and my poor life is gone)
Yet my last effort, as my first desire, shall be
But to approach thy glory; then, having gained
One raptured glance, I'll die content.
For I, the source of beauty, warmth and life
Have in his perfect splendour once beheld. (P. 87)

28. Since *Orlando* was not as "deep" a book as *To the Lighthouse,* Virginia Woolf wrote in her diary: "I never got down to my depths and made shapes square up, as I did in the *Lighthouse*" (p. 136).

29. *Cf.* E. M. Forster's essay on anonymity in *Two Cheers for Democracy* (London, 1951), pp. 93–97.

30. C. G. Jung, *Psychology of the Unconscious* (New York, 1916), p. 248.

31. P. W. Martin, *Experiment in Depth: A Study of the Work of Jung, Eliot and Toynbee* (London, 1960), pp. 110, 151.

CHAPTER III: *The Voyage Out* and *Night and Day*

1. *Virginia Woolf and Lytton Strachey: Letters,* ed. Leonard Woolf and James Strachey (London, 1956), p. 75.

2. *Ibid.,* p. 146.

3. For other references to Helen's embroidery, see pp. 30, 244–246.

4. John Custance, *Wisdom, Madness and Folly* (New York, 1952), p. 37.

5. Sir Walter Ralegh (an earlier spelling of Raleigh), *The Discovery of the Large, Rich, and Beautiful Empire of Guiana,* ed. Sir Robert H. Schomburgk, The Hakluyt Society, No. 3 (London, 1848), p. 57. *Cf.* VO, pp. 341–342. Holtby cites Virginia Woolf's debt to Raleigh for this scene, but she fails to detect the other similarities between *The Voyage Out* and *The Discovery of . . . Guiana.* See Winifred Holtby, *Virginia Woolf* (London, 1932), pp. 78–79 for a comparison of the river scene passages.

6. VO, pp. 1, 367, and Raleigh, *The Discovery of . . . Guiana,* p. 114. Virginia Woolf may have borrowed other details from Raleigh: the idea of the waterfall (pp. 270, 272) may have been inspired by Raleigh (p. 81); the grass in which Rachel rolls (p. 347) may have been inspired by him (p. 92). His account of what he had been told about the Amazon women (p. 28) and his report of the male Indians' atti-

tudes towards the female (p. 39) would certainly have interested Virginia Woolf; and both are relevant to the subject of *The Voyage Out,* namely, the male-female relationship.

7. Other lines from *Comus* suggest a possible connection between *Comus, The Voyage Out,* and Virginia Woolf's personal life. Virginia married Leonard Woolf in 1912 while writing *The Voyage Out.* The name Rachel means "ewe." In *Comus* a spirit comes to inform the brothers that their virgin sister is with Comus. Since the spirit is dressed as a shepherd, the brothers think he has come to them about a lost sheep. But the Spirit replies: "I came not here on such a trivial toy/As a stray'd Ewe, or to pursue the stealth/Of pilfering Woolf" (ll. 501–503).

8. R. C. Trevelyan, "Virginia Woolf," *The Abinger Chronicle,* II (April-May 1941), 23.

9. P. 251. *Cf.* E. M. Forster's remarks in "Not Listening to Music": "It [music] seems to be more 'real' than anything. . . . music which is untrammelled and untainted by reference is obviously the best sort of music to listen to; we get nearer the centre of reality (*Two Cheers for Democracy* [London, 1951], p. 138).

10. London, 1963, p. 87.

11. Sophocles, *The Antigone,* trans. Gilbert Murray (New York, 1941), pp. 37–38, 58, 60.

12. See in particular Erich Neumann's treatment of the subject in *The Great Mother: An Analysis of the Archetype,* trans. Ralph Manheim, Bollingen Series XLVII (New York, 1955). However, Leonard Woolf states in a letter written to me on August 2, 1967, "I do not think that my wife ever read anything of Jung and was not familiar [*sic*] with his works."

13. See Edwin S. Schneidman and Norman Farberow, eds., *Clues to Suicide* (New York, 1957) and Herbert Hendin, *Suicide and Scandinavia* (New York and London, 1964), Ch. III, esp. pp. 21–22, 26.

14. *Beginning Again: An Autobiography of the Years 1911 to 1918* (New York, 1964), p. 80.

15. Aileen Pippett, *The Moth and the Star: A Biography of Virginia Woolf* (Boston and Toronto, 1955), p. 11.

16. For Freud's theory, see his essay "Dostoevsky and Parricide" published with Dostoevsky's *Stravrogin's Confession,* trans. S. S. Koteliansky and Virginia Woolf (London, 1926). Also relevant is Helene Deutsch's "Absence of Grief" (1937) in *Neuroses and Character Types,* ed. John D. Sutherland and M. Masud R. Khan (London, 1965), pp. 235–236.

17. Helen disclaims any power to influence Rachel (p. 143); yet both she and Mrs. Flushing seem to be agents of fate (pp. 347, 283).

18. Virginia Woolf used these terms to compare Katharine with Cassandra (p. 362).

19. See Maud Bodkin, *Archetypal Patterns in Poetry* (London, 1934), pp. 300–307.

20. Jean Guiguet, *Virginia Woolf and Her Works*, trans. Jean Stewart (London, 1965), p. 209.

21. See CE II, 87, and CE I, 244.

22. *Virginia Woolf and Lytton Strachey: Letters*, p. 53.

23. Fyodor Dostoevsky, *The Idiot*, trans. Constance Garnett (New York, 1935), p. 375. N&D, pp. 132, 138.

24. Fyodor Dostoevsky, "Notes from Underground," *White Nights and Other Stories*, trans. Constance Garnett (New York, 1923), p. 75.

25. In 1927 Virginia Woolf published an essay entitled "Life Itself," which she later revised as part of "Two Parsons" in *The Common Reader II*.

26. "Notes from Underground," *White Nights*, p. 76.

CHAPTER IV: *Jacob's Room* and *Mrs. Dalloway*

1. *Virginia Woolf* (London, 1963), p. 101.

2. Josephine Schaefer, *The Three-fold Nature of Reality in the Novels of Virginia Woolf* (The Hague, 1965), p. 68.

3. See VO, pp. 227, 251 for images of the match, flames, and matchbox.

4. Winifred Holtby, *Virginia Woolf* (London, 1932), p. 120.

5. *Ibid.*

6. *Virginia Woolf and Her Works*, trans. Jean Stewart (London, 1965), p. 224.

7. Bernard Blackstone, *Virginia Woolf: A Commentary* (London, 1949), p. 66.

8. For a study of her use of symbols in *Jacob's Room*, see N. C. Thakur, *The Symbolism of Virginia Woolf* (London, 1965), Ch. III.

9. (*Autobiographical Fragment*), "The tea table . . . ," unpublished, in "Articles, essays, fiction and reviews," Vol. 9, dated January 28, 1940, Part I of 1940, pp. 67, 69. Located in the Berg Collection, the New York Public Library.

10. *Neuroses and Character Types*, ed. John D. Sutherland and M. Masud R. Khan (London, 1965), p. 235.

11. See Sigmund Freud, "Dostoevsky and Parricide" published with

Dostoevsky's *Stravrogin's Confession*, trans. S. S. Koteliansky and Virginia Woolf (London, 1926), esp. pp. 96–97.

12. *Wisdom, Madness and Folly* (New York, 1952), p. 72.

13. *Fiction and the Unconscious* (Boston, 1957), p. 130.

14. Schaefer, *The Three-fold Nature of Reality*, p. 86.

15. Virginia Woolf used what Robert Humphrey calls "indirect interior monologue." That is, she as omniscient author "intervenes between the character's psyche and the reader"; she did not present the psychic content directly. See Humphrey's description and analysis of her technique in his book, *Stream of Consciousness in the Modern Novel: A Study of James Joyce, Virginia Woolf, Dorothy Richardson, William Faulkner, and Others* (Berkeley and Los Angeles, 1958), esp. pp. 29–32, 50–52, 58–59, 70–72.

16. Virginia Woolf, "Introduction," *Mrs. Dalloway*, The Modern Library (New York, 1928), p. viii.

17. Josephine Schaefer sees the structure of the novel in a somewhat similar manner (*The Three-fold Nature of Reality*, p. 86).

18. Pp. 6, 45, 54–59, 79, 104, 113, 129–130, 140, 165, 204.

19. New York, 1956, p. 528.

20. *The Fields of Light: An Experiment in Critical Reading* (New York, 1951), pp. 135–136. Brower is right, for example, in criticizing the solitary traveler's vision as "verbally inert matter." See *Mrs. Dalloway*, pp. 64–65. He also criticizes the horse metaphor on p. 50 and Peter's pursuit of the girl, pp. 59–60.

CHAPTER V: *To the Lighthouse* and *The Waves*

1. Virginia Woolf, "Foreword," *Recent Paintings by Vanessa Bell*, February 4th to March 8th, 1930, 92 New Bond Street, The London Artists' Association, pp. 3–4.

2. P. 58. The similarity between this aspect of Bernard's personality and that of Desmond MacCarthy is pointed out by Leonard Woolf in *Beginning Again: An Autobiography of the Years 1911 to 1918* (New York, 1964), pp. 142–143.

3. Trans. Ralph Manheim (New York, 1966), I, 151–152.

4. *A Treasury of the Theatre, Vol. II: Modern European Drama from Ibsen to Sartre*, ed. John Gassner (New York, 1935), p. 388.

5. *Virginia Woolf and Her Works*, trans. Jean Stewart (London, 1965), p. 296.

6. Cox, "The Solitude of Virginia Woolf," *The Free Spirit: A Study of Liberal Humanism in the Novels of George Eliot, Henry*

234   *Virginia Woolf and the Androgynous Vision*

James, E. M. Forster, Virginia Woolf, Angus Wilson (London, 1963),
p. 333. I have inserted in brackets the name of the character to whom
each aspect refers.

7. Leonard Woolf, *The Journey Not the Arrival Matters: An Autobiography of the Years 1939 to 1969* (New York, 1970), p. 75.

8. *The Three-fold Nature of Reality in the Novels of Virginia
Woolf* (The Hague, 1965), p. 155.

9. *The Moth and the Star: A Biography of Virginia Woolf* (Boston
and Toronto, 1955), p. 292.

10. Alfred Lord Tennyson, "The Holy Grail" in "Idylls of the
King," *The Works of Tennyson,* ed. Hallam Lord Tennyson (New
York, 1913), p. 410, 1. 3.

11. Moody, *Virginia Woolf* (Edinburgh and London, 1963), p. 48.

12. Holtby, *Virginia Woolf* (London, 1932), p. 195.

13. Brewster, *Virginia Woolf* (London, 1963), p. 126.

14. *The Three-fold Nature of Reality,* p. 139.

15. *Ibid.,* p. 152.

16. See Chapter I, where I discuss the significance of these lines in
terms of Mr. Ramsay's personality.

CHAPTER VI: *The Years* and *Between the Acts*

1. Linda Thurston, "On Male and Female Principle," *The Second
Wave,* I (Summer 1971), 39.

2. *Ibid.*

3. *Virginia Woolf: A Commentary* (London, 1949), p. 194.

4. Virginia Woolf was, of course, influenced by the feminist movement. The relationship between her art and her feminism is the subject
of Herbert Marder's book, *Feminism and Art: A Study of Virginia
Woolf* (Chicago and London, 1968). Also relevant is Charles G. Hoffmann's article, "Virginia Woolf's Manuscript Revisions of *The
Years,*" *PMLA,* LXXXIV (January 1969), 79–89.

5. *The Three-fold Nature of Reality in the Novels of Virginia
Woolf,* Studies in English Literature, VII (The Hague, 1965), p. 185.

6. John Custance, *Wisdom, Madness and Folly: The Philosophy of
a Lunatic* (New York, 1952), pp. 42–43, 55, 76–81.

7. *Mrs. Dalloway,* p. 100.

8. Aileen Pippett, *The Moth and the Star: A Biography of Virginia
Woolf* (Boston and Toronto, 1955), p. 308.

9. *Downhill All the Way: An Autobiography of the Years 1919 to
1939* (London, 1967), p. 153.

10. *Virginia Woolf and Her Works,* trans. Jean Stewart (London, 1965), p. 308.

11. Leonard Woolf, *Downhill All the Way,* p. 156.

12. Her use of Defoe and Brontë as opposite poles was discussed in Chapter II.

13. For a discussion of the symbolic relevance of these introductory passages see N. C. Thakur's chapter on *The Years* in his book *The Symbolism of Virginia Woolf* (London, 1965).

14. Virginia Woolf's concept of the "moment of vision" was discussed in Chapter II.

15. Virginia Woolf, "Introduction," *Mrs. Dalloway,* The Modern Library (New York, 1928), p. viii.

16. *The Three-fold Nature of Reality,* p. 186.

17. *Mother Goose,* illus. Hilda Miloche and Wilma Kane (Racine, Wisconsin, 1953).

18. *Virginia Woolf and Her Works,* pp. 320–321.

19. Leonard Woolf, *The Journey Not the Arrival Matters: An Autobiography of the Years 1939 to 1969* (New York, 1969), pp. 91, 93.

Selected Bibliography

Annan, Noel. *Leslie Stephen: His Thought and Character in Relation To His Time.* London, 1951.

Beers, C. W. *A Mind that Found Itself,* New York, 1908.

Bell, Clive. *Art.* New York, 1913.

————. *Old Friends.* London, 1956.

————. *Proust.* London, 1928.

————. *Since Cézanne.* New York, 1922.

Bell, Quentin. *Roger Fry.* Leeds University Press, 1964.

Bell, Quentin, *et al. Vision and Design: The Life, Work and Influence of Roger Fry, 1866–1934.* Exhibition arranged by the Arts Council and the University of Nottingham, 1966.

Bellac, Leopold, *et al. Manic-Depressive Psychosis and Allied Conditions.* New York, 1952.

Bennett, Joan. *Virginia Woolf: Her Art as a Novelist.* Cambridge, England, 1964.

Blackstone, Bernard. *Virginia Woolf: A Commentary.* London, 1949.

Bodkin, Maud. *Archetypal Patterns in Poetry: Psychological Studies of Imagination.* London, 1934.

Bowen, Elizabeth. "The Achievement of Virginia Woolf," *Collected Impressions.* New York, 1950. Pp. 78–82.

————. *"Orlando," Seven Winters and Afterthoughts.* New York, 1962.

Bradbrook, Frank W. "Virginia Woolf: The Theory and Practice in Fiction," *The Modern Age,* ed. Boris Ford. The Pelican Guide to English Literature, No. 7. Baltimore, 1964.

Brewster, Dorothy. *Virginia Woolf.* London, 1963.

Brown, E. K. *Rhythm in the Novel.* Toronto, 1950.

Brown, Robert Curtiss. "Laurence Sterne and Virginia Woolf, A Study in Literary Continuity," *The University of Kansas City Review,* XXVI (December 1959), 153–159.

Campbell, John D. *Manic-Depressive Disease: Clinical and Psychiatric Significance.* Philadelphia, London, Montreal, 1953.

Chambers, R. L. *The Novels of Virginia Woolf.* London, 1947.

Cox, C. B. "The Solitude of Virginia Woolf," *The Free Spirit: A Study of Liberal Humanism in the Novels of George Eliot, Henry James, E. M. Forster, Virginia Woolf, Angus Wilson.* London, 1963.

Custance, John. *Adventures into the Unconscious.* London, 1954.

————. *Wisdom, Madness and Folly: The Philosophy of a Lunatic.* Preface by C. G. Jung. Foreword by Canon L. W. Grensted. New York, 1952.

Daiches, David. *Virginia Woolf.* Norfolk, Connecticut, 1942.

Deikman, Arthur J. "De-automatization and the Mystic Experience," *Psychiatry; Journal of the Biology and Pathology of Interpersonal Relations,* XXIX (November 1966), 324–338.

Delattre, Floris. *Le Roman psychologique de Virginia Woolf.* Paris, 1932.

Eliot, T. S., *et al.* "Notes on Virginia Woolf," *Horizon,* III (May 1941), 313–327.

Firestone, Shulamith. *The Dialectic of Sex: The Case for Feminist Revolution.* New York, 1970.

Forster, E. M. *Aspects of the Novel.* London, 1958.

————. *Two Cheers for Democracy.* London, 1951.

Fouchet, Max-Pol. "Evolution de l'esthétique en France de 1789 à 1940." 3 vols. Unpublished course lectures, Paris, 1956–1957.

Frank, Joseph. "Spatial Form in Modern Literature," *Criticism: The Foundations of Modern Literary Judgment,* ed. Mark Schorer *et al.* New York, 1948. Pp. 379–392.

Freedman, Ralph. *The Lyrical Novel: Studies in Hermann Hesse, André Gide, and Virginia Woolf.* Princeton, 1963.

Freud, Sigmund. *Civilization and Its Discontents,* trans. Joan Riviere. The International Psycho-analytical Library, ed. Ernest Jones. No. 17. London, 1951.

————. "The Psychology of Women," *New Introductory Lectures on Psycho-analysis,* trans. W. J. H. Sprott. New York, 1933. Pp. 153–185.

Friedman, Melvin. *Stream of Consciousness: A Study in Literary Method.* New Haven, 1955.

Fry, Roger. "The Artist and Psycho-Analysis," *The New Criticism: An Anthology of Modern Aesthetics and Literary Criticism,* ed. Edwin Berry Burgum. New York, 1930.

Fry, Roger. *Cézanne: A Study of His Development.* New York, 1958.

———. *Last Lectures,* ed. Kenneth Clark. Cambridge, England, 1939.

———. *Transformations: Critical and Speculative Essays on Art.* New York, 1926.

———. *Vision and Design.* New York, 1957.

Gibson, Robert W. "Psychotherapy of Manic-depressive States," *Psychiatric Research Reports of the American Psychiatric Association,* ed. Hassan Azima and Bernard Glueck. No. 17 (November 1963), 91–97.

Giovanni, G. "Method in the Study of Literature in Its Relation to the Other Fine Arts," *Journal of Aesthetics and Art Criticism,* VIII (March 1950), 185–195.

Grant, Duncan. "Virginia Woolf," *Horizon,* III (June 1941), 402–406.

Gruber, Ruth. *Virginia Woolf: A Study.* Leipzig, 1935.

Guiguet, Jean. *Virginia Woolf and Her Works,* trans. Jean Stewart. London, 1965.

Hafley, James. *The Glass Roof: Virginia Woolf as Novelist.* University of California English Studies, No. 9. Berkeley, 1954.

Haftmann, Werner. *Painting in the Twentieth Century: An Analysis of the Artists and Their Work,* trans. Ralph Manheim. 2 vols. New York and Washington, 1965.

Heilbrun, Carolyn. *Toward a Recognition of Androgyny.* New York, 1932.

Hoffmann, Charles G. "Virginia Woolf's Manuscript Revisions of *The Years,*" LXXXIV (January 1969), 79–89.

Holloway, John. "The Literary Scene," *The Modern Age,* ed. Boris Ford. The Pelican Guide to English Literature, No. 7. Baltimore, 1964.

Holtby, Winifred. *Virginia Woolf.* London, 1932.

Hulcoop, John. "Virginia Woolf's Diaries: Some Reflections after Reading Them and a Censure of Mr. Holroyd," *Bulletin of the New York Public Library,* LXXV (September 1971), 301–310.

Johnstone, J. K. *The Bloomsbury Group: A Study of E. M. Forster, Lytton Strachey, Virginia Woolf, and Their Circle.* New York, 1954.

Jung, C. G. *The Archetypes and the Collective Unconscious,* trans. R. F. C. Hull. Collected Works, IX, 1. Bollingen Series XX. New York, 1959.

———. *Psychology of the Unconscious,* trans. Beatrice Hinkle. New York, 1916.

————. *Two Essays on Analytical Psychology,* trans. R. F. C. Hull. Collected Works of C. G. Jung, VII. New York, 1953.

————. *The Undiscovered Self,* trans. R. F. C. Hull. Boston, 1958.

Keynes, J. M. *Two Memoirs.* London, 1949.

Kirkpatrick, B. J. *A Bibliography of Virginia Woolf.* London, 1957.

Laski, Marghanita. *Ecstasy: A Study of Some Secular and Religious Experiences.* Bloomington, 1961.

Leaska, Mitchell. *Virginia Woolf's Lighthouse: A Study in Critical Method.* New York, 1970.

Lederer, Wolfgang. *The Fear of Women.* New York, 1968.

Lesser, Simon O. *Fiction and the Unconscious.* Preface by Ernest Jones. Boston, 1957.

Lewin, Bertram D. *The Psychoanalysis of Elation.* New York, 1950.

Love, Jean O. *Worlds in Consciousness: Mythopoetic Thought in the Novels of Virginia Woolf.* Berkeley, 1970.

Lundholm, Helen. "The Manic-Depressive Psychosis," *Duke University Psychological Monographs.* Vol. I. Durham, North Carolina, 1931.

MacCarthy, Desmond. *Leslie Stephen.* Cambridge, 1937.

Maitland, Frederic William. *The Life and Letters of Leslie Stephen.* London, 1906.

Marder, Herbert. *Feminism & Art: A Study of Virginia Woolf.* Chicago and London, 1968.

Mauron, Charles. *Aesthetics and Psychology,* trans. Roger Fry and Katherine John. London, 1935.

————. *The Nature of Beauty in Art and Literature,* trans. Roger Fry. London, 1927.

Mendilow, A. A. *Time and the Novel.* London, 1952.

Moody, A. D. *Virginia Woolf.* Writers and Critics Series. Edinburgh and London, 1963.

Moore, G. E. *Principia Ethica.* Cambridge, England, 1959.

Nathan, Monique. *Virginia Woolf,* trans. Herma Briffault. New York and London, 1961.

Neumann, Erich. *The Great Mother: An Analysis of the Archetype,* trans. Ralph Manheim. Bollingen Series XLVII. New York, 1955.

Pippett, Aileen. *The Moth and the Star: A Biography of Virginia Woolf.* Boston and Toronto, 1955.

Rantavaara, Irma. "Virginia Woolf and Bloomsbury," *Suomalaisen Tiedeakatemian Toimituksia.* Annales Academiae Scientiarum Fennicae, Series B, Vol. 82. Helsinki, 1953.

Richter, Harvena. *Virginia Woolf: The Inward Voyage.* Princeton, 1970.

Roberts, John Hawley. "Towards Virginia Woolf," *Virginia Quarterly Review,* X (October 1934), 587–602.

————. "Vision and Design in Virginia Woolf," *PMLA,* LXI (September 1946), 835–847.

Rosenfeld, Herbert. "Notes on the Psychopathology and Psychoanalytic Treatment of Depressive and Manic-Depressive Patients," *Psychiatric Research Reports of the American Psychiatric Association,* ed. Hassan Azima and Bernard C. Glueck. No. 17 (November 1963), 73–83.

Schaefer, Josephine O'Brien. *The Three-fold Nature of Reality in the Novels of Virginia Woolf.* Studies in English Literature, Vol. VII. The Hague, 1965.

Schneidman, Edwin S. and Norman Farberow, eds. *Clues to Suicide.* New York, 1957.

Starkie, Enid. *From Gautier to Eliot: The Influence of France on English Literature 1851–1939.* London, 1960.

Stephen, Karin. *The Misuse of Mind: A Study of Bergson's Attack on Intellectualism.* London, 1922.

Stephen, Leslie. *An Agnostic's Apology and Other Essays.* London, 1890.

————. *Essays on Freethinking and Plainspeaking.* London, 1907.

————. *Hours in a Library.* 4 vols. London, 1907.

Stern, Karl. *The Flight from Woman.* New York, 1965. Pp. 1–39.

Stone, Wilfred. *The Cave and the Mountain: A Study of E. M. Forster.* Stanford, 1966.

Sypher, Wylie. *Loss of the Self in Modern Literature and Art.* New York, 1962.

————. *Rococo to Cubism in Art and Literature: Transformations in Style in Art and Literature from the 18th to the 20th Century.* New York, 1960.

Thakur, N. C. *The Symbolism of Virginia Woolf.* London, 1965.

Thurston, Linda. "On Male and Female Principle," *The Second Wave,* I (Summer 1971), 38–42.

Trevelyan, R. C. "Virginia Woolf," *The Abinger Chronicle,* II (April-May 1941), 23.

Verga, Ines. "Virginia Woolf's Novels and Their Analogy to Music," *Argentine Association of English Culture 1943–1945.* English Pamphlet Series, No. 11. Buenos Aires, 1945.

Watts, Alan. *The Two Hands of God: The Myths of Polarity.* New York, 1963.

White, Robert W. *The Abnormal Personality*. New York, 1956.

White, William A., *et al.*, eds. *Manic-Depressive Psychosis: An Investigation of the Most Recent Advances*. Association for Research in Nervous and Mental Disease, Vol. XI. Baltimore, 1931.

Woolf, Leonard. *Beginning Again: An Autobiography of the Years 1911 to 1918*. New York, 1964.

————. *Downhill All the Way: Autobiography of the Years 1919 to 1939*. London, 1967.

————. *Growing: An Autobiography of the Years 1904 to 1911*. New York, 1962.

————. *The Journey Not the Arrival Matters: An Autobiography of the Years 1939 to 1969*. New York, 1969.

————. *Sowing: An Autobiography of the Years 1880 to 1904*. New York, 1960.

Woolf, Virginia. (Autobiographical Fragment), "The Tea Table . . . ," unpublished, in "Articles, essays, fiction and reviews," Vol. 9, dated January 28, 1940, Part I of 1940, pp. 55–69. Located in the Berg Collection, the New York Public Library.

————. *Between the Acts*. London, 1941.

————. *Collected Essays*. 4 vols. London, 1966–1967.

————. *Contemporary Writers*, ed. Jean Guiguet. London, 1965.

————. Diary No. 2. Hyde Park Gate, June 30–October 1, 1903(?) unpublished manuscript in the Berg Collection, the New York Public Library. Pp. 149–150. This is one of seven holograph notebooks written during the years 1899–1919.

————. *Flush: A Biography*, London, 1933.

————. "Foreword," *Recent Paintings by Vanessa Bell*. London, 1930.

————. *A Haunted House*. London, 1944.

————. "Introduction," *Mrs. Dalloway*. The Modern Library. New York, 1928. Pp. v-ix.

————. *Jacob's Room*. London, 1922.

————. *Mrs. Dalloway*. London, 1925.

————. *Night and Day*. London, 1919.

————. *Orlando*. London, 1928.

————. "Pictures," *The Moment and Other Essays*. London, 1947. This essay is not included in *Collected Essays*, 4 vols.

————. *Roger Fry: A Biography*. New York, 1940.

————. *A Room of One's Own*. London, 1929.

————. "Rupert Brooke," *Times Literary Supplement*, August 8, 1918, 371.

————. *Three Guineas*. London, 1938.

————. *To the Lighthouse.* London, 1927.

————. *Virginia Woolf and Lytton Strachey: Letters,* ed. Leonard Woolf and James Strachey. London, 1956.

————. *The Voyage Out.* London, 1915.

————. "Walter Sickert: A Conversation," *Sickert Centenary Exhibition of Pictures from Private Collections.* London, 1960.

————. *The Waves.* London, 1931.

————. *A Writer's Diary,* ed. Leonard Woolf. London, 1954.

————. *The Years.* London, 1937.

Zaehner, R. C. *Mysticism: Sacred and Profane.* London, 1957.

Zorn, Marilyn, "The Pageant in *Between the Acts,*" *Modern Fiction Studies,* II (February 1956), 31–35.

Index

243